R

THIS BOOK BELONGS TO

Khaye Robertson

What's the number one thing you want to learn about money?

_____

Take a look at the table of contents. Which two
chapters are you most excited about?

1. _____

2. _____

Hey! I'm George—your host for this course. You're about to learn money
the fun way, and what you take away from this class will help you for
the rest of your life. (Yes, your whole life.) Now get ready for a page or
two of technical stuff. Then you'll meet the experts.

—George

Acknowledgments

The only way to build a curriculum that's like no other is to work with a team that's like no other. Ramsey Solutions is grateful to each person below for their dedication to creating a financial literacy curriculum that truly empowers students to make sound financial decisions for life.

Educators

Kerri Nevills
Clovis Adult Education
Clovis, CA

Brian Glynn
Lincoln-Way West
High School
New Lenox, IL

Kathy Jarman
Helias Catholic
High School
Jefferson City, MO

Lance Garvin
Pike High School
Indianapolis, IN

Dara Schmoe
Marysville Getchell
High School
Marysville, WA

Wendy Pitlik-Plehn
Sheboygan South
High School
Sheboygan, WI

Amanda Wilson
Bremen High School
Bremen, GA

Eric Lambert
North Bullitt
High School
Shepherdsville, KY

Melinda Byers
South Haven
High School
South Haven, KS

Alex Short
St. Mary's High School
St. Louis, MO

Nikki Flinn
Lincoln Jr/Sr
High School
Lincoln, KS

Alex Todd
Elizabethtown
High School
Elizabethtown, KY

Credits

Executive Vice President
Jim King

Chief Creative Officer
Luke LeFevre

Chief Marketing Officer
Jennifer Sievertsen

Executive Marketing Director, B2B
Walt Yates

Executive Creative Director, Video
Lara Johnson

Senior Creative Director, B2B
Jameson Sheppard

Director of Curriculum Products
Ryan Haedge

Instructional Designer
Rebecca Curry

Creative Design
Jason Miller
Sarah Sperry
Brittany Foster
Kaitlyn Marken

Content Development
Michelle Grooms
Rick Prall
Mary-Kate Tucto
Scott Chaney
George Kamel
Eva Daniel
Ara Vito
Jessa Sexton
Naomi Parton
Rachel Sims

Content Editing/ Proofing
Rachel Knapp
Jessica Sly
Jordan Russ
Becca Krese
Madison Sullivan
Andrea Pace

Photography
Seth Farmer

Project Management
Jenn Norton
Maria Katz
Jenny Paschall
Emily Kemp

Marketing
Jacqueline Garneau
Kate Flynn
Luke Sammons
Palmer Reynolds
Dan Stevenson

Digital Product Manager
Kelsi Clymer

Digital Development
Scott Bradley
Ethan Dowler
Stephanie Sauder
Bryson Rafael
Shawn Murry
Jim Ebert
Brendan Wovchko

Video Production
Leo Gonzalez
David DiCicco
Melissa Fitzgerald
Chad Stembridge
John Smith
Ian Collins
Tony Marx
Ike Elgard
Colin Smith
Makaila Haase
Eleny Burton
JB Waggoner
Nick Byble
Bryan Raitt
Bengy del Villar
Jonna Covert
Josh Myers
Randy Clark
Sarah Mack
Shane Emerson
Josh Fulton
Jeff Gideon
Jenna Coletta
Connor Bowser

Meet the Experts

No one is born knowing all there is to know about money. It takes time, experience, and a few lessons learned the hard way to figure it all out. The experts you'll meet in this course have been there and done that—and now you get to learn from them!

Dave Ramsey, Chris Hogan, Anthony ONeal, Ken Coleman, and Rachel Cruze are passionate about helping people succeed in their finances, careers, and everyday lives. They're all #1 bestselling authors and speakers who have already helped millions of people win with money—and they want you to win too. Because when you understand how money works, the possibilities are endless. Let's do this!

Contents

1 **Introduction to Personal Finance** 1

2 **Budgeting Basics** 29

3 **Saving Money** 57

4 **Credit and Debt** 87

5 **Consumer Awareness** 115

6 **Career Readiness** 143

7 **College Planning** 171

8 **Financial Services** 199

9 **The Role of Insurance** 219

10 **Income and Taxes** 247

11 **Housing and Real Estate** 275

12 **Investing and Retirement** 295

13 **Global Economics** 323

For this curriculum, you'll find your course materials and additional resources in RamseyClassroom at **ramseyclassroom.com**.

Introduction to Personal Finance

This chapter introduces the topic of personal finance, explores the evolution of credit and consumerism in America, and highlights the importance of both knowledge and behavior when it comes to managing your money.

LESSON VIDEO GUIDE

There are no secrets of the rich. Personal finance is all about common sense. — Dave Ramsey

GUIDED NOTES   While you watch the video, complete the section below.

1. The problem with anyone's money is the person in the *Miroor*.

2. It's hard to be disciplined and have *Self control*.

3. Self-control is *emosional* maturity.

4. You can make the *life* you want to make in America today.

ANALYZE AND REFLECT   After you watch the video, respond to the question(s) below.

1. How do you think learning about personal finance can help you in your future—*and* right now?

   _____

   _____

   _____

2. You can start life after high school with a clean slate. How does knowing this affect your perspective of learning about personal finance?

   _____

   _____

   _____

LEARNING OBJECTIVES

- Describe what personal finance is.
- Analyze personal finance as it relates to the normal American family.

MAIN IDEA

Learning how to manage your money now will help you avoid the financial mistakes most people make—and that's how you win with money!

Welcome to the course that has the power to change the trajectory of your future! In some classes, you might wonder if you'll ever use what you're learning once you leave school. But not in this class. Sure, we'll talk about some stuff that's a long way off—like buying a home or investing for retirement. But you can start using a lot of what you're about to learn right now—in your real life! Sounds great, right?

What Is Personal Finance?

Personal finance is just that—*your* personal finances and what you choose to do with *your* money. It's all the money decisions you make every day—like figuring out when and where to save and spend your cash. When you make the right choices, you're managing your money. But the wrong choices can lead to your money problems managing you.

Once you understand how earning, budgeting, saving, spending, and giving affect your money, you'll have all the tools you need to make the right choices. And that's what good personal finance is all about. Being financially literate is having the knowledge and skills you need as a **consumer** to be able to manage your money well.

> **You'll either manage your money or the lack of it will always manage you.**
> — Dave Ramsey

Just think about your current money situation. You might have an income from a part-time job, or your parents may pay you for doing chores. What are you doing with your money? If you just put it in your pocket and spend it without a plan, you'll probably end up running out of money—fast. But if you make it a habit to plan and set goals for your money, it will last longer. And you could end up actually paying cash for your own car or paying for college—debt-free!

A Giant Debt Problem

Does the idea of buying a car or going to college without borrowing money shock you? Of course it does! That's because

Personal Finance: all the financial decisions an individual or family must make in order to earn, budget, save, spend, and give money over time

Consumer: a person or organization that uses a product or service

almost everyone you know uses debt to pay for those things—and more.

Here's the deal. On the surface, it looks like most people are doing really well with money. They have nice houses, fancy cars, expensive jewelry, and all the latest technology. But they can't really afford those things. They're using **debt** to pay for it all just to keep up the appearance of success. That's what's known as "keeping up with the Joneses," and it traps people in a cycle of debt.

Debt: money owed to another person or company

Paycheck to Paycheck: an expression used to describe a person or household whose monthly income is devoted to expenses and has little to no savings

Debt doesn't open doors. It closes them.

— Anthony ONeal

In America, 72% of people say they're burdened by consumer debt. The average borrower has over $34,000 of debt—not including a mortgage![1] As the chart below shows, debt is definitely a problem. But debt doesn't have to be a problem for you!

Living Paycheck to Paycheck

All that debt leads to another big problem: **paycheck-to-paycheck** living. Almost 80% of Americans use all of the money they get from one paycheck just to make it to the next.[2]

Because a big chunk of every paycheck goes to their monthly debt payments, they can't save any money for emergencies or big purchases. So they go even deeper in debt to pay for those things too. It's a never-ending cycle that's difficult for many people to break.

Debt Isn't the Only Problem

Let's get real for a moment: Personal finance does involve some math. But personal finance is mostly about behavior. Life and money habits like budgeting, investing, goal-setting, giving, establishing healthy boundaries in personal relationships, and furthering your skills and education all impact your finances. How's that possible? Because personal finance is only 20% head knowledge and 80% behavior.

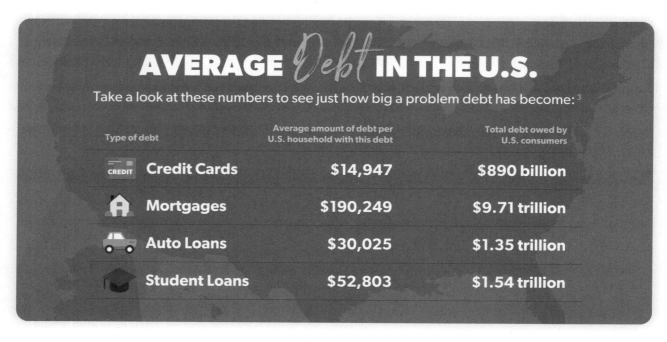

AVERAGE *Debt* IN THE U.S.

Take a look at these numbers to see just how big a problem debt has become:[3]

Type of debt	Average amount of debt per U.S. household with this debt	Total debt owed by U.S. consumers
Credit Cards	$14,947	$890 billion
Mortgages	$190,249	$9.71 trillion
Auto Loans	$30,025	$1.35 trillion
Student Loans	$52,803	$1.54 trillion

That means knowing what to do with money isn't the real problem. It's actually making smart money choices that's hard for most people.

In this course, we'll focus on both head knowledge and behavior. You'll learn the right way to manage your money, and you'll learn how to build good money habits that you can use now and build on in the future. Remember, for most American families, normal is being broke and living in debt. You don't have to be normal!

Debt is normal. Be weird!

Did You Know?

85% of parents are interested in their kids taking a course on personal finance to learn how to better handle money.[4]

Your JOURNAL

What will make the biggest impact on your financial future? Explain your answer.

_____

_____

_____

REMEMBER THIS   Add a ✓ next to each completed learning objective below.

◯ You can describe personal finance as all the money decisions a person or family makes in order to earn, budget, save, and spend money.

◯ You recognize that the normal American family struggles with overwhelming debt and living paycheck to paycheck.

THIS LESSON MAKES ME FEEL   (Circle) your response to what you learned.

 CONFUSED   SURPRISED   THOUGHTFUL   CONFIDENT

LESSON VIDEO GUIDE

The caliber of your future will be determined by the choices you make today.

— Anthony O'Neal

GUIDED NOTES

While you watch the video, complete the section below.

1. Write down three key takeaways from the history of credit in America.

   _____

   _____

   _____

2. Take _____ off the table.

3. Have a _____ account.

4. Start _____ early.

ANALYZE AND REFLECT

After you watch the video, respond to the question(s) below.

1. Now that you've learned about the history of credit and debt in America, how does this impact the way you think about money? What will you do differently as a result?

   _____

   _____

   _____

MAIN IDEA

Using credit and being in debt have become accepted money behaviors. It hasn't always been like that—and you don't have to live this way.

How Did We Get Here?

What if we told you it wasn't long ago that using credit, or borrowing money to buy things, was frowned upon in the United States? We're not kidding! It was even illegal in many cases.

Credit and debt are part of our culture. Today, 83% of American adults have at least one credit card.[5] That's because credit companies spend a lot of money to convince us that credit is the normal way to get what we want. Just like companies advertise their new line of basketball shoes, credit card companies, banks, and other lenders promote credit to get us to buy.

> ## Debt is the biggest thief of your financial future.
>
> — *Dave Ramsey*

The result is the huge debt problem we talked about in Lesson 1. Instead of avoiding debt, many Americans now believe debt is a necessary part of their financial lives! That kind of culture shift doesn't happen overnight. So, how did we get here?

Credit As We Know It

Prior to 1920, the only way for banks to make money by loaning money was to charge sky-high **interest rates**. But that was illegal, so most banks stayed out of the credit business.

Loan sharks were individuals and small organizations that offered credit—also with incredibly high **interest**—to people in desperate financial situations who had nowhere else to turn. These shady, illegal operations were not socially acceptable. But today, we don't think twice about carrying a credit card that charges 21% interest. What a difference a century makes!

After World War I, the country entered "the Roaring Twenties," a decade-long economic boom. Americans wanted the new, mass-produced products—like home appliances and cars—but they didn't always have the money. Because of the demand, credit laws were relaxed and lending became profitable for banks. The average person could get credit without turning to loan sharks, so buying on credit became more socially accepted—though not as much as it is today. This was the beginning of what we now know as the credit industry.

Credit: the granting of a loan and the creation of debt; any form of deferred payment

Interest Rate: the percentage of principal charged by the lender for use of its money

Loan Shark: person or entity that charges borrowers interest rates above an established legal rate

Interest: the additional cost a lender charges for borrowing their money

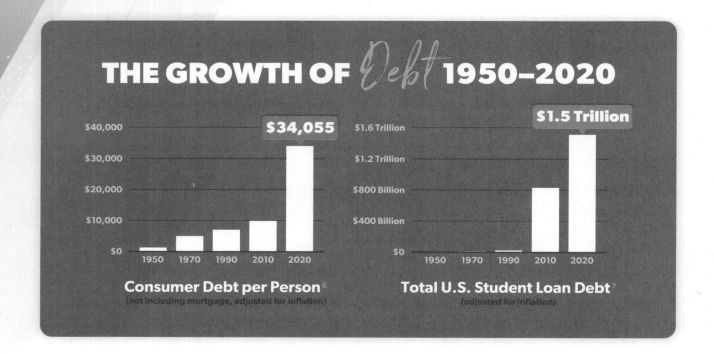

THE GROWTH OF *Debt* 1950–2020

$34,055

$40,000
$30,000
$20,000
$10,000
$0

1950 1970 1990 2010 2020

Consumer Debt per Person[6]
(not including mortgage, adjusted for inflation)

$1.5 Trillion

$1.6 Trillion
$1.2 Trillion
$800 Billion
$400 Billion
$0

1950 1970 1990 2010 2020

Total U.S. Student Loan Debt[7]
(adjusted for inflation)

Going Into Debt

When the stock market crashed in 1929, it launched the country into the Great Depression in the 1930s. Millions of people were out of work, and many people lost everything. President Franklin D. Roosevelt passed the New Deal, a program designed to promote economic recovery and social reform and help working-class Americans get back on their feet.

World War II ultimately helped end the Great Depression by creating a lot of new jobs. As Americans returned to work, the economy strengthened. Once again, people became comfortable with the idea of borrowing money and going into debt.

The chart above shows how Americans have become comfortable with debt. In 1950, the average debt per person was under $1,500 (adjusted for inflation).[8] But now, it's over $34,000 in nonmortgage debt.[9] Keep in mind that back in 1950, credit cards and student loans weren't what they are now.

Credit cards (Mastercard, Visa, and American Express) weren't even introduced to the public until the late 50s. Before that, in 1950, the average credit card debt was *zero*. Now, the national average is $3,366 per person.[10] When you narrow it down to people who actually have credit cards, the average amount of debt rolls up to over $14,900 per family.[11]

Student Loans

In less than 50 years, our national student loan debt has gone from zero to a crisis level of more than a trillion dollars. The turning point was in 1972 when the Student Loan Marketing Association (SLMA, known as Sallie Mae) began offering government-funded federal loans to college students. It was a huge change that made borrowing money to go to college easy—practically automatic.

On the chart, you can see that in 1950, student loans weren't even a blip on the map. In fact, the total debt figure was zero.

Did You Know?

In 1924, General Motors launched the General Motors Acceptance Corporation (GMAC) so consumers could finance a car purchase. By 1930, three out of four cars were bought with car loans.[12]

But now, the national student loan debt has ballooned to over $1.5 trillion![13] That's absolutely insane!

Today's Reality

So, what's the takeaway? Americans are drowning in debt because they've made debt a "normal" way of life. That much is clear just from looking at the stats and the history of credit and debt in America. The highest debt level is among 45–54-year-olds, with the 35–44 age bracket coming in a close second.

Studies show that young Americans—those under age 36—are carrying over $26,000 in debt![14] And how are they racking up all that debt? Mostly from student loans. But like we talked about in Lesson 1, Americans also have a problem with buying way too much stuff. Credit and debt have made all that possible. That's why it's the norm today.

But there's good news! You don't have to continue this cycle and feel like you're drowning in debt. All of this can end with your generation!

You control your future. You decide where your money goes and how much of it you save for later.

— Chris Hogan

It's time to realize that just because debt has become an American norm, that doesn't mean it has to become your reality. You can make the choice to avoid the trap of using credit to buy things!

Did You Know?

For their daily purchases:[15]

54% of Americans prefer to use debit cards.

14% of Americans prefer to use cash.

Your **JOURNAL**   How does understanding the history of credit make you think differently about credit cards and other forms of debt?

_____

_____

_____

REMEMBER THIS   Add a ✓ next to the completed learning objective below.

◯   You recognize that using credit has become normal in American culture.

THIS LESSON MAKES ME FEEL   Circle your response to what you learned.

 CONFUSED   SURPRISED   THOUGHTFUL   CONFIDENT

LESSON VIDEO GUIDE

When it comes to your money, YOU are in charge.   — Anthony O'Neal

GUIDED NOTES   While you watch the video, complete the section below.

1. Write down three takeaways from Anthony's discussion with the students.

   _____

   _____

   _____

2. Have a _____ .

3. Live on _____ than you make.

4. Stay away from _____ .

ANALYZE AND REFLECT   After you watch the video, respond to the question(s) below.

1. After hearing Anthony tell his story, what are some things you can do to start right with your financial future?

   _____

   _____

   _____

LEARNING OBJECTIVES

- Describe how avoiding debt can give you financial freedom and a sense of hope for the future.
- Recognize that personal finance is mostly a series of behavioral decisions.

MAIN IDEA

You're responsible for how you handle your money. You need to have a plan, spend less than you make, and stay out of debt.

You're in Charge

Over the past 100 years, Americans have gone from believing debt was socially unacceptable to relying on debt to pay for everything from a new home to a new pair of jeans. But you can change the game.

If you make up your mind to stay away from debt, and then follow through by making decisions that keep you from going into debt, you'll have hope for your financial future.

> **Your decisions from today forward will affect not only your life, but your legacy.**
>
> — *Dave Ramsey*

This is really all it takes to avoid the cycle of debt that so many people are trapped in. Remember, personal finance is 20% head knowledge and 80% behavior.

You're in charge of your money, your attitude, and your behavior—that's why it's called *personal* finance. It's your money and your decisions. With a few basic money principles to guide you as you budget, spend, save, and give, you *can* do this. Take control of your money!

Lifetime Money Principles

First, make sure to always have a budget. A budget is just a written game plan for your money (that's what Chapter 2 is all about). Next, stay out of debt. We've given you plenty of reasons why. But it boils down to the fact that when you don't have debt payments, you'll actually have money to save, spend, and give.

Here's another principle: Live on less than you make. That will keep you out of debt and help you save money. Sure, it seems like common sense, but all the stats on debt show it's a hard principle to follow. Then you'll want to save and invest money for your future. Finally, without any debt, you can be outrageously generous!

Simple, easy to understand, and easy to put into practice, right? They're the kind of principles that can make a huge difference in your future—the kind of principles Anthony ONeal wishes he'd learned about when he was in high school.

> To give anything less than your best is to sacrifice the gift.
>
> **Steve Prefontaine**
> Olympic long-distance runner

Did You Know?

44% of Americans report they have less than $1,000 in savings.[16]

ANTHONY ONEAL

Fifteen years ago, I remember having my high school diploma in my left hand and my college ID in my right hand. With a scholarship and my father's GI Bill, college was paid for. I stepped onto the college campus and thought, "Yes! Freedom!"

One day, I was walking on campus and a guy stopped me and asked, "Hey! How'd you like a free T-shirt and two free large pizzas?" I was like, *Yeah, I'm in college and I'm broke. All they're asking me to do is fill out a credit card application—I can do that!* Not even thinking I'd get approved for the credit card, I filled it out.

That was absolutely the worst financial decision I've ever made in my entire life.

In just a few months, I'd charged $15,000 in credit card debt, $10,000 in furniture, and $10,000 in student loans. And there I was, $35,000 in debt before my 19th birthday!

But it didn't stop there. A series of bad decisions eventually got me kicked out of college. I lost my scholarship, the GI Bill, and my apartment. I lost everything.

So, at age 19, I was homeless and in debt—a lot of debt. Over the next six months, most of my nights were spent living in my car. Until one day I looked in the rearview mirror and thought, *Why am I here? I need to get my life together!* I wept and prayed that if I could just get out of there, I would make it my life's work to help other young people not make the same stupid mistakes I'd made. And that's the day that changed my life.

Fast forward to today. Of course I'm still learning as I go, but I'm standing on the foundation of my faith and a lot of good, quality choices. I'm debt-free, living in a home that I built, and traveling around the world helping young people. I'm literally living my dream while becoming a better person.

I always tell young people that the caliber of your future will be determined by the choices you make today. How are you going to graduate high school? How are you going to graduate college? What's your career path? That's all going to be determined by your choices. *Your* choices are what matter—not the choices of your friends or your family.

> ## There I was, $35,000 in debt before my 19th birthday.

Live Like No One Else

If you live by these basic money principles now, you can live and give like no one else later. That means if you make smart financial decisions today, you'll have the money you need in the future to do all the things you want—without any debt.

There will be times when it's tough to live out these principles. While you're making sacrifices to live the lifestyle you can afford, your friends, even your family members, may live like they have no money problems at all. Don't let that get to you. Their lives may seem perfect on the outside: the perfect family, in the perfect house, in the perfect neighborhood, driving the perfect cars, and wearing the perfect clothes. But that "perfect" family is usually drowning in debt.

Start Right

Over half of teens and young adults associate money with stress and worry.[17] So chances are, you're already stressed out about finances. But learning how to manage money the right way can put an end to all that and help you avoid future financial mistakes.

Ultimately, this course isn't about anyone telling you what to do with your money. It's about you learning how to tell your money what it can do for you.

With the right knowledge, behavior, and the money principles we just covered, you really can make good choices with your money, stop stressing about it, and build a future filled with financial peace and confidence. That's what we call *winning with money!*

> Today, there are three kinds of people: the haves, the have-nots, and the have-not-paid-for-what-they-haves.
>
> **Earl Wilson**
> American columnist

 Your JOURNAL How does knowing you're in charge of your money change your perspective of your financial future?

_____

_____

_____

REMEMBER THIS Add a ✓ next to the completed learning objective below.

○ You can describe how avoiding debt can lead to financial freedom and hope.

○ You understand that personal finance is 20% head knowledge and 80% behavior.

THIS LESSON MAKES ME FEEL Circle your response to what you learned.

 CONFUSED   SURPRISED   THOUGHTFUL   CONFIDENT

LESSON VIDEO GUIDE

It doesn't take a lot of income to become a millionaire if you start investing early and if you are steady.

—Dave Ramsey

GUIDED NOTES   While you watch the video, complete the section below.

1. Two measures of wealth: income and _____.

2. Your net worth is what you _____ minus what you owe.

3. A negative net worth is when you _____ more than you own.

4. You want a high income, but it is more _____ to have a high net worth.

ANALYZE AND REFLECT   After you watch the video, respond to the question(s) below.

1. Write down one goal that you set and then successfully accomplished in your life. How did you accomplish it?

    _____

    _____

    _____

2. What are some future goals you have for your life?

    _____

    _____

    _____

LEARNING OBJECTIVES

- Understand the basics of building a financial plan.
- Identify assets and liabilities to be able to calculate a person's net worth.
- Develop short-, medium-, and long-term financial goals.

MAIN IDEA

If you want to win with money, you need to know how much money you have to work with, where you want to get to, and then create a plan to get there.

Building a Financial Plan

Now that you've learned some solid money principles, it's time to create your **financial plan**. Everyone—no matter how old they are or how much money they have—needs a clear picture of their personal finances so they can reach their money goals. To do that, you need to know where you stand financially, how much income you have to work with, what goals you want to set, and how you'll reach those goals. Your financial plan will guide your money decisions.

Net Worth

When it comes to money, your personal **net worth** will show you where you are financially. It's a starting point for your financial plan. Here's how to determine your net worth:

- Calculate your **assets**. This is the total value of everything you own such as a car, house, jewelry, and money in savings and investments.
- Calculate your **liabilities**. This is the total of all your debt, such as balances on credit cards, student loans, personal loans, car loans, and home mortgages.

To calculate your net worth, simply subtract what you owe (liabilities) from what you own (assets). If the value of your assets is greater than your liabilities, you'll have a **positive net worth**! If the amount of your liabilities is larger than the value of your assets, you'll have a **negative net worth**. You may not own much right now, but you're probably not in debt either. Keep it that way and build your net worth without debt!

> **Net worth is what you own minus what you owe.**
>
> — *Chris Hogan*

Your Income

Once you have your starting point with your net worth, you need to know how much money you can put toward your goals. You'll need to:

- Calculate your **net income**. That's the money you bring home after taxes are taken out. This includes *all* sources of income and ways you get money.

Financial Plan: a plan of action that allows a person to meet not only their immediate needs but also their long-term goals

Net Worth: the amount by which the value of a person's assets exceeds or falls behind the value of their liabilities

Asset: anything that is owned by an individual, including money in the bank or investments

Liability: financial debts or obligations

Definitions continued on the next page

Positive Net Worth: the dollar value of a person's assets is greater than the dollar value of their liabilities

Negative Net Worth: the dollar value of a person's liabilities is larger than the value of their assets

Net Income: what a person earns after payroll taxes and other deductions are taken out; often referred to as take-home pay

Expense: the cost of goods or services; money paid out

- Calculate your **expenses**. This is what you spend money on each month, such as your bills and any debt payments.

The income you have left after paying your expenses determines how quickly you'll reach your money goals. The more money you have, the faster your progress. But if you don't have enough money to cover your expenses, you'll need to increase your income or cut your spending.

Setting Solid Financial Goals

Now you're ready to start setting money goals. A lot of people have good intentions about their money, but they rarely follow through. That's why you need crystal-clear, actionable goals that are:

- *Specific:* Don't say, *I'm going to save for a car.* Have an amount in mind. Say, *I'm going to save $4,000 for a car.*
- *Measurable:* Break your big goal into smaller chunks (daily, weekly, or monthly). If you want to save $4,000 for

a car, plan to save $500 a month for eight months or $250 a month for 16 months.

- *Time-Sensitive:* If your goal has no deadline, you'll get discouraged or distracted. Plan to accomplish your goals by a specific date.
- *Yours:* These must be your goals, not someone else's. You can get input about your goals from people you trust, but ultimately, you need to choose goals you're passionate about.
- *Written:* You need to write down your goals, including all the steps it will take for you to reach them. A written goal provides clarity and serves as a powerful reminder to keep you on track. A written goal keeps you accountable.

Double-check your money goals with these three questions:

1. Are these your personal goals?
2. Who will hold you accountable?
3. What specific steps are needed for you to achieve your money goals?

3 TYPES OF *Financial Goals*

A good financial plan includes a mix of short-, medium-, and long-term goals.

SHORT-TERM
takes up to two years to reach

MEDIUM-TERM
takes two to five years to reach

LONG-TERM
takes longer than five years to reach

Goals keep you focused!

| 0 years | 1 | 2 | 3 | 4 | 5 | 6 |

Developing a Money Plan

So, why are we talking about creating a financial plan before you've even learned money basics like budgeting and saving? Great question! Like the money principles we talked about in Lesson 3, your financial plan is a big-picture framework for all of the money skills you're going to learn in this course.

Without that framework, there's not much point to budgeting, is there? It's just another skill to learn—and potentially forget. But when you have a solid money philosophy pointing you in the right direction, those money skills become a real game changer, now and in your future!

In the next lesson, we're going to take this framework to the next level, and you'll learn about a simple, proven action plan you can start following right now. We call it **The Five Foundations**.

A financial plan is your map to get from where you are to where you want to be with your money.

— Dave Ramsey

Is all of this starting to come together for you? With solid money principles, a financial plan with money goals, and proven money practices for your personal finances,

You can win with money!

Did You Know?

The top three financial concerns of teens:[18]

47%
Paying for college

45%
Not being able to live on their own

43%
Paying taxes

 Your JOURNAL What are some action steps you can take now that will put you on a path to win with money?

_____

_____

_____

REMEMBER THIS Add a ✓ next to each completed learning objective below.

○ You understand the basics of building a financial plan.

○ You can explain how to calculate net worth.

○ You know how to develop short-, medium-, and long-term financial goals.

THIS LESSON MAKES ME FEEL Circle your response to what you learned.

 CONFUSED   SURPRISED   THOUGHTFUL   CONFIDENT

LESSON VIDEO GUIDE

YOU have the choice of what kind of person you're going to become. —Dave Ramsey

GUIDED NOTES While you watch the video, complete the section below.

1. The First Foundation: Save _____ for an emergency fund.

2. The Second Foundation: Get out of debt and _____ out of debt.

3. The Third Foundation: Pay _____ for your car.

4. The Fourth Foundation: Pay cash for _____.

5. The Fifth Foundation: Build wealth and be outrageously _____.

6. Generosity is not just about giving money, it's a _____ quality.

7. Being generous means you are ready to give _____ of something than is expected.

ANALYZE AND REFLECT After you watch the video, respond to the question(s) below.

1. How will following The Five Foundations help you start your financial future off right?

_____

_____

_____

The Five Foundations

Dave Ramsey has taught millions of people how to manage their money for more than 30 years. **The Five Foundations** are based on his teachings—with a few changes to make them useful for high school students.

Like the money principles we covered, The Five Foundations probably don't sound like most of the financial advice you've heard before. That's okay. You already know that normal in America is broke—and you don't want to be normal. To make the most progress, it's important to follow these in order:

THE FIRST FOUNDATION
Save a $500 emergency fund.

THE SECOND FOUNDATION
Get out and stay out of debt.

THE THIRD FOUNDATION
Pay cash for your car.

THE FOURTH FOUNDATION
Pay cash for college.

THE FIFTH FOUNDATION
Build wealth and give.

Get Started Now

If you don't already have $500 saved for an emergency fund, that's your First Foundation. Start saving part of your income or come up with a way to earn some extra money—yep, get a job! Throw all your extra money toward your goal to get $500 in the bank and knock this step out as fast as you can. Why? Because emergencies are going to happen, so you need to be prepared.

> **The caliber of your future is determined by the choices you make today.**
> — *Anthony O'Neal*

After putting $500 in the bank, it's time for The Second Foundation: Get out of debt. Don't have any debt? Great! Make the decision that debt will never be a part of your money plan. That's one of the most important money principles you can live by. If you do have debt—maybe a car loan or money you owe a friend or family member—don't let it hang over you any longer. Pay it off!

Words of Wisdom

You should have an emergency fund because unexpected things are going to happen.

Smart people have known this for centuries and used to say, "In the house of the wise are stores of choice food and oil, but a foolish man devours all he has" (Proverbs 21:20).

In other words, having some money saved up can turn a crisis into an inconvenience.

The Third Foundation is to save up and pay cash for your car. Yes! You heard that right—pay cash for a car. No loans and no leases. Ever. Remember, you're not going into debt for anything.

Saving money for college is The Fourth Foundation. We're not talking about saving up extra spending money. We're talking about paying for your entire college education with cash. There are plenty of ways to graduate debt-free. You just have to be willing to work hard to reach that goal.

Finally, you'll be ready for The Fifth Foundation: Build wealth and give. The Fifth Foundation is the ultimate financial goal, and it's where you're headed!

The Path Forward

You'll see **The Five Foundations** a lot in this course. Following them will save you from learning some big money lessons the hard (and expensive) way. These money principles will act as your guardrails to keep you on course with your financial action plan.

Here's a Tip:

Don't freak out when you read The Fourth Foundation. Chapter 7 is all about how to go to college and graduate debt-free.

Remember: Your financial future will be determined by your choices. The Five Foundations aren't always easy to live by, but they'll set you up to win with money if you choose to follow them.

Down the Road

When you're out of school, working full time, and no longer depend financially on your parents, you'll begin a different action plan for your money called the 7 Baby Steps. They're similar to The Five Foundations, with a few differences to help adults win with money.

For example, with the 7 Baby Steps, instead of a $500 emergency fund, you'll save $1,000 and then work up to saving 3–6 months of your living expenses. That's super important as an adult because there are so many unknowns that can impact your finances. The COVID-19 pandemic caused a lot of American workers to lose their jobs in 2020. That's just one reason why having an emergency fund is such an important part of your financial plan.

Take Time to Be *Generous*

SOMETIMES, in our fast-paced world, we can become so focused on ourselves that we forget we're a part of a larger local, national, and global community. What does it mean to be a member of a community? More than just having a shared locality (region, nation, or planet), community refers to a feeling of fellowship with others, which comes from sharing common interests, challenges, and goals. Empathy and a desire to help those in need come naturally when we feel connected with others. When you think about it, being a member of a community comes with both privileges and responsibilities. Find ways to get involved in your community: Volunteer at a charity you really care about, become a mentor and friend to a kid in need, or regularly visit with a person in a nursing home. Be generous with your time.

Like The Five Foundations, the 7 Baby Steps provide a clear path to get you where you want to be financially. They'll serve as a guide for the rest of your life—a guide that's worked for millions of people. The best part? Since you're starting with The Five Foundations, you'll already be ahead of the game when you move into the 7 Baby Steps as an adult.

Financial Literacy

All of this talk about money principles, goals, and Foundations may feel like a lot right now. The idea of saving a $500 emergency fund may seem impossible—and what does it even mean to build wealth for the future?

Well, that's why you're in this **financial literacy** course—to learn, understand, and apply the skills, words, and concepts that will help you make wise decisions with your money. No one is born with this financial knowledge—everyone has to learn it.

The problem isn't really that we don't know what to do—we choose not to do it.

— Dave Ramsey

We'll cover it all, from big-picture personal finance concepts to the language of finances. That way, you can talk with financial professionals about your money and know when they're trying to make a deal that's good for their finances, not yours. And you'll learn the skills you need to reach your money goals, starting with your $500 emergency fund all the way to a million-dollar retirement.

> Money is a guarantee that we may have what we want in the future. Though we need nothing at the moment, it insures the possibility of satisfying a new desire when it arises.
>
> **Aristotle**
> Greek philosopher

Financial Literacy: the knowledge and skill base necessary for people to be informed consumers and manage their finances effectively

---

Your JOURNAL

How can each of The Five Foundations help you make wise decisions with your money?

_____

_____

_____

REMEMBER THIS   Add a ✓ next to the completed learning objective below.

◯ You can explain how The Five Foundations provide a personal financial action plan.

◯ You can describe what it means to be financially literate.

THIS LESSON MAKES ME FEEL   Circle your response to what you learned.

😓 CONFUSED   😮 SURPRISED   🙂 THOUGHTFUL   🤩 CONFIDENT

LESSON VIDEO GUIDE

Being aware of whether you are a saver or a spender allows you to take control of your money.

—*Rachel Cruze*

GUIDED NOTES   While you watch the video, complete the section below.

1. We all have _____ personalities.

2. When it comes to money, you are either a _____ or a saver.

3. Neither one is right or _____.

4. It's important that you _____ your money personality.

ANALYZE AND REFLECT   After you watch the video, respond to the question(s) below.

1. Are you a spender or a saver? Give an example of a situation where you exhibit the behavior of your money personality.

_____

_____

_____

2. Identify at least three reasons why knowing your money personality will benefit you.

_____

_____

_____

LEARNING OBJECTIVES

- Understand that your money personality will impact how you handle money.
- Recognize how to talk about and handle money as a single adult and in marriage.

MAIN IDEA

Whether you're a saver or spender, you need to learn how to manage your money and how to talk about it with others.

Your Money Personality

Money and relationships go hand in hand, which means the way you handle your money affects everyone around you. Whether you save, overspend, give, or borrow from friends, people notice. We're not kidding when we say all your relationships will be influenced by how you handle money. No pressure, right?

While you probably still depend on the adults in your life, you're developing your own money personality. You may have a lighthearted view of money. Or thinking about money may make you feel stressed or anxious. You could be naturally good at saving or carefree about spending.

We're all wired differently, but generally people identify with one of two main money personalities: saver or spender. If security and structure are important to you, you're more likely to be a saver. If you tend to be spontaneous, you're more likely to be a spender.

There are positives and negatives for both money personalities. On the positive side, savers generally take fewer risks with their money and are more likely to have a plan to save money for their retirement.

But one negative is that savers can be so strict with their money that they never spend any of it.

> ## We all have to work on our money skills.
> — Dave Ramsey

Spenders don't have that problem. They love to spend money on new experiences and enjoy the things they buy, which is a positive. However, they generally don't think about the future or save money for retirement, and that's a big negative. Also, if they're not careful, they can overspend easily.

Knowing your money personality—saver or spender—can help you create a financial plan that plays up your strengths and helps balance your weaknesses.

Talking About Money

When you talk to others about money—especially family members—it's important to consider their money personality and values too.

Did You Know?

54% of teens said their parents were always worried about money.[19]

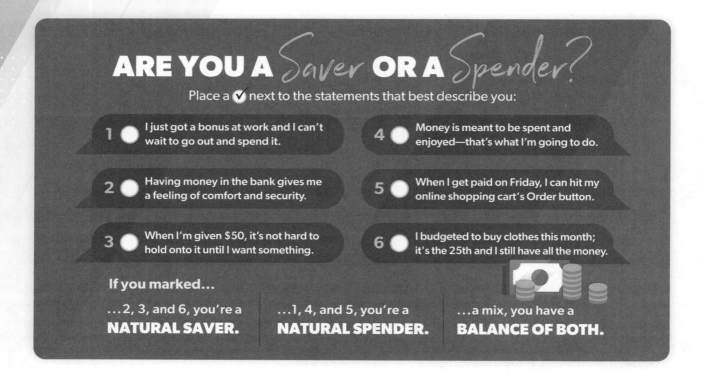

ARE YOU A *Saver* **OR A** *Spender?*

Place a ✔ next to the statements that best describe you:

1 ○ I just got a bonus at work and I can't wait to go out and spend it.

2 ○ Having money in the bank gives me a feeling of comfort and security.

3 ○ When I'm given $50, it's not hard to hold onto it until I want something.

4 ○ Money is meant to be spent and enjoyed—that's what I'm going to do.

5 ○ When I get paid on Friday, I can hit my online shopping cart's Order button.

6 ○ I budgeted to buy clothes this month; it's the 25th and I still have all the money.

If you marked...

...2, 3, and 6, you're a **NATURAL SAVER.**

...1, 4, and 5, you're a **NATURAL SPENDER.**

...a mix, you have a **BALANCE OF BOTH.**

Talking about money with your parents can be really uncomfortable. Here are some guidelines to help you communicate better:

- ***Pick the right time and place.*** Starting a conversation about money with your mom or dad two minutes before they need to leave for work is not ideal. Leave plenty of time for both of you to have a relaxed and complete conversation.

- ***Be honest.*** When it comes to money and relationships, honesty is the key. Share your thoughts and listen to theirs. Ask questions if you don't understand.

- ***Seek counsel.*** One of the best ways to avoid costly mistakes is to get advice from an adult you trust. They might not always give you the answer you want to hear, but they'll always have your best interests at heart.

- ***Share your goals.*** Share your money goals with an adult you trust and ask them to hold you accountable and encourage you along the way.

Did You Know?

39% of teens said their parents never or rarely (less than once a month) or never discussed financial topics with them.[20]

Managing Money

It won't be long before you're managing your own budget and paying your own bills. Balancing your financial obligations with your money goals can be challenging. But with the right approach, you can totally do this!

AS A SINGLE ADULT

Young singles who are in college or just starting a career tend to pour all of their time and energy into school or work. It's easy to let your busy life distract you from managing your bank account or creating and sticking to a monthly budget. Even when you're busy, managing your money must remain a priority.

Beware of impulse buying—you know, buying something as soon as you see it. It usually happens when you're stressed or when the I-owe-it-to-myself syndrome kicks in. With no one's opinion or input to worry about, single adults can rationalize almost any expense. It's up to you to stay financially disciplined!

Develop an accountability relationship with someone you trust and can talk to about major purchases and your budget. Accountability friends must love you enough to be brutally honest and promise to do so for your own good.

> ## When you understand how you're wired, it affects your money and relationships.
> — Rachel Cruze

AS A MARRIED COUPLE

If you think managing money is difficult on your own, it's even more complicated when you get married. And when you start adding kids to the mix, it can get crazy! A sad reality is that money fights between husbands and wives are a leading cause of divorce in America.[21] The best time to discuss your money values and goals is before you get married to make sure you're both on the same page.

So, who should be in charge of the financial decision-making in a marriage? That's not a trick question. Both spouses need to decide how they're going to manage their money—together. Although one person might have a natural gift for budgeting, the decision-making has to be done together. Teamwork makes the dream work—especially with family finances and money goals! Consistency and communication help too.

Did You Know?
94% of couples with great marriages discuss their money goals and dreams together.[22]

Your JOURNAL

Why is it important to understand if you're more of a natural saver or a natural spender?

_____

_____

_____

REMEMBER THIS   Add a ✓ next to each completed learning objective below.

○ You can identify your money personality and explain how you interact with money.

○ You recognize how to talk about money and how to handle money both as a single adult and as part of a married couple.

THIS LESSON MAKES ME FEEL   Circle your response to what you learned.

😓 **CONFUSED**   😮 **SURPRISED**   🙂 **THOUGHTFUL**   🤩 **CONFIDENT**

Chapter 1 Review

Personal Finance	Interest Rate	Net Worth	Negative Net Worth
Consumer	Loan Shark	Asset	Net Income
Debt	Interest	Liability	Expense
Paycheck to Paycheck	Financial Plan	Positive Net Worth	Financial Literacy
Credit			

1. Having a(n) _____ means the amount of your liabilities is larger than the value of your assets.

2. _____ means having the knowledge and skills to manage your personal finances.

3. As a(n) _____, it's up to you to make choices about what you buy and use.

4. _____ is a fee charged for using borrowed money for a purchase.

5. American culture and businesses have convinced consumers that using _____ is normal.

6. _____ relates to all of the different money decisions you make each day.

7. Knowing your _____ is the starting point for a financial plan.

8. A(n) _____ is anything you own that has value.

FINISH THE SENTENCE   Use what you've learned in this chapter to complete these sentences.

1. When talking about personal finances, Dave Ramsey says, "You will either manage your money or the lack of it will _____ _____."

2. When it comes to your money goals, in order to have clarity and a powerful reminder to keep you on track, you need to _____ _____.

1. The percentage of Americans who are living paycheck to paycheck is almost . . .

    A. 60%   C. 80%

    B. 70%   D. 90%

2. Personal finance is 20% head knowledge about money. What's the other 80%?

    A. Cash in the bank   C. Experience

    B. Behavior   D. Relationships

3. Living on less than you make means not . . .

    A. Buying a car at 16 years old

    B. Going to college after high school

    C. Budgeting to eat out with friends

    D. Spending all of your money

4. The total student loan debt owed in the U.S. is currently about how much?

    A. $1.5 million   C. $1.5 trillion

    B. $1.5 billion   D. $1.5 quadrillion

5. Almost half of all Americans report having less than _____ in savings.

    A. $500   C. $5,000

    B. $1,000   D. $10,000

6. The Five Foundations provide a simple _____ to help you win with money.

    A. Action plan   C. Suggestion

    B. Guide for investing D. Educational course

Review **QUESTION**   List The Five Foundations in order. Explain how they can help you make wise choices with your money.

_____

_____

_____

_____

_____

_____

Give Every Dollar a Name!

Budgeting Basics

This chapter dives into why budgeting is key to taking control of your money—and how you can get started right now.

The Benefits of Budgeting

LESSON VIDEO GUIDE

You are going to have to handle money. So you can choose to handle it well, or not so well.

— *Rachel Cruze*

GUIDED NOTES   While you watch the video, complete the section below.

1. A budget is a _____ for your money.

2. Your budget gives you _____ to spend.

3. Money _____ in two ways: in and out.

4. Money flows out in three ways: Giving, Saving, and _____.

5. 95% of people agree that budgeting is _____.

6. Only _____ of people do a budget every month.

ANALYZE AND REFLECT   After you watch the video, respond to the question(s) below.

1. What are some benefits of learning to budget now? What are some financial and emotional consequences you might face later if you don't start budgeting?

   _____

   _____

   _____

   _____

LEARNING OBJECTIVE

Understand the purpose and importance of budgeting as part of your personal financial plan.

MAIN IDEA

Your biggest wealth-building tool is your income—and the best way to make the most of your income is to create and stick to a monthly budget.

The Purpose of a Budget

Think about the last time you got money from your job or as a gift. You probably had a lot of ideas for how to spend it, right? Maybe you planned a date night at the movies, a trip to the nail salon, or pizza with your friends. Maybe you needed to pay for some essentials like getting the oil changed in your car or buying a new pair of sneakers.

But then, you stopped at the coffee shop for a mocha on the way to school, ordered the latest video game on your break at work, and went to the basketball game with your friends on Friday night. In the meantime, your car was still waiting for that oil change, and your new shoes—they're still at the store. Your plans for a big date night, a shiny manicure, or pizza with your friends faded away as fast as your money!

It's no fun running out of money before you get to spend it on the things you need or want. No fun at all! That's why it's so important to use a budget—so you're in control of your money, and you don't have to wonder where it all went.

What Is a Budget?

A **budget** is a plan for how you spend your money. And it's not just for adults with full-time jobs—it's for you too. Even if you don't have a lot of money right now or if you're just making minimum wage, you still need to have a plan for how you're going to spend your money every month. You need a budget!

This is your wealth we're talking about here! Get excited! Make those dollars dance!

— Dave Ramsey

Money flows two ways: in and out. A budget simply shows you what your income is (the money coming in) and what your expenses are (the money going out) for a set period of time. A good budget also breaks down your income and spending into specific categories so you know exactly where your money comes from and where you plan to spend it.

Budget: a written plan for giving, saving, and spending

There are plenty of ways to get ahead. The first is so basic I'm almost embarrassed to say it: Spend less than you earn.

Paul Clitheroe
Australian financial advisor

Only 35% of Americans budget **BUT** 95% of Americans say **BUDGETING IS IMPORTANT**[1]

IT'S NOT A *KNOWLEDGE* PROBLEM!

Budgeting Provides Freedom

A budget is one of those things that most people know they should do, but few of them actually create and stick to a budget—as you can see in the graphic above. So, what's the deal?

The truth is, a budget doesn't *limit* your freedom—it *gives* you freedom to spend money on what you want.
— *Rachel Cruze*

A lot of people don't budget because they think it will keep them from having fun with their money. But a budget doesn't tell you not to spend—it gives you permission to spend!

Here's how: When you create your budget at the beginning of the month, you'll know exactly what you can afford. You'll tell your money where to go—whether it's to pay for gas, trips to the coffee shop, or your cell phone bill—because you're in control. That's the whole purpose of a budget! You don't have to worry if you can pay your bill at the restaurant with your friends or if you'll be able to make your car insurance payment. Your budget already knows! You just need to stick to it.

Creating a budget sounds pretty simple, right? It really is. We've already talked about personal finance being 20% head knowledge and 80% behavior. So, no, you don't have to be a financial expert to create and live on a budget—but you do have to put in the effort to make budgeting a habit!

Did You Know?

Students who have taken a personal finance course report higher confidence than students who did not when it comes to:

95% Budgeting

87% Investing

94% Saving[2]

Winning With Money

Your biggest wealth-building tool is your income—and the best way to make the most of your income is to create and stick to a monthly budget. That's why our first money principle is to always have a budget. It's the key to making all your financial goals a reality—like saving, paying off debt (if you have it) and, one day, building wealth for retirement.

Plus, if you've ever wanted to be generous with your money—to help out a friend, donate to a charity, or give something to your church—but weren't sure if you could, your budget also gives you permission to support causes that are important to you.

Research shows that nearly half of Americans (46%) say their personal debt level creates stress and makes them anxious. Yet 33% of those without debt say they never worry about their finances. [3] The difference is often the budget—getting on a budget and sticking to a budget.

We're not kidding when we tell you that budgeting can change your entire financial outlook—even right now when you don't have a ton of money to budget. That's actually when a budget can have the most impact.

Don't worry if you've got no idea how to get started creating a budget—we'll show you the way. Every journey begins with the first step. That may sound cliché, but it's true. In the rest of this chapter, we'll introduce you to everything that goes into a budget and the most effective way to budget your money each month.

You've got this!

Did You Know?

Nearly 80% of students who complete a personal finance course create a monthly budget for their money. [4]

 Your JOURNAL How does having a monthly budget help you achieve your money goals?

_____

_____

_____

REMEMBER THIS Add a ✓ next to the completed learning objective below.

○ You understand the purpose and importance of budgeting as part of your personal financial plan.

THIS LESSON MAKES ME FEEL Circle your response to what you learned.

 CONFUSED   SURPRISED   THOUGHTFUL   CONFIDENT

LESSON VIDEO GUIDE

The more organized your budget is, the better it will work for you. — *Rachel Cruze*

GUIDED NOTES   While you watch the video, complete the section below.

1. The first component of a budget is _____.

2. The second component is _____.

3. The third component is _____.

4. The fourth component is _____.

5. The way you break up your _____ is up to you.

6. Your income, savings, and _____ can also have categories.

7. Find creative ways to be _____ with your time and money.

ANALYZE AND REFLECT   After you watch the video, respond to the question(s) below.

1. The way you use your money reveals your true priorities. Knowing that, how could having budget categories help you prioritize your money?

   _____

   _____

   _____

MAIN IDEA

Once you understand what goes into a budget and how different expenses work, you'll be ready to create your own budget.

Basic Budget Components

Now you know what a budget is, what it's for, and that everyone needs a plan for how they spend their money. You also know it's a simple habit a lot of people avoid—but it's so worth the effort!

Before you dive in and create your own budget for your money, you need to know what goes into one. Don't worry, it's not complicated.

The Four Parts of a Budget

Every budget starts with four basic parts: income, giving, saving, and spending.

Your **income** is any money you earn or receive as a gift. So, if you have a part-time job, your paycheck is considered income. When your birthday rolls around or you get cash for a graduation gift, that's considered income too, because it's money coming in.

The other parts of a budget—giving, saving, and spending—are expenses or money that's going out.

- Giving is the first priority in your budget. This is where you decide how you'll be generous with the money you have.
- Saving, your next priority, is the part of your budget where you set aside money for your savings goals.
- Spending includes everything else you spend money on, like bills, food, gas—you get the idea.

> **If you will happen to your money, then you'll have some. If you just let all your money happen to you, then you'll never win.**
> — Dave Ramsey

To keep your budget on track, you'll need to break your budget down even further into separate categories. All that means is, if you have more than one source of income—like your after-school job and a babysitting gig—list them separately.

Then, when it comes to your expenses, break them down into as many categories as you need. For example, transportation is a spending category that could include money for both gas and oil changes for your

Did You Know?

The most common budget categories for using cash are:
- Groceries
- Restaurants
- Gas
- Entertainment
- Personal

Income: money received for work, as a gift, or through investments

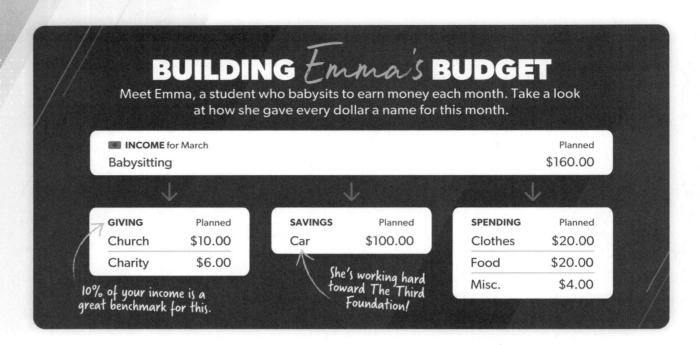

BUILDING *Emma's* BUDGET

Meet Emma, a student who babysits to earn money each month. Take a look at how she gave every dollar a name for this month.

💳 INCOME for March	Planned
Babysitting	$160.00

GIVING	Planned
Church	$10.00
Charity	$6.00

10% of your income is a great benchmark for this.

SAVINGS	Planned
Car	$100.00

She's working hard toward The Third Foundation!

SPENDING	Planned
Clothes	$20.00
Food	$20.00
Misc.	$4.00

Fixed Expense: expense that remains the same from month to month

Variable Expense: expense that varies in dollar amount from month to month, but that you can expect to have every month

Intermittent Expense: expense that occurs at various times throughout the year and tends to be in large, lump sums

Definitions continued on next page

car. Just list those expenses separately too. Check out how Emma, a typical sophomore, used these categories to create her budget in the example above.

Why go to all that trouble? Detailed categories will help you make better spending decisions. When you're running low in one category, you'll know to slow down your spending. Then, when you're out of money in a category—that's it! No more spending in that category.

Don't get hung up on the number of categories you have—or don't have. Start by writing down where you're spending your money. It's the first step in taking control of your money and telling it what to do.

Four Types of Expenses

It only takes a couple of months of budgeting to see that your expenses don't all work the same way. And that really becomes obvious once you're on your own and start adding expenses like rent and groceries.

Here's what we mean. Rent is an expense you pay once a month, and it's the same amount every month. That makes it a **fixed expense**. You also pay your electric bill once a month, but the amount varies from month to month. That makes it a **variable expense**. Groceries and gas are also variable expenses.

Intermittent expenses come up at certain times of the year—like when you buy a yearbook or pay your car insurance premium four times a year.

Then there are **discretionary** (or **non-essential) expenses** that are wants—not needs. And they can be fixed, variable or intermittent. Eating out at restaurants (a variable expense) or an online gaming subscription (a fixed expense) are good examples of discretionary expenses.

While it's important to know the different types of expenses, it's more important to make room for them in your budget. Some of your numbers will be rock solid, and some will be estimates—and that's okay. It's one more reason to take your time and really think through all the ways you spend money each month.

The Importance of Giving

We talked a lot about how your budget helps you make good saving and spending decisions. But don't forget: Your budget helps you decide how to be generous with your money too.

Giving something that seems small to you could be something big to the person you help and bless.

— Anthony O'Neal

Giving is your first priority in your budget—even before you set aside money to save. Why? Simple—when you approach your money in a spirit of generosity, you're more grateful and content with what you have. Contentment naturally leads you to serve and help others.

Whatever your income might be, set aside 10% to give to those less fortunate than you are. That can be done through a charity, a nonprofit organization, or even a church. Ten percent might seem like a lot, especially if you don't make a lot of money. But living off of 90% of your income is not much different than living off of 100%. And what might seem like a small amount of money to you can make a big difference to someone else.

Make giving a part of your budget starting today. You'll set yourself up for a lifelong habit of generosity. As you have more money, you'll be able to give more. And you'll discover another one of the secrets about money: Giving truly is the most fun you'll ever have with money!

Discretionary (Nonessential) Expense: expense for things you don't need

---

Your JOURNAL

What is the most common type of expense you have in your life right now?

_____

_____

_____

REMEMBER THIS   Add a ✓ next to the completed learning objective below.

○ You can identify the basic components of a budget, sources of income, and the four different types of expenses.

THIS LESSON MAKES ME FEEL   (Circle) your response to what you learned.

 CONFUSED   SURPRISED   THOUGHTFUL   CONFIDENT

LESSON VIDEO GUIDE

People who are successful in life work hard and are intentional with their money.

— Rachel Cruze

GUIDED NOTES   While you watch the video, complete the section below.

1. A zero-based budget is when your income minus your giving, saving, and spending equals _____.

2. Prioritize your _____: shelter, utilities, transportation, and food.

3. A zero-based budget does not mean zero dollars in your _____ account.

4. The best kind of budget is a _____ budget.

5. Make sure you have a miscellaneous _____.

6. Use a budgeting app that works for _____.

ANALYZE AND REFLECT   After you watch the video, respond to the question(s) below.

1. You need to give every dollar a name. Why is this important? What might happen if you don't have a plan for every dollar you make?

   _____

   _____

   _____

LEARNING OBJECTIVE

Define *zero-based budget* and understand why it is the most effective way to budget.

MAIN IDEA

A zero-based budget helps you be intentional in paying your bills and planning for spending—and it helps you reach your financial goals.

Not All Budgets Are Effective

Budgeting really is a simple process. But if you're going to take the time to do it, you want it to actually work, right?

You could budget a lot of different ways. But the best way—the one that will make the most of every dollar you have—is the **zero-based budget**. All that means is, you want your income minus your expenses to equal zero. That doesn't mean you don't end up with any money! It means you're giving every dollar you make a job to do—whether it's giving, saving, or spending.

When you give every dollar a job to do in your budget, you're not just making sure your bills are covered or you have enough set aside for shopping. You're being intentional about reaching the goals you set in your financial plan.

And you don't have to make a lot of money to start working toward your goals. You can start making real progress today on **The Five Foundations**! Saving an emergency fund, paying cash for a car, and paying cash for college are doable goals. A zero-based budget is the perfect place to start because it will help you stretch your money as far as it will go!

Create a Zero-Based Budget

You can create your zero-based budget in just a few steps. And you have plenty of options for how you do it. You can start with pencil and paper—super old-school. If you like working with spreadsheets, awesome! Go for it. Budgeting apps on your phone are also a great choice. They do the math for you and are super convenient when you need to do a quick check on your spending or track an expense (we'll talk more about that in the next lesson).

> **When your income minus your expenses equals zero, you know for sure you've accounted for every dollar.**
> — Rachel Cruze

Bottom line, the best method for budgeting is the one you feel most comfortable with and the one you will use. It really doesn't matter where or how you budget as long as you do it! So, what are you waiting for? Let's get started!

Zero-Based Budget: a cash-flow plan that assigns an expense to every dollar of your income; the goal is for the total income minus the total expenses to equal zero

The Five Foundations:

 Save a $500 emergency fund.

 Get out and stay out of debt.

 Pay cash for your car.

 Pay cash for college.

 Build wealth and give.

LET'S BUILD *Your* BUDGET

1 ADD UP YOUR MONTHLY INCOME.

Write down your planned monthly **net income** (or your take-home pay). Remember, that's any money you earn or receive during the month. This is how much you can spend for the month. Simple!

📷 INCOME	Planned
Total	

2 WRITE DOWN EVERY EXPENSE.

Start with giving, then savings. Your budgeted savings should take into account your short-, medium-, and long-term savings goals. Then, list all remaining planned expenses in order of priority—essentials like your cell phone bill first and nonessential expenses last.

Leave a little room in your budget for unexpected expenses. This shouldn't be much—aim for 5–10% of your income. This miscellaneous category comes in handy for those moments when you realize you forgot to buy your cousin a birthday gift or you didn't budget money for a school field trip. If you don't use all the money in this category, put it toward one of your savings goals.

Remember, your budget gives you permission to spend your money on things you want. So, leave some room for fun after the essentials are covered!

🏠 EXPENSES	Planned
Giving	
Saving	
Spending	
Total	

3 SUBTRACT YOUR EXPENSES FROM YOUR INCOME TO EQUAL ZERO.

Don't be surprised if your income and expenses don't balance out right away. That just means you need to adjust how much money you're budgeting in your categories until the bottom line comes to zero. It will take a while for you to really get the hang of budgeting. Your first monthly budget may be way off, but by the third month you'll be pretty good at it—so don't give up!

📷	INCOME
− 🏠	EXPENSES
=	**$0**

41

Looking Toward the Future

After high school and college, your income and budget will change. You'll have more money, more expenses, and maybe even a spouse and family who depend on your income. Those life changes will affect your finances, your goals, and your priorities.

Learning to budget will pay off in your future.

— Anthony O'Neal

When you add expenses like rent, utilities, food, cell phone, and car insurance to your budget, it will be more important than ever to prioritize your spending well.

Giving and saving will always come first in your budget. Then, you'll focus on what's called the Four Walls: food, utilities, shelter, and transportation. With those things covered, you can focus on other goals, like getting out of debt (if you have any), saving up a full emergency fund of 3–6 months of expenses, and even saving for a down payment on a home.

Then, when you have no debt other than a mortgage, you should budget 15% of your **gross income** to invest for retirement. That's **The Fifth Foundation**!

That picture—a debt-free family who's got their bills covered, has money in the bank for emergencies, and is building wealth for the future—is completely different than the picture of the "normal" American family you saw in Chapter 1.

The simple—but powerful—zero-based budget is the secret to making all of your money goals a reality!

Net Income: what a person earns after payroll taxes and other deductions are taken out; often referred to as take-home pay

Gross Income: the amount you earn before taxes and other payroll deductions

The Fifth Foundation: Build wealth and give.

$\mathcal{Y}\text{our}$ **JOURNAL**   Why is the zero-based budget the most effective type of budget?

_____

_____

_____

REMEMBER THIS   Add a ✓ next to the completed learning objective below.

◯   You can define what a zero-based budget is and explain why it is the most effective type of budget.

THIS LESSON MAKES ME FEEL   (Circle) your response to what you learned.

 CONFUSED   SURPRISED   THOUGHTFUL   CONFIDENT

LESSON VIDEO GUIDE

You are responsible for knowing where your money is coming from and where it is going each day.

— Rachel Cruze

GUIDED NOTES

While you watch the video, complete the section below.

1. After you make a budget, you need to _____ every expense.

2. Keeping track of your expenses will help you _____ your budget.

3. A budget is never going to be a _____ process.

4. One of the best ways to track your expenses is the _____ system.

5. When you use _____, you end up spending less.

6. Don't underestimate the emotional _____ you get when using cash.

ANALYZE AND REFLECT

After you watch the video, respond to the question(s) below.

1. Tracking your money will allow you to reach your financial goals. How does tracking your expenses help you fine-tune your goals? How can you plan for unexpected expenses?

    _____

    _____

    _____

LEARNING OBJECTIVE

Understand the purpose, importance, and process of tracking your expenses to help you stick to and evaluate any needed adjustments in your budget.

MAIN IDEA

Tracking your expenses is the best way to stick to your budget and recognize if you need to make adjustments to your budget.

Successful Budgeting

You've walked through all the steps to create your budget: You've identified your income and listed out all your expenses. You added it all up, subtracted, made a few adjustments, and finally got it to zero. That's awesome!

Now what?

Creating your budget is just the first half of successful budgeting. Now that you have a budget, you need to put your budget to work and stick to it. The second half of successful budgeting is tracking your expenses to make sure you're sticking to your plan—and know where to adjust your budget when you need to. Yes! You can do that!

How to Track Your Expenses

Tracking your expenses is even simpler than creating a budget. When you spend money, just record how much you spent and subtract it from the budget category. You can instantly see how much money is still available in that category.

Sometimes you'll make a purchase that falls into more than one category.

For example, if you buy a $20 T-shirt for yourself and one as a gift for your friend at the same store, you'll need to split that transaction so that $20 comes out of your Gifts category and $20 comes out of your Clothing category.

Are you spending money on things that don't matter at the expense of things that do?

— Anthony O'Neal

The hardest part of tracking expenses is just getting into the habit. It can be a hassle to pull out a pencil and paper every time you spend money. You could also collect all your receipts each day and update your budget all at once. The most convenient way to track your expenses is with a budgeting app that connects to your bank account. Then you can digitally log each transaction into one of your categories. It's usually as simple as dragging and dropping. And no math necessary!

Did You Know?

The average household spends about $370 on groceries and $290 on dining out each month.[5]

TRACKING *Emma's* EXPENSES

Let's check in with Emma! She spent $34.32 on food, which is $14.32 more than she had budgeted for this month. It's time to adjust the budget.

SPENDING	Planned	Remaining
Clothes	$20.00	$20.00
Food	$20.00	–$14.32
Misc.	$4.00	$1.76

CLOTHES
$20.00
– $14.32
—————
$5.68

SPENDING	Planned	Remaining
Clothes	$20.00	$5.68
Food	$20.00	$0.00
Misc.	$4.00	$1.76

HERE'S WHAT SHE DID: Emma hasn't spent any of her budgeted money on clothes, so she shifted $14.32 from that category over to her food category to cover what she overspent.

What if You Go Over?

You'll have times—especially when you're new to budgeting—that you go over your budget in a category. It's not a huge deal as long as you deal with it right away.

Unless you work overtime or bring in some extra income, you'll need to adjust your budget for the month. That means you'll have to cut back on how much you planned for one category to balance out what you overspent in another. Then, when you make your budget for next month, review everything you spent.

When we fail to plan, we plan to fail—and so there is always too much month left at the end of the money.

— Dave Ramsey

If you planned to spend $100 on food this month but you've already spent $120, you'll have to move $20 from one of your other categories to cover the extra you spent. That means you'll have $20 less to spend in that category. And you won't be able to buy food again until next month.

Remember Emma from Lesson 2? In the example above, check out how tracking her expenses showed where her spending was off. When you're on top of it like Emma, you simply decide which category to cut back on. And you can make the adjustment to your budget next month so you don't go over budget again.

It might not sound like a fun thing to do, but you know what's even less fun? Running out of money because you weren't paying any attention to how much you were spending on what.

The Envelope System

For instant budgeting accountability, there's nothing like the envelope system! With it, you use cash for categories you tend to overspend on. Food, gas, entertainment, and shopping are all good categories for the envelope system.

Here's how it works: Go to the bank (weekly or monthly) and get some cash. Put the amount of cash you've budgeted for each category in its own envelope labeled with the category's name. Any time you buy something from a category, just use the cash from its envelope. Once the cash is gone, no more spending!

The envelope system has been around for a long time—mostly because it works! You can use the envelope system no matter how you choose to set up your budget. It even works well with budgeting apps.

Tracking Expenses Over Time

If you really want to dig in to how you spend money and see if it lines up with the money goals you've set, you can create a cash-flow statement. It's not the same thing as a budget, though it's easy to get them confused. While a budget is a written plan for giving, saving, and spending, a **cash-flow statement** summarizes all of your income and expenses over a certain time period. In other words, a budget tells you what *will* happen with your money while a cash-flow statement shows you what *has already* happened with your money.

Cash-flow statements are most often used in business, but you can create one to see where you're spending money so you can adjust your budget to reach your goals faster. For example, your cash-flow statement might show you that you've spent half of your income eating out over the last three months. (Oh, yeah! It's possible!) If you have any savings goals at all, you might—and by might, we mean definitely—want to adjust your spending so it matches your priorities. It's that easy!

Cash-Flow Statement: a record that summarizes all of the income and outgo (spending) over a certain time period

---

Your JOURNAL

If you notice that you're spending too much in a certain budget category, what are some things you could do to fix the shortfall?

_____

_____

_____

REMEMBER THIS   Add a ✓ next to the completed learning objective below.

○   You understand the purpose, the importance, and the process of tracking your expenses throughout the month.

THIS LESSON MAKES ME FEEL   (Circle) your response to what you learned.

 CONFUSED   SURPRISED   THOUGHTFUL   CONFIDENT

LESSON VIDEO GUIDE

When you control your money instead of your money controlling you, you will win in life.   — *Rachel Cruze*

<u>**GUIDED NOTES**</u>   While you watch the video, complete the section below.

1. You need to do a budget every single _____.

2. The first month you do your budget will be a _____, and that's okay.

3. Give your budget _____ months to start working.

4. _____ your budget with someone you trust.

5. When budgeting becomes a habit in your life, it will become easier and _____.

6. Every month is going to be _____.

<u>**ANALYZE AND REFLECT**</u>   After you watch the video, respond to the question(s) below.

1. Why is it worth the time and effort to create and fine-tune your budget and make budgeting a habit?

   _____

   _____

   _____

LEARNING OBJECTIVES
- Define irregular income.
- Develop a plan for budgeting with an irregular income.

MAIN IDEA

Budgeting is a habit you have to work at—but it's worth it even if you don't have a lot of money to budget or if you have an irregular income.

Your Monthly Budget

Now you know everything that goes into creating your own zero-based budget—and how to stick to it so all that effort literally pays off!

Budgeting isn't a "set it and forget it" activity. The budget you make for this month won't work for next month. You need to make a new budget each month before the month begins. We like to call that "on paper, on purpose." (Don't sweat the "on paper" part—using an app works just as well, maybe even better!)

Every dollar you spend is a reflection of your values.

— Rachel Cruze

Remember, it will take practice to get the hang of budgeting. The first month, you may not know how much to budget in some of your categories. You may leave some categories out completely. That's okay—just make adjustments during the month so you'll have a better starting point next month.

Simply *knowing* you should budget is very different from *doing* a budget. You've got to make budgeting a habit! And the only way to make anything a habit is to just keep doing it. But it helps if you can see some results, right?

After budgeting for a couple of months, a lot of people say they feel like they got a raise. They're able to save more, and they don't feel nearly as stressed about running out of money before their next payday. So keep at it! Unless you actually like to have more stress and less money. No? We didn't think so.

Do I Budget in High School?

Now, maybe you're wondering if you even have enough money to budget right now because you're in high school. Yes, you do!

Even if you don't have a part-time job, you might get money from your parents or get paid for odd jobs every now and then, like babysitting. Plus, you probably get money for your birthday or Christmas. You get money, so you need a budget!

You definitely *spend* money! Maybe you pay for your gas, clothes, or your cell phone bill. So, you need a budget!

Did You Know?

65% of students who took this course talked to their family about money or finances this month.[7]

The First Foundation: Save a $500 emergency fund.

Did You Know?

The average American household spends more than 90% of their annual income.[8]

Irregular Income: income that comes in at different amounts or at different times, or both

Commission: earnings based on a percentage of the sales made

Even if you have just $100 a month to budget, you want to make the most of it, right? A budget will help you do that.

As you get into the habit of monthly budgeting, don't forget to save part of your income every month. It's your second budgeting priority right after giving. In the next chapter, we'll talk more about what kinds of things to save for and how to make savings goals.

Maturity is the ability to delay gratification.

— *Dave Ramsey*

There are some pretty simple savings goals you can start budgeting for now. Think about some expenses you know will come up during the year. Birthdays and holidays don't sneak up on you—they happen the same time every year, so you can start planning for them now. Are you going to prom? Decide how much you want to spend, divide it by the number of months until prom, and build that into every budget! And don't forget about **The First Foundation**: Saving a $500 emergency fund!

That probably sounds like a lot of money—especially if you don't have a regular income. Don't worry. You can do a zero-based budget and meet your goals even with an irregular income!

What's an Irregular Income?

If you work mostly odd jobs or you have a part-time job and the number of hours you work varies from week to week—you earn what's called an **irregular income**. You get paid different amounts or at different times, or both. The same is true if you work a seasonal retail job, cut grass during the summer, or have a baking side hustle.

You're not alone! Many Americans are self-employed or work in sales on straight **commission**—making money based on a percentage of the total sales they make. That means they also deal with an irregular income.

Budgeting an irregular income can feel like you're aiming at a moving target. But it really is just as simple to plan for an irregular income as it is for a regular one.

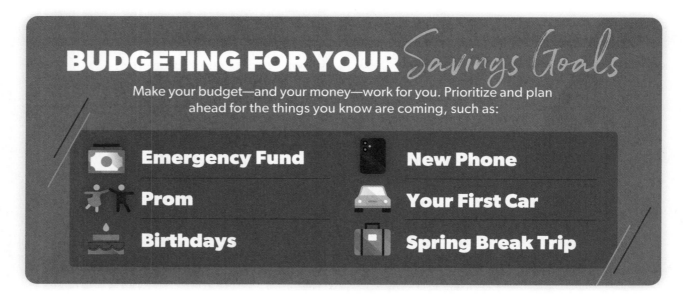

BUDGETING FOR YOUR *Savings Goals*

Make your budget—and your money—work for you. Prioritize and plan ahead for the things you know are coming, such as:

- Emergency Fund
- Prom
- Birthdays
- New Phone
- Your First Car
- Spring Break Trip

How to Budget With an Irregular Income

Budgeting when you have an irregular income starts with your expenses. Make a list of everything you'll spend money on next month—car insurance, gas, savings, weekend entertainment, clothing and anything else. Write it *all* down.

Next, prioritize your expenses, starting with the most important, and work your way down to the least important. Giving is at the top, next is saving, and then your essential expenses—any bills you're responsible for.

Then, when you get paid, you assign the money to the expenses as far as you can down the list. Anything you don't get to on your list will have to wait until the next time you get paid.

If you're not getting as far down your list as you need to, think about how you can boost your income. Can you find more odd jobs? Ask for more hours at work? Get creative and think of things you're good at that you could turn into a side hustle, like tutoring or teaching piano lessons.

If you make it all the way down your list and you have money left over—awesome! You can increase the amounts in some of the categories you have (saving more money is always a good option) or add categories. The point is for you to decide how to spend that extra money instead of letting it go to waste!

You really are in control of how much money you earn and where it goes. That's the power of a monthly budget!

Did You Know?

More than 15 million Americans are self-employed and many others work on straight commission. All of them deal with an irregular income that makes budgeting all the more important.[9]

Your JOURNAL

Why is it important to create a budget even if you don't get a lot of money or if you have an irregular income?

_____

_____

_____

REMEMBER THIS   Add a ✓ next to each completed learning objective below.

◯ You understand what it means to have an irregular income.

◯ You know that while budgeting for an irregular income involves a slightly different process, it can be done.

THIS LESSON MAKES ME FEEL   (Circle) your response to what you learned.

😟 CONFUSED   😮 SURPRISED   🙂 THOUGHTFUL   🤩 CONFIDENT

LESSON VIDEO GUIDE

Talking and communicating about money is often more valuable than money itself.

— *Rachel Cruze*

GUIDED NOTES   While you watch the video, complete the section below.

1. You will be inclined to budget one way or another way based on your money

    _____ .

2. Ask a parent or find a _____ to help keep you accountable.

3. Be _____ with yourself about your spender or saver tendencies.

ANALYZE AND REFLECT   After you watch the video, respond to the question(s) below.

1. How does your specific money personality (whether you're a saver or a spender) play into your relationships now? How will it affect your future relationships?

    _____

    _____

    _____

2. What is one way learning to budget now will affect your future?

    _____

    _____

    _____

LEARNING OBJECTIVES

- Evaluate your money personality as it relates to the task of budgeting.
- Recognize the importance of sharing money goals and budgeting in marriage.
- Understand that budgeting is a money habit that promotes financial security and a lifestyle of giving.

MAIN IDEA

Budgeting will help you reach your money goals, help you talk about money with others, and lead you to become outrageously generous.

Personality and Budgeting

Back in Chapter 1, we talked about the two types of people when it comes to money—spenders and savers.

It's probably no surprise that your money personality—a spender or a saver—can affect your attitude toward budgeting. Savers usually really like the idea of budgeting. They love having a defined plan for their money so they can save, save, save!

Spenders, on the other hand, need some convincing that budgeting is a good thing. They don't want to feel restricted about when and where they can spend their money. If that's how you're feeling right now, it's okay. You'll just need to try a little harder to give budgeting a chance to work for you.

Remember that your budget really does give you permission to spend. If you budget $100 to spend on clothes, you actually get to spend $100 on clothes— guilt- and stress-free! You can ignore that voice in the back of your head that's telling you you're getting yourself into a financial

bind. Eventually, that voice will go away completely when you're used to spending the money you budget on the things you want! Doesn't that sound great?

Making Time to Budget

To help you get into the habit of budgeting, it helps to schedule time every month to work on the next month's budget. It might sound weird to schedule time with yourself. But if you set aside a specific day and time to work on your budget, you're more likely to actually do it.

Did You Know?

The average family spends over $1,800 per year on clothing.[10]

> If we don't plan ahead, we will never get ahead. Those who stay behind get left behind.
>
> — Anthony ONeal

When you're single, whether that's now or as an adult, you call the shots about where you spend your money, when you

How to Stick With Your Budget

CONGRATS! By now you've learned how to create a zero-based budget—but you're also probably learning that it can sometimes be hard to stick to it. Check out these tips to help you stay on track.

1 KEEP IT REAL. Make sure your saving and spending goals are realistic. If you only make $300 a month, you know you won't be able to save all $300 when you've also got a cell phone bill to cover.

2 THINK WEEKLY. Break a few of your budget categories into weekly amounts. That will keep you from ending up with too much month at the end of your money.

3 CHECK YOUR SOCIAL CALENDAR. Plan for events and celebrations that are coming up.

4 LEARN TO SAY NO (OR NOT NOW). Sometimes you just need to hold off until you have enough money to do it.

5 FIND A BUDGET BUDDY. Everyone can benefit from having a friend who can keep you on track with your money goals.

spend your money, and what you spend your money on. That's a lot of freedom, but it's also a big responsibility.

Why not invite someone you trust to give you advice about your budget? A parent or someone you know who's good with money will help you make the right decisions about spending and saving. And it never hurts to have a friend hold you accountable and give you honest feedback to help you stay on track and meet the money goals you set.

Budgeting in a Marriage

When you get married, budgeting takes on a whole new kind of intensity. Both spouses have equal say in the budget, after all. So, you both need to work on it together in a Budget Committee Meeting.

That's the time both spouses decide together how they will give, save, and spend their money. And you can probably guess that your money personalities—saver

Did You Know?

94% of couples in "great" marriages say they discuss their personal finances together.[11]

or spender—will play a big part in those money conversations.

Many married couples say that one person tends to be the saver, while the other is more of a spender. One might love to do budgets, while the other likes making money decisions on the fly. One may have a long-term focus, while the other enjoys living in the moment. That's pretty normal—and it's a good thing that couples often balance each other out like that.

If you're married, there should be no such thing as my money or your money. It's our money.

— *Rachel Cruze*

But that doesn't mean it will be easy to agree on your budget without a lot of open, honest communication. In a marriage or any close relationship, you can't avoid talking about money—even when it's hard. Approach money as a team so when you win, you win together!

Budgeting for a Lifetime

For savers and spenders alike, getting the habit of budgeting down early in life will help you find—and keep—peace of mind. And once you've gotten the hang of creating a new budget each month, you'll be surprised how natural it becomes to make a plan and live according to it.

Whether you've got big plans like saving for college, dreams to start your own business one day, or hopes of retiring early, budgeting is the first step to getting your financial life on track for the future. It's how you take control of your money!

When you're in control of your money, you get to live life on your terms instead of the bank's terms. You'll have the freedom to build wealth and buy the things that are important to you—instead of the burden of sending out a big portion of your money to debt payments. And, best of all, you'll have the opportunity to live a life of outrageous generosity and be a blessing to others!

And, remember, no matter how much or how little you earn, you can start today!

What are you waiting for?

Did You Know?

Money fights are a leading cause of divorce in America.[12]

Your **JOURNAL**   How does the habit of creating a budget—and sticking to it—reflect financial maturity and responsibility?

_____

_____

_____

REMEMBER THIS   Add a ✓ next to each completed learning objective below.

○ You can evaluate your money personality and accommodate for your strengths and weaknesses through the task of budgeting.

○ You recognize the importance of sharing money goals and budgeting in marriage.

○ You understand that budgeting is a money habit that promotes financial security and a lifestyle of giving.

THIS LESSON MAKES ME FEEL   (Circle) your response to what you learned.

😓 CONFUSED   😮 SURPRISED   🙂 THOUGHTFUL   🤩 CONFIDENT

Chapter 2 Review

Budget	Variable Expense	Zero-Based Budget	Cash-Flow Statement
Income	Intermittent Expense	Net Income	Irregular Income
Fixed Expense	Discretionary Expense	Gross Income	Commission

1. Taxes and withholdings impact your _____ _____, which is the amount of money you take home on your paycheck.

2. The cost of groceries and gas is considered a(n) _____.

3. To budget with a(n) _____ _____, prioritize expenses from most to least important so your most important expenses are covered first.

4. A(n) _____ _____ needs to be evaluated in light of your other expenses for the month.

5. A(n) _____ stays the same from month to month.

6. A(n) _____ _____ should account for fixed, variable, intermittent, and discretionary expenses based on income.

FINISH THE SENTENCE   Use what you've learned in this chapter to complete these sentences.

1. A budget doesn't tell you not to spend. A budget actually _____ _____.

2. The envelope system is especially helpful for expenses like _____ _____.

3. The three priorities in your budget, after listing income, are _____ _____.

4. Specific categories are important to consider when creating a budget so you can _____ _____.

1. What is it called when you make money on the percentage of the total sales you make?

    A. Irregular income   C. Gross income

    B. Commission   D. Overtime

2. Which of the following is not a type of discretionary expense?

    A. Fixed   C. Variable

    B. Intermittent   D. Depreciation

3. What's your biggest wealth-building tool?

    A. Income   C. Savings account

    B. Investments   D. Inheritance

4. When you're creating your monthly budget, what's the first priority under "Expenses"?

    A. Saving   C. Spending

    B. Giving   D. Entertainment

5. If you approach money with a generous spirit, you'll be . . .

    A. Able to save   C. More grateful

    B. Less content   D. Free of stress

6. What will tracking expenses help you do?

    A. Stick to a budget   C. Make adjustments

    B. Catch errors   D. All of these

Review **QUESTION**   What's a zero-based budget, and why is it important?

_____

_____

_____

_____

_____

_____

Pay Yourself First.

Saving Money

This chapter emphasizes the importance of saving and explains three reasons why you should save money: emergencies, large purchases, and wealth building.

Saving Money Takes Discipline

LESSON VIDEO GUIDE

The secret to saving money is controlling the person in the mirror. —Dave Ramsey

GUIDED NOTES   While you watch the video, complete the section below.

1. What causes you to have money is you _____ some of it.

2. Murphy's Law: If it can go _____, it will.

3. Saving is _____ a part of your budget.

4. In America, nearly _____ out of 10 people live paycheck to paycheck.

5. You will have a financial _____ at some point in your life.

6. Saving gives you the freedom to be super _____ with your money.

ANALYZE AND REFLECT   After you watch the video, respond to the question(s) below.

1. Why is self-discipline the key to becoming a good saver?

    _____

    _____

2. What are some long-term consequences of not learning to save while you are young?

    _____

    _____

LEARNING OBJECTIVE

Understand the importance of saving money to avoid a variety of financial problems.

MAIN IDEA

Saving your money isn't easy, but if you start making it a priority in your money plan right now, it will make your financial life a lot easier in the future.

Are Americans Good Savers?

Picture this: You're out with friends and just finished seeing a movie or checking out that new smoothie shop. As you drop one of your friends off—*crash!*—you back into their family's mailbox. You broke the taillight on the car, and the mailbox is more horizontal than it should be.

What do you do? Well, if you don't have any money saved up, you're likely panic-texting your parents asking for help. You've just gotten a taste of how awful an emergency feels when you don't have any money to cover it.

But what if you had $500 in the bank? Sure, it stinks to see the money you saved go out the window to fix a mailbox and your taillight. But you don't have to stress—because you have an emergency fund! You've got the money for the repairs. *Phew.*

The thing is, even though people know saving is important, it isn't easy. If it were, everyone would do it. When Americans got comfortable after WWII and used debt to buy all kinds of things, they also stopped saving as much. Fast forward to today, and many Americans are *really* bad at saving money—no matter what the overall economy is doing.

A recent study shows that 39% of Americans couldn't cover a $400 financial emergency without going into debt.[1] In fact, 47% of Americans have less than $1,000 saved for an emergency.[2] That's a whole lot of people who aren't putting any money away! So, why aren't people saving more?

Debt steals your future, but saving secures your future.

— *Rachel Cruze*

Some people say, "I just bought a house," or "I have too many bills," or "I don't make enough money to save." Others think a financial emergency will never happen to them. The reality is, it's not *if* an emergency will happen—it's *when.*

Choosing Not to Save

Have you ever heard of Murphy's Law? It says that anything that can go wrong will go wrong. And when you don't make saving money a part of your financial plan, you invite Murphy to make a mess of your finances. We're talking about things like stress from unexpected expenses, living

Did You Know?

14% of Americans have $0—yes, zero—saved.[3]

Save a part of your income and begin now, for the man with a surplus controls circumstances and the man without a surplus is controlled by circumstances.

Henry Buckley
Australian politician

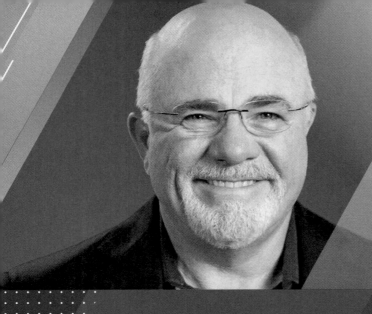

The reporter's question hung in the air for a minute while I searched for an answer: "How did you bounce back from bankruptcy?" Bounce back? Honestly, there was no bounce. Just a splat! I had made a complete mess of things while chasing the American Dream.

Of course, things were great at first. At 26, I had more than $4 million in real estate. I was driving a nice car and making an awesome salary. I was buying my wife jewelry and taking cool vacations. We were having a blast!

But it was all built on debt. I had borrowed money up to my eyeballs. And when one bank demanded I pay back all the money (because it was theirs to begin with), the others quickly followed. Before I knew it, my American Dream had become a total nightmare. We lost everything. I was so devastated—I could hardly breathe. *Scared* doesn't begin to cover it. But crushed comes close.

I worked really hard to avoid losing it all, but it wasn't enough. Finally, with a baby, a toddler, and a marriage hanging on by a thread, we signed the bankruptcy papers. I'll never forget that day: Thursday, September 22, 1988.

> ## Before I knew it, my American Dream had become a total nightmare.

You know the definition of insanity, right? Doing the same thing over and over and expecting different results. Well, that day I stopped the insanity. I had tried it my way and ended up crushed! It was time to change.

So, I went on a quest to find out how money really works. I wanted to know how to control my finances—and make sure I was the last Ramsey to ever mess up with money! I read everything I could get my hands on. I interviewed wealthy people who didn't use debt but actually made money and kept it. Eventually, my journey led me to a really uncomfortable place: my mirror.

The bad news was that the guy looking back at me had been the problem in the past. But the good news was that he would be the solution moving forward. I could change. I could learn to grow my character, control my behavior, and make smart decisions. And if I did, I would win with money.

You can make the same choices for the person you see in your mirror. I wished I'd known this information in high school. It will help you avoid a life of money nightmares and set you on the path to your American Dream. So get ready!

It's game on!

61

paycheck to paycheck, or not being able to pay your bills because of debt.

When you don't save money, you may even have to put off your dreams. Things like traveling, education, and buying a house all take money. When you have money saved, you'll be able to afford to travel, get a quality education, and build your dream home.

Not saving has many downsides. One of the worst is when people who don't save run into tough spots. And when they do, they turn to debt. But debt isn't a tool to use to make you wealthy—and it definitely isn't a replacement for cash in the bank.

Start Saving Now

Dave's story is proof that you can start making good money decisions no matter where you are in life. You have to *choose*

to make saving a priority now and then continue to develop the habit.

Stop throwing your money away. Stack your cash.

— Anthony O'Neal

Think of saving like working out at the gym: Getting started is tough and sometimes you just don't feel like doing it. But the longer you stick with it, the stronger and better you feel. It's the same with saving—the more you do it, the more it becomes natural. Because with money in the bank, you can handle emergencies. And imagine how much more you'll be able to do when you're in your dream career earning a much larger income.

It was character that got us out of bed, commitment that moved us into action, and discipline that enabled us to follow through.

Zig Ziglar
Bestselling author and motivational speaker

Did You Know?

The following have started saving money:[4]

63%
Millennials

56%
Gen Z

Your **JOURNAL**   What has prevented you from saving money in the past? Based on what you've learned, what can you do to change this?

_____

_____

_____

REMEMBER THIS   Add a ✓ next to the completed learning objective below.

◯   You understand that saving money will help you avoid a lot of money problems.

THIS LESSON MAKES ME FEEL   Circle your response to what you learned.

 CONFUSED   **SURPRISED**   **THOUGHTFUL**   **CONFIDENT**

LESSON VIDEO GUIDE

If you start saving now while you're young, you'll be able to do so much more later on in life.

— Anthony O'Neal

GUIDED NOTES   While you watch the video, complete the section below.

1. The first reason to save money is to build your _____ fund.

2. The second reason to save is for _____ purchases.

3. The third reason to save is for _____ building.

4. Write down two key takeaways from the student discussion:

   _____

   _____

ANALYZE AND REFLECT   After you watch the video, respond to the question(s) below.

1. What struggles or victories have you experienced when it comes to saving money?

   _____

   _____

2. In the previous chapters, we discussed being a natural spender or a natural saver. How can your money personality affect your ability to save?

   _____

   _____

LEARNING OBJECTIVES

- Explain the three basic reasons to save money.
- Understand how you can start saving now.

MAIN IDEA

There are three basic reasons to save money: to build an emergency fund, to pay cash for purchases, and to build wealth.

Three Basic Reasons to Save

In Lesson 1, we talked about why many Americans struggle with saving money and how you can get ahead by making saving a habit while you're still in high school. Now, let's take a closer look at the three basic reasons you should make saving money a priority in your financial plan.

REASON #1: EMERGENCIES

The first reason to save money is to build an emergency fund. Remember, this is **The First Foundation**! An **emergency fund** is money you save to cover the cost for emergencies when they happen. And they *will* happen. For you, a financial emergency might look like replacing a lost cell phone or paying a car insurance deductible if you back into your friend's car. *Yikes!*

If you have cash on hand when those unexpected situations pop up, you solve two big problems at once: First, you won't have to turn to a credit card or get a bank loan to cover the expenses. This is a big part of following the principle of staying out of debt. When you have debt, you're always paying money for things in the past. Owing other people means you have less freedom with your money. Second, cash has the power to turn an emergency into an inconvenience. You just pay what you need to, build your fund back up, and move on with your life. No lingering debt and no stress. What a relief!

> **One of my biggest mistakes at 18: I didn't save. I didn't have a plan for my money.**
>
> — *Anthony ONeal*

REASON #2: LARGE PURCHASES

The second reason to save is to pay for **large purchases**—or anything you don't have enough money to pay for now with cash. We live in a culture of instant gratification. We want everything *now*. And like we talked about in Chapter 1, it's really easy to use debt to buy stuff you can't afford. Why wait and save when you can just put it on a credit card, right? That's how people end up in a financial hole.

If you really want to save money, you've got to live on less than you make. While this seems like an easy concept, people

Did You Know?

94% of millionaires said they live on less than they make.[5]

The First Foundation: Save a $500 emergency fund.

Emergency Fund: a savings account set up specifically to be used to cover financial emergencies

Large Purchase: a purchase that requires a significant amount of money

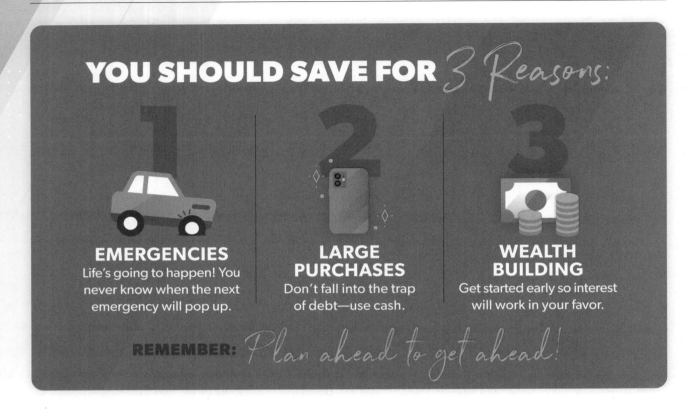

YOU SHOULD SAVE FOR *3 Reasons:*

1 EMERGENCIES
Life's going to happen! You never know when the next emergency will pop up.

2 LARGE PURCHASES
Don't fall into the trap of debt—use cash.

3 WEALTH BUILDING
Get started early so interest will work in your favor.

REMEMBER: *Plan ahead to get ahead!*

get it wrong all the time. In Lesson 4, we'll dig into why saving up and paying cash for purchases (like a new laptop) is a much wiser decision.

REASON #3: WEALTH BUILDING

The third reason for saving money is to build wealth. Now, this one takes time. There's no get-rich-quick button that will instantly build wealth. But while it takes patience, it's not difficult if you have long-term financial goals and stick to a plan. The key is to start planning and saving for your future as soon as possible.

When you put in the work to start building wealth early, you'll be able to really live and give like no one else. And that really is the most fun you can have with money!

Can you imagine being a millionaire—or even a multimillionaire? You might be shocked to learn that one-third of all

millionaires earned less than $100,000 per year—but they saved regularly. It's possible for you too! In this course, you'll learn how to start saving and investing for the future—and you'll see how anyone can become a millionaire in America.

How to Start Saving

So, you understand *why* you need to save—now what? No matter how much you make, you *can* start saving today! First, like we talked about back in Chapter 2, you'll want to include saving in your budget. It's your second priority after giving. Make it a habit to budget money for savings *before* you cover the rest of your spending categories.

And you'll want to be sure you set a realistic savings goal. For example, if you make $600 a month at your part-time job, it's not reasonable to say you're going to save all $600 each month. That wouldn't leave you any money to give or to pay for that cell phone bill, a night at the movies, or dinner with your friends. You'd only be setting yourself up for a busted budget—and that's a surefire way to get discouraged with the whole process.

To really stack up cash, you'll have to make sacrifices here and there, so it won't always be easy. Just be sure to look at all your expenses and set a goal that you can actually reach.

You will only save money when it becomes an emotional priority.

— Dave Ramsey

To get into the habit of setting money aside, you could put part of your income, whether it's from a job like babysitting or doing chores—or even just spare change—into a jar in your room. Then, when you've built up a good-sized stash, move it to your savings account.

If you already have a checking account, you can set up an automatic transfer to move money from your checking account to your savings account each week. You'll pile up cash in your savings account *and* create an automatic savings habit, especially if you get paid through direct deposits to your checking account.

Regardless of how you decide to save, it's important to keep a routine. Every time you earn money, put some of it in savings. If you just create this one habit now, you won't believe how big an impact it will have on *your financial future!*

Did You Know?

94% of students who complete this course feel much more confident in being able to save money.[7]

Your JOURNAL

What's one large purchase that you want to save for? What's your plan to save the money you need?

_____

_____

_____

REMEMBER THIS   Add a ✓ next to each completed learning objective below.

○ You can explain the three basic reasons to save money.

○ You recognize how to start saving right away.

THIS LESSON MAKES ME FEEL   Circle your response to what you learned.

☹ CONFUSED   😮 SURPRISED   🙂 THOUGHTFUL   🤩 CONFIDENT

LESSON VIDEO GUIDE

An emergency is something you couldn't see coming and you are not ready for. — Dave Ramsey

---

GUIDED NOTES   While you watch the video, complete the section below.

1. The First Foundation: Save a _____ emergency fund.

2. An emergency is an _____ expense.

3. Money comes from _____.

4. An emergency fund turns a crisis into an _____.

ANALYZE AND REFLECT   After you watch the video, respond to the question(s) below.

1. Contrast the difference between a financial emergency and nonemergency.

_____

_____

_____

2. Having an emergency fund reduces drama and stress. Give two real-life examples of how an emergency fund could help reduce stress in your life.

_____

_____

_____

LEARNING OBJECTIVE

Understand the importance of always having an emergency fund as part of your financial plan.

MAIN IDEA

The purpose of an emergency fund is to have enough cash on hand to cover an unexpected expense. This protects you from having to pile up debt or going without a necessity when something goes wrong.

Emergencies Do Happen

The First Foundation is simple: Save a $500 emergency fund. That will put a cash cushion between you and a financial emergency—and you won't have to go into debt to cover the expense. Great idea, right?

You learned in Lesson 1 that a lot of adults don't save because they think a financial emergency won't happen to them. Remember Murphy's Law? Well, not having cash on hand for emergencies is like setting up a big, flashing sign outside your home inviting Murphy and his friends to stop in, stay awhile, and wreak havoc on your finances. Don't let that be you!

> **Discipline is the bridge between who you are now and who you want to be in the future.**
>
> — *Anthony O'Neal*

The coronavirus pandemic in 2020 is just one example of how unexpected the unexpected really is. In America, our economy took a huge hit as businesses closed—temporarily at first—in an effort to prevent the spread of COVID-19. A lot of people lost their jobs, and the unemployment number skyrocketed in just a week. No one expected a pandemic—but it happened.

The people who were prepared with an emergency fund were in a much better place financially to weather that storm. That's why it's so important to save for emergencies. Not because you're afraid of another pandemic, but because you never know what will happen. We just know that something *will* happen. That's life—and your emergency fund will help keep you on solid footing so you can get through it and move on.

Emergency Fund Basics

Your emergency fund is your first savings priority, so get $500 in the bank before you save for those new shoes. Keep your emergency fund in a separate savings account—not in your checking account where you could spend it and not know it.

The First Foundation: Save a $500 emergency fund.

Did You Know?

One out of every three Americans experienced a job loss or income disruption during the COVID-19 pandemic.[8]

WAYS YOU CAN *Save $500*

You may already have $500 stored away, which is great! But if you don't, it's easier than you might think to save $500 quickly. Here are a few simple ideas:

Sell Stuff
Sell stuff you don't use or need anymore, like clothes, games, and electronics.

Find a Job
Look for a part-time job at local businesses, summer camps, or golf courses.

Tutor
Tutor younger students in your strongest school subjects.

Start a Biz
Hand out fliers for your own babysitting, dog-sitting, or yard work business.

Earn Cash
Ask your parents or grandparents if you can do some extra chores for cash.

Teach
Offer lessons in what you're good at, like piano or horseback riding.

Remember This:

39% of Americans said they would be unable to cover a $400 emergency.[9]

Here's a Tip:

When you have your $500 in the bank, don't think about what you could do with that $500. Forget about that money until you have an emergency.

Keep in mind that $500 is just your beginner emergency fund. Once you're out of school, have started your career, and have zero debt, you'll want to build your emergency fund to 3–6 months of living expenses. That means you'll take the estimated dollar amount it takes to pay for the Four Walls we talked about in Chapter 2—food, utilities, shelter, and transportation—and multiply it by three to six. That way, you'll be prepared for an emergency or even a temporary job loss.

Now when you've got that fully funded emergency fund in place as an adult, some people will tell you that you should invest that money. *Don't fall for it.* Your emergency fund isn't meant to be an *investment*—it's meant to be *insurance*. You need that money to be there for you in case of an emergency. And it needs to be easy to get to. A savings account or a money market account—which we'll cover in Chapter 8—are the only places you should keep your emergency fund.

Emergency or Not?

Now here's where things can get fuzzy. Once you have $500 in your savings account, when's it okay to use that money? What actually counts as an emergency? Here are three questions to ask before you spend your emergency fund:

IS IT UNEXPECTED?

Life has a few surprises we could all live without. And that's the key word when it comes to emergencies: *surprise*. An emergency is an unexpected event. You had no idea it was coming. Your tire blew out on the way to school? That's an emergency. Christmas is not an emergency. It happens the same day every year. The same goes for one-off events like birthdays or the prom—you know when they're coming, so budget and save for them.

IS IT NECESSARY?

People often confuse wants and needs. Once you have your driver's license and are driving by yourself, you and your parents may consider a cell phone a need. But the latest and greatest smartphone is a want. It's simple: If your cell phone breaks or is lost and you don't have another reliable way to get in touch with your parents, it's okay to use your emergency fund to buy an *affordable* replacement phone. But if you just want to upgrade to the newest model because it has a better camera, that calls for a large-purchase savings plan. Never use your emergency fund for a want.

IS IT URGENT?

A real emergency needs to be taken care of immediately. So, if your car's radiator hose has a leak in it, go get it fixed so your car is safe to drive. On the other hand, a sale at your favorite gaming store, though it can *feel* urgent, is not an emergency. If you have some spending money in your budget, go for it! But don't dip into your emergency fund just because there's a limited-time offer sign in the window—a video game sale has never been declared a state of emergency.

> **A crisis becomes an inconvenience when you have an emergency fund.**
> — *Dave Ramsey*

So, what happens if you need to use the money in your emergency fund? Great question! Just get focused and get $500 back in the bank as quickly as you can so you're ready for the next emergency. If you use it, replace it. It's that simple.

By failing to prepare, you are preparing to fail.

Benjamin Franklin
Author, inventor, and political theorist

Did You Know?

Of teens (16–19) who work, their median wage is $477 per week.[10]

 Your **JOURNAL**   What's the purpose of the three questions you should ask before using your emergency fund?

_____

_____

_____

REMEMBER THIS   Add a ✓ next to the completed learning objective below.

◯   You understand the importance of always having an emergency fund as part of your financial plan.

THIS LESSON MAKES ME FEEL   ⬭Circle⬭ your response to what you learned.

 CONFUSED   SURPRISED   😊 THOUGHTFUL   CONFIDENT

LESSON VIDEO GUIDE

The larger the purchase, the more planning and vision you have to have. —Dave Ramsey

GUIDED NOTES   While you watch the video, complete the section below.

1. Save up and pay for things with _____.

2. Avoid _____ payments for life.

3. If you invested _____ per month in mutual funds from age 25 to 65, you could have $3.6 million in a mutual fund.

ANALYZE AND REFLECT   After you watch the video, respond to the question(s) below.

1. If you need to save $1,000 for a new laptop and you'll need it in six months, what would your weekly savings goal need to be?

_____

2. If you start saving and paying cash for large purchases early in life, how will that help you later in life?

_____

_____

3. Other than a car, what are some common large purchases that offer financing or payment options you should avoid? List at least two examples.

_____

_____

LEARNING OBJECTIVE

Evaluate the benefits of saving up for large purchases instead of borrowing money for them.

MAIN IDEA

Planning ahead for large purchases and saving over time means you'll never need to go into debt to buy something.

Save Up and Pay Cash

The second reason to save money is to be able to pay cash for large purchases—anything you don't have enough money to get right now with cash. That one habit alone will keep you out of debt forever!

When you know you have a large purchase coming up—like a prom dress or tux or maybe a new phone—your budget will help you reach your savings goal. Saving for a large purchase is simple. First, decide how much you'll spend and how long you have to save. Then divide the total cost by the number of months you have to save and work that amount into your budget. For instance, if prom is five months away and you plan to spend $200 on it, you'll need to save $40 a month ($200 ÷ 5 = $40).

Planning ahead and saving over time means you'll never need to go into debt for a large purchase. Saving $40 a month is basically like paying yourself. And that's way better than using a credit card and paying a credit card company $40 a month *plus interest!* That's right—prom will end up costing you more than $200 if you pay for it with plastic instead of cash.

Buy Your Car With Cash

There's nothing quite as exciting as getting your driver's license and sliding behind the wheel of your first car. But before you hit the lot and let a slick-haired salesman talk you into a shiny, new 72-month car loan, let's look at the facts. The average monthly car payment for a new car is $554.[11] That's serious cash to shell out each month for something that will lose 60% of its value within five years!

> **Rich people ask, "How much?" Broke people ask, "How much down and how much per month?"**
> — *Dave Ramsey*

It's crazy how many people believe car payments are just part of life—that's a myth! Remember, **The Third Foundation** is to pay cash for your car. It just takes a plan.

Instead of dropping by the dealership and signing that deal, put that $554 in savings each month. In just 10 months, you'd have $5,540 saved up to buy a used

Did You Know?

Total U.S. auto loan debt at the start of 2020 was $1.35 trillion.[12]

The Third Foundation: Pay cash for your car.

Words of Wisdom

It's important to know how much things cost before you buy.

A smart doctor once wrote, "Suppose one of you wants to build a tower. What is the first thing you will do? Won't you sit down and figure out how much it will cost and if you have enough money to pay for it?

Otherwise, you will start building the tower, but not be able to finish. Then everyone who sees what is happening will laugh at you. They will say, 'You started building, but could not finish the job'" (Luke 14:28–30).

car to get you from point A to point B—without borrowing a dime!

If you keep up the saving habit, in another 10 months you'd have $5,540 more saved. If you sold your car for around what you paid for it, you'd have about $11,000 to spend on an even nicer used car after less than two years of saving. If you keep it up, you could find yourself in a downright fancy set of wheels in just a few years!

And if you can't swing $554 a month, don't worry. Set an amount that you can consistently save and budget based on that. Look at the chart on this page. If you only set aside $250 a month, you'll still have $3,000 in your car fund after a year. You *can* do this!

Before You Buy

Whether it's your first car or a new laptop, you want to be very intentional any time you plan to drop a serious chunk of change

on a purchase. Here are some ways you can avoid getting a case of buyer's remorse:

NEVER RUSH INTO A BIG PURCHASE

Don't let yourself get caught up in the moment and blow your hard-earned cash on something you don't actually want or need. Take some time and walk away from the store display—or computer screen—and sleep on it before you buy.

DON'T FALL FOR ZERO INTEREST

If you're in the market for a big-ticket item like a car, you'll see lots of **interest rate** deals like "zero-percent interest" or "12 months same-as-cash" promotions. They make you think you can get a loan to finance your wheels without paying any extra interest. That really is too good to be true. Why? Because if you don't have enough money to pay the cash up front, odds are you'll struggle to make monthly

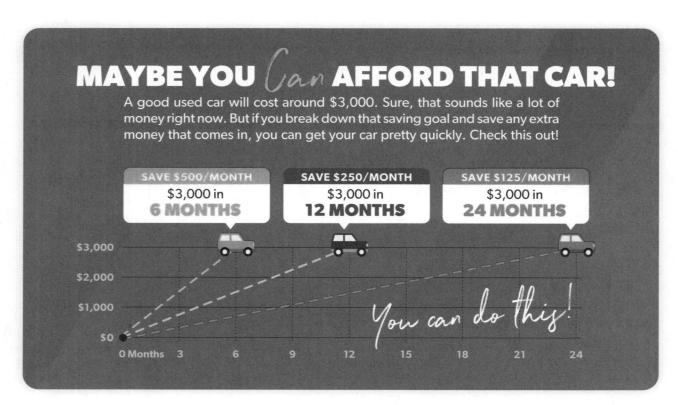

MAYBE YOU *Can* **AFFORD THAT CAR!**

A good used car will cost around $3,000. Sure, that sounds like a lot of money right now. But if you break down that saving goal and save any extra money that comes in, you can get your car pretty quickly. Check this out!

SAVE $500/MONTH	SAVE $250/MONTH	SAVE $125/MONTH
$3,000 in **6 MONTHS**	$3,000 in **12 MONTHS**	$3,000 in **24 MONTHS**

You can do this!

payments on time. And that's what the businesses are counting on. If you make even one late payment or fail to pay off the balance before the zero-interest period ends, you'll have to pay interest back to the date you made the purchase. That's called **accrued interest**. It may not seem fair, but the details are in the contract most buyers overlook.

> ## It's okay to own nice stuff. Just don't let your nice stuff own you.
> *— Rachel Cruze*

PAY UP FRONT

Stores rarely advertise the full price of things like smartphones these days. It's always something like, "Starting at $30 a month." You have to do some digging to find out that the full price is actually a whopping $720. That's a lot of money, right? But by only showing you the monthly payment, companies make their products *seem* affordable.

It's much easier to think, *Oh, I can do $30 a month!* than to shell out the $720 up front. But that $720 price tag is enough to make you *really* think about if that phone is worth it, isn't it? Don't get us wrong—it's okay to have nice things. Just be sure you can cover the purchase with cash and not monthly payments.

So, when it comes to making large purchases, it's always a good idea to remember what Dave Ramsey says:

"Cash is king!"

Interest Rate: the percentage of principal charged by the lender for use of its money

Accrued Interest: the amount of interest charged on a debt but not yet collected; interest accumulates from the date a loan is issued

---

Your JOURNAL

What are the advantages of saving up for large purchases?

_____

_____

_____

REMEMBER THIS Add a ✓ next to the completed learning objective below.

○ You can explain the benefits of saving up for large purchases instead of borrowing money for them.

THIS LESSON MAKES ME FEEL ⬭Circle your response to what you learned.

😓 CONFUSED   😲 SURPRISED   🙂 THOUGHTFUL   🤩 CONFIDENT

LESSON VIDEO GUIDE

The best friend your money could ever have is called compound interest. — Chris Hogan

GUIDED NOTES   While you watch the video, complete the section below.

1. $100 _____ per month from age 25 to 65 is $1,176,000.

2. _____ of Americans have less than $10,000 saved for retirement.

3. Adults devise a plan and follow it. Children do what _____ good.

4. Compound interest causes your money to _____.

5. Interest that you pay is a penalty. Interest that you earn is a _____.

ANALYZE AND REFLECT   After you watch the video, respond to the question(s) below.

1. Think about the Jack and Blake example. If you were Blake, what would your reaction be? What would you wish you had done differently?

   _____

   _____

   _____

2. What are two reasons Americans don't save more for retirement?

   _____

   _____

MAIN IDEA

When it comes to building wealth for the future, you need two things: money consistently invested and time for it to grow.

Building Wealth

Okay, now that you've got your emergency fund and you're saving for all your large purchases, it's time for the exciting part of saving: building wealth. Since you're in high school, before you start focusing on building wealth, you'll want to make sure you have **The Fourth Foundation** taken care of, which is to pay cash for college.

It doesn't make sense to invest *and* take out loans for college. So, use all your extra money to cover your education costs first. Once you're out of college, living debt-free, and have 3–6 months of living expenses in savings, that's when you'll start building wealth.

> **Building wealth is a marathon, not a sprint.**
>
> — *Chris Hogan*

Building wealth is the third reason for saving money, and it's also **The Fifth Foundation.** When you get serious about saving to build wealth, you can look forward to the day when you can live and give like no one else! Keep in mind that this won't happen overnight. Building wealth is a marathon, not a sprint. That means it's going to take some time—a long time—and you may not enjoy every second of it (just like running a marathon). You'll have to work at it consistently over years—even decades.

You Can Be a Millionaire

Really—it's true! Even if you've never stepped foot inside a bank, it just takes a little effort and a lot of patience for you to build wealth. Millionaire status isn't just for celebrities and CEOs, and you definitely don't have to have a six-figure salary to reach it. In America, there's absolutely no reason why you can't become a millionaire as an adult!

So, what does it take to build wealth and become a millionaire? Two things: money consistently invested and time for the money to grow. As a high school student, you have the second part covered—you've got time. To show you what can happen when you add money to the equation, check out the story of Jack and Blake (on the next two pages) to get an idea of how the money you invest can grow over time.

The Fourth Foundation: Pay cash for college.

Did You Know?

25% of Americans have $0 saved for retirement.[13]

The Fifth Foundation: Build wealth and give.

The Story of JACK & BLAKE

AND THE POWER OF COMPOUND GROWTH

JACK

At age 21, Jack decided to invest $2,400 every year ($200 per month) for nine years. He picked investment funds that had an average annual return of around 11% over the long term. Then, at age 30, Jack stopped putting money into his investments. So all together, he put a total of $21,600 into his investment funds, then left them alone.

BLAKE

Blake didn't start investing until age 30—nine years after Jack got started. And just like Jack, Blake put $2,400 into his investment funds every year—but he invested until he turned 67. His investments had the same average annual return of around 11% as Jack's, but he invested for 29 more years. Blake invested a total of $91,200 over 38 years.

When both Jack and Blake turned 67, they decided to compare their investment accounts. Who do you think had more? Jack, with his total of $21,600 invested over nine years, or Blake, who invested $91,200 over 38 years? Check this out:

Jack starts investing money at 21 years old.

$0 $0 $0 $0 $0 $0 $0 $0 $0 $0 $0

$0 $0 $0 $0 $0 $0 $0 $0

21 • • • • • • • • 30 • • • • • • • 40 •

Blake starts investing money at 30 years old.

JACK

Total invested over 9 years:	Return:
$21,600	**$2,547,150**

He never caught up!

BLAKE

Total invested over 38 years:	Return:
$91,200	**$1,483,033**

$0 $0 $0 $0 $0 $0 $0 $0 $0 $0 $0 $0 $0 $0 $0 $0 $0 $0 $0 $0 $0 $0 $0 $0 $0

50 • • • • • • • • • **60** • • • • • • **67**

Blake invests $2,400 a year until
age 67—almost his entire life.

THE SECRET IS TO START EARLY!

Isn't that amazing? Believe it or not, Jack came out ahead—more than $1 million ahead! Blake ended up with a total of $1,483,033 while Jack ended up with a total of $2,547,150. How did Jack do it? *He started early.* Jack put in less money but started nine years earlier.

As a result, Jack had more time for the magic of **compound growth** to do its thing. Compound growth is a millionaire's best friend! It's essentially *free money*.

Compound Growth: the average rate of growth for an investment over time; often expressed as an annual figure

Millionaires don't make excuses. They make progress.

— *Chris Hogan*

Keep in mind, Jack and Blake were investing, which is different than saving. We'll talk about that difference a little later—and all about investing in Chapter 12.

So, is there a secret or trick you need to know in order to become a millionaire? Nope! The key is to get started as soon as possible—and invest consistently for years.

The Millionaire Reality

Sure, having a six-figure salary can make it a lot easier to invest and build wealth. But in a Ramsey Solutions survey, 93 percent of the 10,000 millionaires interviewed said their wealth came from hard work, *not* because they had big salaries.[14] Even more surprising? The top three careers reported among those millionaires were accounting, engineering, and teaching. That's right—teachers. That means with hard work, discipline, and patience, there's no reason why *you* shouldn't become a millionaire too.

So, what's the difference between saving and investing? Good question. Investing is different in a couple of ways. The first has to do with time. You save money you plan to use in five years or less—for a phone, a car, or even college (if you're planning to go less than five years from now). When you invest, on the other hand, you do it for longer than five years— like 20–30 years or even longer.

The second difference is where you put your money. When you save, a simple savings account or money market account

The Real Reason to *Build Wealth*

ON THE SURFACE, it may seem selfish to build wealth. Does that make you greedy—just focused on making the next dollar? No way! Sure, there are people like that in the world. But like everything else to do with money, you have a choice. You can choose to be a wealthy person *and* a generous person. That's the real reason to build wealth: So you can use your money to help people in need, whether they're sick, lost their job, need help paying for college—you name it. Imagine the impact you can have on your community—and even the world—because you've chosen to build wealth and be generous with it! Hang on to that goal and let it motivate you to keep making smart choices with your money.

at your bank is all you need. But when you invest your money, you need to put it somewhere else. Again, we'll cover the details in Chapter 12.

How to Get Started

Building wealth starts with building solid money habits right now. For over 30 years on his radio show, Dave Ramsey has taught a lot of people how to build wealth. You know what most of them say? They wish they had known all this stuff while in high school because it would have made a huge difference. So you're already ahead! But if you aren't supposed to start investing yet, how does this apply to *you*?

Believe it or not, you can start forming wealth-building habits today. It all begins with being intentional with saving money. Seriously, time is on your side—and that's

an advantage a lot of adults don't have. Start with a commitment to save money and make it a priority. Then you'll be on your way to building wealth.

I want you to invest as early as you possibly can.

— Anthony O'Neal

The next time you wonder if saving money and building wealth will actually make a difference, just look back at what Jack and Blake were able to do with some money and some time. That's incredible! And that's the same formula—money and time—that will help you be able to

build wealth and give!

Here's a Tip:

When you allow your investments to grow for 20, 30, and even 40 years, you really see growth happen. That's why you need to start early!

It takes as much energy to wish as it does to plan.

Eleanor Roosevelt
First Lady of the United States, 1933–1945

Your JOURNAL   Why is it important to start investing as early as possible?

_____

_____

_____

REMEMBER THIS   Add a ✓ next to the completed learning objective below.

◯   Starting early and being consistent are the keys to building wealth.

THIS LESSON MAKES ME FEEL   (Circle) your response to what you learned.

😓 CONFUSED   😗 SURPRISED   🙂 THOUGHTFUL   🤩 CONFIDENT

We've got to be able to grow money to live the lives we want to live.

— *Chris Hogan*

GUIDED NOTES   While you watch the video, complete the section below.

1. Everyday people can build _____.

2. You need a _____ to become a millionaire.

3. If you invest _____, you will have nothing.

4. Your money combined with interest over time creates _____

    _____.

5. What is the secret to becoming a millionaire?

    _____

    _____

ANALYZE AND REFLECT   After you watch the video, respond to the question(s) below.

1. You shouldn't take your investments out early. What do you think are some consequences of taking money out of your retirement early?

    _____

    _____

    _____

LEARNING OBJECTIVE

Understand and be able to calculate compound interest and compound growth.

MAIN IDEA

Compound interest and compound growth are two ways your money earns more money over time in a savings or investment account.

What Is Compound Interest?

In Lesson 5, you learned about compound growth—and it's pretty powerful stuff when it comes to investing! Compound interest is really similar—so similar that people often use the two terms interchangeably.

Compound essentially means you're putting money on top of money. **Compound interest** is just interest paid on interest you've already earned. That means your **principal** (the original amount of money you invested) plus the interest it earns during a certain time equals a new total investment amount. Essentially, your money earns money on its own.

But wait—*why* does this happen? Well, when you put money into a savings account at a bank, for example, the bank pays you interest because they use your money to do business. But don't worry—there are tons of rules and regulations to make sure you don't lose your money.

Sounds like a sweet deal, right? So, how can that be bad? Well, the reverse is true as well. When you borrow money (aka use credit and debt), you pay interest as a fee for using that money. Credit cards and student loans often have compounding interest rates that make money for them.

That means when you borrow money, you'll pay back *more* money than what you borrowed. That's why you always want compound interest working for you instead of working against—as it does with debt.

> ## Interest that you earn is a reward. Interest that you pay is a penalty.
> — *Chris Hogan*

Compound Interest Works

So, what exactly makes compound interest so powerful? Two things: time and the interest rate. The longer your money earns interest, the more it will grow. The interest rate determines how quickly your money will grow over time.

Let's say you make a one-time deposit of $1,000 in a savings account with a 10% interest rate. (Note: A typical savings account at a local bank will have an interest rate that is much lower than 10%, but using this rate will be easier to show the math.) At the end of the first year, you would earn $100 in interest and have $1,100 total. At the end of the next year, you'd

Compound Interest: interest paid on interest previously earned

Principal: the initial amount of money invested or borrowed

HOW TO CALCULATE *Compound Interest*

To calculate how much money you'll have after several years of compound interest, you can use a compound interest formula. When you use this formula, be sure to follow the mathematical order of operations (look it up if you forget how it works).

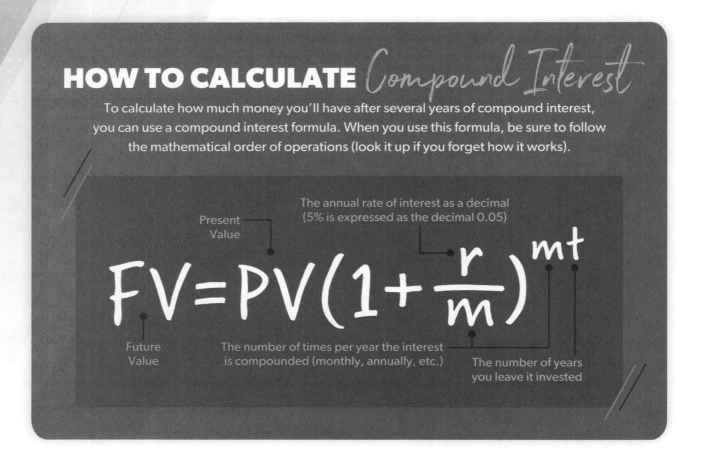

$$FV = PV\left(1+\frac{r}{m}\right)^{mt}$$

Present Value

The annual rate of interest as a decimal (5% is expressed as the decimal 0.05)

Future Value

The number of times per year the interest is compounded (monthly, annually, etc.)

The number of years you leave it invested

> The most powerful force in the universe is compound interest.
>
> **Albert Einstein**
> German physicist

have $1,210—not just $1,200—because your interest from the previous year ($100) would also earn $10 in interest. Your interest would compound—or build upon itself.

Year	Start of Year	Return Rate	End of Year
1	$1,000	10%	$1,100
2	$1,100	10%	$1,210
3	$1,210	10%	$1,331
10	$2,357	10%	$2,594
20	$6,115	10%	$6,727

Using the formula at the top of this page, in 10 years, you would have $2,594 and $6,727 in 20 years! That growth came from compound interest on your original $1,000.

Compound Growth

In Lesson 5, the Jack and Blake story showed how compounding really hits a

Rate of Return: the measure of an investment's profit or loss, usually expressed as a percentage of the initial investment

new level when you invest. But in their case, rather than compound interest, that is compound growth. What's the difference?

Compound interest is earned at a fixed rate, while compound growth—or the compound annual growth rate—is an average based on an investment's past performance (because investments don't grow at the same rate all the time).

Even though mutual funds and stocks will go up and down in value, their compound annual growth rate can be used to estimate the **rate of return.** That's how much your investment could grow (or lose value) over time. When you know the rate of return, all you have to do is plug it into the compound interest formula above to estimate what the investment could be worth decades from now. Very cool!

Inflation and the Time Value of Money

There are two more factors to keep in mind when you start investing. One is **inflation**, or the rise in the price of goods and services over time. For example, if inflation averages 3% per year over the next five years, that means $500 today would only buy the equivalent of $425 five years from now. That stinks!

Start paying yourself and investing in your future.

— Anthony ONeal

So, in order to outpace inflation, your investments need to have a higher rate of return than the average inflation rate over time. We'll go into more detail about investing in Chapter 12. For now, just know that saving, investing, and compound growth will help you win with money!

The second factor to keep in mind is the **time value of money**. This principle says that a certain amount of money today is worth more than the same amount in the future. Why? Because if you invested that money today, you could earn interest on it and end up with more than you started with in the first place.

Plus, inflation will drive prices up and lower the value of the same amount of money in the future. Think about it this way: If you invest $500 today with a 10% rate of return and leave it alone for five years, that $500 would turn into $800. And that's much better than having that $500 turning into $425 due to inflation!

Inflation: the persistent rise in the cost of goods and services over time

Time Value of Money: concept that an amount of money is worth more today than in the future due to earning potential

---

Your JOURNAL — Explain the differences and similarities between compound interest (for money saved) and compound growth (for money invested).

_____

_____

_____

REMEMBER THIS Add a ✓ next to the completed learning objective below.

◯ You understand how to calculate compound interest and compound growth, the keys to growing your savings and investments exponentially over time.

THIS LESSON MAKES ME FEEL (Circle) your response to what you learned.

 CONFUSED   SURPRISED   THOUGHTFUL   CONFIDENT

Chapter 3 Review

Fill in the blanks below using the correct key terms from this chapter.

Emergency Fund	Large Purchase	Interest Rate	Accrued Interest
Compound Growth	Compound Interest	Principal	Rate of Return
Inflation	Time Value of Money		

1. 47% of Americans have less than $1,000 saved for a(n) _____.

2. An investment's _____ is its percentage gain or loss over time.

3. _____ is the average rate of growth for an investment over a period of time.

4. The price of goods and services increases over time due to _____.

5. The initial amount of money you deposit or invest is called the _____.

6. You save for a(n) _____ when you don't have the cash to buy it now.

7. _____ deals—such as 90-days-same-as-cash—are often used to get you to buy higher-priced items.

8. The _____ refers to the earning potential of money.

FINISH THE SENTENCE Use what you've learned in this chapter to complete these sentences.

1. When talking about saving money, Anthony ONeal says, "Start paying yourself and _____ _____."

2. The First Foundation is: Save _____ _____.

3. If you make a late credit payment, you might see the lender add _____ _____.

4. The three reasons to save money are _____ _____ _____

1. Which of the following would be considered an emergency fund expense?

   A. Lost cell phone

   B. Video game sale

   C. Blown car tire

   D. Sale on shoes

2. "Rate of return" is a phrase used to describe what aspect of investing?

   A. Compound growth

   B. Accrued interest

   C. Risk and return ratio

   D. Inflation

3. In The Five Foundations, what is The Third Foundation?

   A. Pay cash for college

   B. Save a $500 emergency fund

   C. Pay cash for your car

   D. Get out and stay out of debt

4. When you make a purchase but later wish you hadn't done so, you experience . . .

   A. Selfishness

   B. Buyer's remorse

   C. Impulse purchase

   D. Time value

5. Which of the following questions helps you determine if something is actually an emergency expense?

   A. Is it urgent?

   B. Is it unexpected?

   C. Is it necessary?

   D. All of the above

6. What two elements do you need to build wealth through compound growth?

   A. An inheritance and a lawyer

   B. Money invested and time

   C. Money invested and good stocks

   D. Time and a wealthy relative

 **QUESTION**   Why is it important to make an emergency fund your first financial priority?

Debt is Dumb.
Cash is King!

Credit and Debt

This chapter identifies the dangers of debt, debunks some credit myths, explains the credit report and score, and provides practical strategies to get out of debt—and stay out.

Beware of Credit and Debt

LESSON VIDEO GUIDE

More marketing dollars are spent to sell you to go into DEBT than any other category.

— Dave Ramsey

GUIDED NOTES   While you watch the video, complete the section below.

1. Debt is the most aggressively marketed product _____.

2. Visa, Mastercard, Discover, and American Express spend over _____ a year on marketing alone.

3. There were no credit cards prior to _____.

4. Write down two of the four key years mentioned in the brief history of debt and why they were important.

   _____

   _____

ANALYZE AND REFLECT   After you watch the video, respond to the question(s) below.

1. What's the main reason our culture has normalized credit cards over the past 60 years? What can we do to change the normalization of debt in the future?

   _____

   _____

   _____

   _____

LEARNING OBJECTIVES

- Define debt and evaluate the financial burden and risk that debt presents.
- Understand the relationship between credit and debt.
- Understand that credit is a financial product that's heavily marketed to us.

MAIN IDEA

You might think debt is normal and the only way to have everything you want. But the reality is, debt makes businesses a lot of money—and you're stuck with the bill.

Debt Defined

Have you ever watched a commercial for a credit card? (Who are we kidding? Of course you have—they're *everywhere*!) But next time, really pay attention. Those people are just swiping their way to happiness, right? Spa trips, surprise beach vacations, fancy dinners—all made possible with a little plastic card.

You know what those ads don't show? They don't show people making payments for months or years for all that stuff. That's what it really means to use a credit card. Buy now, live with debt, and pay big later.

But the credit industry is way too savvy to just tell you that. They've worked for decades to convince all of us that they're simply offering a service. And that "service" allows you to have all the things you want. Need a new wardrobe? Just swipe a card. Time for a new car? Use easy financing! Need to pay for college? Just sign up for thousands of dollars in student loans.

But you know the truth! In Chapter 1, you learned about the debt crisis in our country. You know debt causes financial insecurity and stress, which often leads to problems in relationships. That's why one of your money principles is to stay out of debt. You *can* live a debt-free life! But you'll need to know the myths from the truths.

Debt is a dream killer and a nightmare maker.

— Anthony O'Neal

Here's just one example: How many times have you heard that student loans are "good debt" because they'll help you get a good-paying career? That might seem like a strong argument, but who wants to start life after college with tens of thousands of dollars of debt? Student loans are *not* the only way to pay for college—and we'll talk more about that in Chapter 7. But here's what you need to know right now: There's no such thing as good debt. All debt is bad for you. That's why we say debt is dumb—credit cards, students loans, and car loans or leases. Stay away from all of it.

What is **debt**? Any time you owe any money to *anybody*—for any reason—that's

Words of Wisdom

When someone borrows money from another, we understand he or she has an obligation to repay. A study in the dictionary will show you what this really means. A definition of obligation is "bound," which is defined as "tied; in bonds: a bound prisoner."

"The rich rule over the poor, and the borrower is slave to the lender" (Proverbs 22:7). Don't become a prisoner or slave to debt!

Debt: money owed to another person or company

debt. We say "debt is dumb," but that doesn't mean someone with debt is dumb. It just means they got sold by marketing tactics. Debt has become normal. In reality, debt is a huge financial burden that stands in the way of financial peace and security. Why? Because your income is your greatest wealth-building tool.

Think back to Chapter 2. If you had to budget hundreds of dollars for a car loan payment every month, how much would you be able to give, save, or spend on other things? (Hint: not much!)

Credit: A Consumer Product

Let's get one thing clear: Credit is *not* a tool that makes your life better. Credit is a big business that makes lots of money for credit card companies, banks, and other lenders. Credit is a product those companies sell—and *you're* their target.

When a lender offers you credit through a credit card, car loan, or student loan, they're offering you the opportunity to borrow their money. The offer is free, but as soon as you accept the offer, you go into debt and start making money for them.

Credit card companies make their biggest profits when people carry a balance from one month to the next. That's when a customer pays only a part of their debt each month instead of paying the entire amount. The balance starts building (or accruing) interest—so now the customer owes more than they originally spent! We'll talk more about how credit card companies make money in Lesson 4.

> **Our great-grandparents thought debt was a sin. Our grandparents thought debt was dumb. Our parents borrowed on a few things. We borrow on everything.**
>
> — *Dave Ramsey*

The Marketing of Credit

Once you turn 18, you become a target of credit card marketing. Credit card companies know people are super loyal to their first credit card. And if you start using debt at an early age, you're likely to make paying with plastic a way of life.

Rather go to bed supperless than rise in debt.

Benjamin Franklin
Author, inventor, and political theorist

A Message From ANTHONY

I mean, I gotta admit: Credit card companies have done a really good job of marketing. Not only do they get you hooked on their products, but they also do it in a way that makes you feel cool, powerful, and like you have access to anything you want. But really, what they're selling you will weigh you down and hold you back from reaching your goals. It's pretty scary how good they are at selling you something that's terrible for you. So here's the solution: Don't use their cards! Be the generation that finally puts an end to the debt crisis in America.

To hook you, credit card companies have several tried and true marketing tactics you need to watch out for:

OFFERING A LOW- OR ZERO-INTEREST INTRODUCTORY RATE

Credit with low or no interest sounds like free money right? Not so fast. Your low or no-interest time period is temporary—that's what "introductory rate" means. Later, you'll get hit with a much higher interest rate, hidden fees, and a bunch of rules.

REQUIRING ONLY THE MINIMUM MONTHLY PAYMENT

Minimum monthly payments cover your interest charges—but you're barely making a dent in the actual amount of debt. Credit card companies love this because it keeps you in debt for years. They win, you lose!

OFFERING CASH BACK AND OTHER REWARDS

Don't be fooled by cash back or airline rewards. Just do the math: If a card "gives you back" 1.5% of every dollar you spend, that's only $1.50 for every $100 spent or $15 for every $1,000. That's not a reward! These companies aren't going to give you something for nothing. They're in business to *make money*—and they're very good at it. Stick with cash and skip the interest, risk, and payments of credit. True rewards come with building wealth.

Did You Know?

People under the age of 18 cannot legally get their own credit card. And between 18–21, you may need a cosigner and proof of income first.

Your JOURNAL

What are some of the common marketing tactics credit card companies use to market to young adults?

_____

_____

_____

REMEMBER THIS   Add a ✓ next to each completed learning objective below.

◯ You understand the financial burden and risk that comes with debt.

◯ You can explain the relationship between credit and debt.

◯ You understand that credit is a financial product and can identify marketing strategies used to promote using credit.

THIS LESSON MAKES ME FEEL   (Circle) your response to what you learned.

😓 CONFUSED   😮 SURPRISED   🙂 THOUGHTFUL   🤩 CONFIDENT

LESSON 2 | Sources and Types of Credit

Normal is broke. You don't want to be normal—you want to be weird. —Dave Ramsey

GUIDED NOTES   While you watch the video, complete the section below.

1. There are four types of credit you need to watch out for. List them below.

_____

_____

_____

_____

2. Myth: You need a student _____ to go to college.

3. Truth: You can go to college _____.

4. Choose a school you can _____.

ANALYZE AND REFLECT   After you watch the video, respond to the question(s) below.

1. You can work and apply for scholarships to help pay for college. How will avoiding student loans help set the tone for avoiding using credit and taking on debt in your life?

_____

_____

_____

LEARNING OBJECTIVES

- Identify sources and types of credit.
- Understand the difference between revolving and installment credit.
- Recognize a predatory lender.

MAIN IDEA

To live a debt-free life, it's important to understand the industry. In other words, if you want to beat the system, you need to understand it first.

Sources of Credit

As much as the credit industry would like you to believe differently, our country wasn't founded on easy financing and 90-days-same-as-cash. If you're going to avoid debt, you need to know what you're dealing with. That begins with knowing the sources and types of credit.

CREDIT CARDS

A Ramsey Solutions study showed that 80% of Americans have a credit card. Credit cards work as a **revolving credit** account. That just means you have a credit limit and you can buy multiple things at different times—as long as you don't exceed your limit. Every time you spend with a credit card, you add to your debt. And the more you add, the harder it is to pay off. You'll learn more about credit cards in Lesson 4.

SECURED AND UNSECURED LOANS

When a borrower is required to put up **collateral**—something they own like a car or house—for a loan, it becomes a *secured* loan. If the borrower fails to make payments on the loan as outlined in the contract, the lender can take and sell the collateral to recoup their costs. So, there's always the danger of losing the loan collateral if you fail to make the payments on time. Credit or loans that don't require collateral (like a credit card) are called *unsecured* debt.

Let me be very clear. Debt is not inevitable!

— Anthony O'Neal

PERSONAL LOANS

Personal loans from a bank, credit union, or other lender are often used to pay for anything from a vacation to debt consolidation (a loan used to move several debts into one payment). They're usually for a fixed amount and have fixed payments. But anything you'd pay for with a personal loan, you can save up and pay for with cash.

Personal loans often come with higher **interest** rates and fees. Some even charge a penalty if you pay them off early. Borrowers usually don't have to put up collateral to get a personal loan.

Revolving Credit: credit that automatically renews whenever a payment is made to reduce the debt

Collateral: something owned (that has value) offered as security on a debt; if the debt is not repaid as agreed, the item is forfeited to the lender

Interest: the additional cost a lender charges for borrowing their money

HOME MORTGAGE

A mortgage is a loan that typically lasts for 15–30 years and is used to buy a house (more on that in Chapter 11). A mortgage is a financial **lien** against a property—and the house is the collateral. That means the lender actually owns the house until the debt is paid. A house is an **appreciating asset**—it goes up in value—and can be a good financial move, as long as you don't buy more house than you can afford.

Lien: a legal claim (or right to own) against an asset until the debt (loan) is repaid

Appreciating Asset: an asset that increases in value over time

HOME EQUITY LOANS

Most homes increase in value over time as the mortgage is paid. This produces **equity**—which is the difference between the amount owed and the current market value of the home. Owners can borrow against their equity with a home equity loan or a home equity line of credit (HELOC).

With a home equity loan, the owner cashes out a portion of their equity in a lump sum. A HELOC—much like a credit card—lets the owner spend their equity when they want, as long as they don't spend over their credit limit.

Borrowing against your home equity might be common, but it's a bad idea. Why? If you **default**—or can't repay the

Equity: the increase in value of a home over time; the difference between the amount owed and what the home could be sold for

Default: failure to repay a loan on time

loan on time—the bank could take your home. So you're risking your home if you can't repay the debt. Not smart!

> *A home equity loan is the credit card of the mortgage world. Don't do that!*
>
> — *Dave Ramsey*

STUDENT LOANS

A student loan is money borrowed from the federal government or private lenders to pay the cost of going to college. Student loans are paid back over 10–20 years—or more. We're experiencing a financial crisis in our country because of student loans—primarily because students don't completely understand what they're signing up for.

We get it—education is important for success, and students and parents will do whatever it takes to get that degree. But going into debt to make that happen is a huge mistake. We'll talk a lot more about student loans in Chapter 7. For now, just understand that the "borrow money or skip college" dilemma is a myth.

PUTTING *Life* ON HOLD

Due to unpaid student debt, millennials are choosing to delay major life decisions, like:[1]

21% GETTING MARRIED

21% HAVING CHILDREN

40% SAVING FOR RETIREMENT

47% BUYING A HOME

AUTO LOANS

A car loan is an example of **installment credit**. That means you make monthly payments on the original loan amount until it's paid off. Almost 90% of new cars are purchased with borrowed money. Wow! The average new car loan is more than $32,000 and has monthly payments of about $550—for 69 months![2] That's more than five and a half years of car payments!

And a car is a **depreciating asset**—meaning it goes down in value. In fact, it loses value the moment you drive it off the lot! But the sad story doesn't end there, does it? After you've spent years paying on the car, it's lost its new-car smell. So, you go out and get another new car—and the car payments start all over again.

This never-ending cycle means you've permanently dedicated a chunk of your income to a car payment. That's a bad idea!

Predatory Lenders

Payday loans, title loans, and pawn shops are all examples of **predatory lenders.** They're called "predatory" because of their reputation for *preying* on desperate people and charging outrageously high interest rates and fees for loans.

Their fees keep people in a terrible cycle of debt. Unfortunately, unbanked Americans—people who can't or choose not to have a bank account—often rely on these types of financial services for their banking needs. The best advice is to stay far away from these types of lenders!

Installment Credit: a loan for a fixed amount of money that's paid back in monthly installments

Depreciating Asset: an asset that loses value over time, such as a car that's worth less every year

Predatory Lender: a lender who uses deceptive, unfair, or fraudulent practices on borrowers who are desperate for cash

---

Your **JOURNAL**   What is debt? How does debt create financial risk and instability?

_____

_____

_____

REMEMBER THIS   Add a ✓ next to each completed learning objective below.

○ You can identify types and sources of credit as well as the financial risk associated with any type of debt.

○ You understand the difference between revolving and installment credit.

○ You can recognize a predatory lender.

THIS LESSON MAKES ME FEEL   (Circle) your response to what you learned.

😓 CONFUSED   😮 SURPRISED   🙂 THOUGHTFUL   🤩 CONFIDENT

LESSON VIDEO GUIDE

 A debit card can do every single thing a credit card can, except build your credit. — Dave Ramsey

GUIDED NOTES   While you watch the video, complete the section below.

1. Myth: I need to have a _____ score.

2. Truth: A credit score is an "I _____ debt" score.

3. A FICO score is not an indicator that you are _____ with money.

4. Your most powerful wealth-building tool is your _____.

5. You _____ rent an apartment without a FICO score.

6. Without a FICO score, an extra _____ may be required.

ANALYZE AND REFLECT   After you watch the video, respond to the question(s) below.

1. A credit score does not factor in your income or the amount of money in your bank account. Knowing that, why do you think so many people believe a credit score is a good measure of financial health?

_____

_____

_____

LEARNING OBJECTIVES

- Identify and evaluate the information used in determining a person's credit score.
- Understand the purpose of a credit score and the components of a credit report.
- Explain the importance of monitoring your credit report.

MAIN IDEA

The FICO credit score is an "I love debt" score and is not a measure of winning with money. You *can* live without a credit score!

What's a Credit Score?

You've probably heard: "As soon as you get out of high school, you need to get a credit card and start building your credit score." Not only is that a horrible idea—it's *a total myth!* You don't need a credit score!

But let's start at the beginning. What's a credit score? A **credit score** is a three-digit number that tells banks and lenders how likely someone is to repay debt. This number comes from a formula that uses information found on a person's credit report.

Unpacking a Credit Score

You may have heard a credit score referred to as a *FICO score*. The FICO score is simply a person's credit score that's calculated with software from Fair Isaac Corporation (FICO). It's the score most lenders use.

Agencies called **credit bureaus**—such as Experian, TransUnion, and Equifax—gather information about your credit history and sell it to creditors who use it to decide if they will lend money to you.

Most of America has bought into the myth that a good FICO score is a big deal— even something to brag about. But the

FICO score doesn't gauge how well you handle money, how wealthy you are, or how successful you are. All it really says is how good you are at making payments to lenders.

Still in doubt? Take a look at the five components of a FICO score:

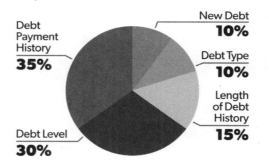

See what we mean? The FICO score is all about debt! How much you have, how much you've had, what kind it is, how long you've had it, and how well you pay it off. Your income, savings, or other financial assets aren't even considered in the calculation. Don't miss that! Even if you became a millionaire tomorrow, your credit score wouldn't change.

Don't be fooled into thinking a FICO score measures how well you handle money. It doesn't. It's just an "I love debt" score.

Did You Know?

Formerly known as the Fair Isaac Corporation, FICO was founded in 1956 by Bill Fair and Earl Isaac.

Credit Score: a statistical number used to represent a consumer's creditworthiness

Credit Bureau: a company that collects credit rating information and makes it available to creditors

UNDERSTANDING *Credit Reports*

This section has any personal information that could be used to identify you.

CHECK THIS:
- ✓ Everything refers to you and not someone else who happens to share your name.
- ✓ The Social Security number is correct.
- ✓ All the addresses are places you've really lived.

This is the largest section. Make sure everything listed is correct. Then, check again. Seriously.

CHECK THIS:
- ✓ Make sure no lines of credit have been opened in your name without your consent—that might mean you've been a victim of identity theft.

Personal Information

Name: John Doe   Social Security Number: 123-45-6789
Date of Birth: Jan 1, 2000   Phone Number: 555-765-4321
Address: 123 Seventh Street, Los Angeles, CA 54321

Credit Summary

Open and Paid Credit Accounts	Available Credit	Remaining Loan Balances	Payment History			
Chart Credit	$3,000	$870	✓	✓	✓	✓
M&X Finance	$30,000	$23,456	✓	✓	✓	30
US Dept of Ed		$38,450	✓	✓	✓	✓

Most credit bureaus make you pay to see this.

689
CREDIT SCORE
300   850
580 670 740 800

Looks like John is 30 days late on this payment!

Accounts Shared with Someone Else	Accounts that Have Been Sent to Collections
None	None

This is a detailed list of every business that has requested your credit report.

Hard inquiries are made when you apply for a credit card, loan, or mortgage.

Soft inquiries come from companies that want to send you promotional materials or creditors checking your account.

CHECK THIS:
- ✓ Be sure that any hard inquiries are correct. If not, it could mean that someone is trying to steal your identity to open a new line of credit.

The items here—bankruptcy, judgments (lawsuit decisions), and tax liens (for unpaid taxes)—are taken from public records.

CHECK THIS:
- ✓ Some things can stay on your report for 7–10 years.
- ✓ Clear up any mistakes in this section ASAP.

Public Records

Bankruptcies: You currently have none in your file.
Judgments: You currently have none in your file.
Liens: You currently have none in your file.

Credit Inquiries

Hard Inquiries

Date	Company
Aug 1, 2021	WB&T Dealer Finance
July 3, 2021	Sesame National Bank

Soft Inquiries

Date	Company	Description
July 5, 2021	Allstop Ins Co	Promotional Inquiry
June 23, 2021	Rillards	Promotional Inquiry

Recognize these? If not, someone might be trying to impersonate you!

How to Dispute Inaccuracies

If you find any mistakes on your credit report, contact the agency that shows the error. Write a letter describing the error and share any evidence you have to prove it's a mistake. Send all of this by certified mail with return receipt (to prove it was delivered). The agency has only 30 days to respond, so you should see some movement pretty quickly to get the error corrected.

The Importance of Monitoring Your Credit Report

A credit report is kind of like a report card for your credit history. While you don't need a credit score to survive, you do need to know what's in your credit report. Yes—even if you're living completely debt-free! Many credit reports have errors. And checking your credit report regularly can help you spot signs of fraud or identity theft.

Once you turn 18, you can request a copy of your credit report from each of the three main credit bureaus for *free* every year. You have to request it, though, because they won't just send you a copy of your report. Don't fall for a website that asks you to pay a fee for your credit report. Go directly to the credit bureaus' websites or go online to annualcreditreport.com. Since each bureau tracks your credit history in a slightly different way, it's a good idea to check all three.

In order to build up your credit score, you have to rack up debt. That's completely foolish!
— Anthony O'Neal

If you see errors or suspect identity theft, contact the credit bureaus to have a fraud alert placed on your report. Then report any suspicious activity to your bank and credit issuers as soon as you can. Monitoring your credit report is important!

Did You Know?

Myth: You need to build a credit score to survive financially.

Truth: You don't need a credit score. People who "need" a credit score are people who plan to take on more debt. That's not what we want for you! Debt-free people don't need a credit score!

Your **JOURNAL**

Why is your credit score not a good indicator of how well you handle money? What does your credit score indicate?

_____

_____

_____

REMEMBER THIS Add a ✓ next to each completed learning objective below.

○ You understand the purpose of a credit score.

○ You can identify and evaluate the information used in determining a person's credit score.

○ You understand the importance of monitoring your credit report.

THIS LESSON MAKES ME FEEL (Circle) your response to what you learned.

😓 CONFUSED   😯 SURPRISED   🙂 THOUGHTFUL   🤩 CONFIDENT

LESSON VIDEO GUIDE

I believe the credit card is the cigarette of the financial world. The truth is, it's killing you. — Dave Ramsey

GUIDED NOTES   While you watch the video, complete the section below.

1. Myth: I need a _____ card to rent a car and make purchases online.

2. Truth: You can do both of these things with a _____ card.

3. Most credit cards will charge you an _____ fee.

4. The average college student's credit card debt is _____.

ANALYZE AND REFLECT   After you watch the video, respond to the question(s) below.

1. What are at least two ways credit card companies make money?

    _____

    _____

2. The credit card industry works similar to the cigarette industry. What reasons caused culture to change its view of cigarettes over the past few decades? What do you think would need to happen to change America's view of credit cards?

    _____

    _____

    _____

LEARNING OBJECTIVES

- Evaluate the increased costs that come with using a credit card to make purchases.
- Identify all the ways the credit card industry makes money.
- Understand the financial impact of choosing to use credit to make purchases.

MAIN IDEA

Credit cards are *not* the same as cash or debit cards. Between interest and fees, a credit card is virtually guaranteed to cost you more money.

Americans and Credit Cards

We've talked about how people use credit cards to buy pretty much anything without giving it much thought. You've probably seen people you know do that. And since credit card debt is so common, you've probably heard someone you know say they're worried about how much credit card debt they have or that they're dreading their next credit card bill.

> **Debt slowed down my dreams. I spent too much time paying for my past instead of enjoying my present and planning for my future.**
>
> — *Anthony O'Neal*

How do people end up overwhelmed by their credit card debt? When most people get their first card, they make promises to themselves like, *I'll only use this for emergencies.* Or, *I'll only charge what I can pay off every month.*

But those promises rarely last. Why? Life happens. Unexpected expenses derail even the best intentions. When you allow credit to be an option for getting what you want or need *now*, instead of waiting and saving up for it, it's easy to cave into the temptation of instant gratification.

Credit card companies make money when you use their product. So, they bombard you with relentless marketing that encourages you to use their card, go into debt, and stay in debt. They make most of their money from three things: interest, fees they charge cardholders, and transaction fees businesses pay to accept credit cards.

The High Cost of Using Credit Cards

Interest charges and countless fees—that's how credit card companies make a lot of money off of you and off of the businesses where you shop.

Buying something with a credit card is *not* the same as spending cash for the same item. Between the interest, the fees, and the ongoing mind games that come with paying with plastic, a credit card is virtually

Seven Common Credit Card Fees

1. Annual fee
2. Balance transfer fee
3. Cash advance fee
4. Finance charge (interest accrued on the revolving balance)
5. Late payment fee
6. Over-limit fee
7. Returned payment fee

CREDIT CARD DEBT IS *on the Rise*

As young adults grow older, they often rack up more and more credit card debt. Take a look at how America's average credit card debt changes by age. [3]

guaranteed to cost you more money—and make money for the credit card companies. Here's how those companies make money from their credit cards:

INTEREST CHARGES

When you buy something with a credit card, you're borrowing money—with interest. Young people, those with lower paying jobs, or those who have bad or no credit scores pay much higher interest rates. The interest builds over time, so you pay more the longer you carry a balance.

Did You Know?

When someone borrows money and has to pay it back, it's called an obligation—a binding course of action.

CASH ADVANCE FEES

A cash advance is a loan you take with a credit card—kind of like an ATM withdrawal with interest. You'll pay a higher interest rate on an advance and have a finance fee.

ANNUAL FEES

Some credit cards charge an annual fee. Cards with perks like airline miles or a low introductory rate often have higher annual fees. Remember: Nothing is free. Skip the card and fees and buy your plane ticket the old-fashioned way—with your money.

OVER-THE-LIMIT FEES

Credit card companies set spending limits on each account based on a person's income, credit score, and any other outstanding debt. If you spend over the credit limit—you guessed it—you have to pay a penalty.

> **If you can't pay cash, you can't afford it.**
> — *Dave Ramsey*

LATE PAYMENT FEES

Any time you miss a payment—whether you lost your job or just plain forgot to make your payment that month—credit card companies don't care. You'll have to pay a late fee.

MERCHANT FEES

Every time a credit card is used to buy something, the credit card company charges the store or merchant a processing fee. That 2–3% fee is built into the prices at most stores to offset the transaction fee.

Spending More Money

When you buy with credit, you spend more money. Why? Because you don't feel the pain that comes with spending—of trading money for something. Think about it, when you have to pull out a $10 bill to pay for the chips and guacamole you ordered, you exchange your money to get food. But when you pay with plastic, you pay and get to keep both—the card and the food.

So, what does that mean? If you don't feel that slight pain of spending money, can you guess what happens 10 times out of 10? Bingo! You spend more money.

Spending with a debit card is the closest thing to using cash because the money is withdrawn directly from your checking account. If you must use plastic (to make purchases online or to rent a car while you're traveling), use a debit card. You'll spend less money in the long run.

Credit Card Myths

A lot of people believe you need a credit card for certain kinds of purchases. Don't fall for those myths! A debit card can do anything a credit card can do. With it, you can shop online, travel, and rent a car or hotel room. The only thing you can't do with a debit card is go into debt!

People also believe credit cards are more secure than debit cards. Again, not true! Debit cards have all the same fraud and security protections as credit cards. There's simply no reason to have a credit card.

Did You Know?

The CARD Act of 2009 put limits on credit card tactics:

- They can't hide fees or interest rate hikes.
- They can't give credit cards to anyone under 21 (with a few exceptions).
- They can't set up tables to market to college students within 1,000 feet of a college campus.

Your JOURNAL What are all the ways you spend more money when you pay with a credit card?

REMEMBER THIS Add a ✓ next to each completed learning objective below.

◯ You've evaluated the increased costs of using a credit card to make purchases.

◯ You can identify all the ways the credit card industry makes money.

◯ You can explain the financial impact of using credit to make purchases.

THIS LESSON MAKES ME FEEL Circle your response to what you learned.

CONFUSED   SURPRISED   THOUGHTFUL   CONFIDENT

LESSON VIDEO GUIDE

*I want you to own a nice car. I just
don't want your nice car to own you!* — Dave Ramsey

GUIDED NOTES   While you watch the video, complete the section below.

1. Myth: Car _____ are a way of life.

2. Truth: Avoid car _____ now and always.

3. The average new car payment in America is _____ a month.

4. Take notes during the car salesman interview. What should you be on the lookout for when buying a car? How should you prepare when you're getting ready to buy a car?

    _____

    _____

    _____

ANALYZE AND REFLECT   After you watch the video, respond to the question(s) below.

1. Consider the statement: Car dealerships make more money on financing than they do on the car. What does that tell you about the value of financing? Who wins and who loses when a car is financed? Why?

    _____

    _____

    _____

LEARNING OBJECTIVES
- Understand why car loans and leases are horrible ways to purchase a car.
- Understand why paying cash for cars and avoiding car loans is not only possible, but the best way to own a car.

MAIN IDEA

Buying a car with cash means you own the car without debt—and you don't have to worry about car loan or lease payments. That's a huge win!

How Do Car Loans Work?

Despite what many Americans think, your car is *not* a status symbol. Yup, we said it. Too many people buy into the myth that they need a sweet new ride. Don't get sucked into the idea that people will have a better opinion of you if you're driving a certain type of car. Having a nice car doesn't mean you're a successful person—just like having an older car doesn't mean you're flat broke.

If you buy into the belief that a shiny new car is a symbol of success, you're measuring success with the wrong end of the ruler.

— *Chris Hogan*

So, what's a car loan and how does it work? Great question. There are two major ways to finance a car: direct financing (a loan) and leasing. But let's just say right up front that neither of these is a good idea. Why? Because each one just puts you into years of debt.

Direct Financing

Many people believe you just can't have a car without a car loan. That's one of the biggest money myths today! The truth is that using credit to buy a car (aka financing) will cost you way more than the car's actual sticker price.

That's because, just like with any loan, you don't just pay back the money it costs to buy the car—you pay interest too!

A car loan payment is determined by three main things:

1. **Principal:** This is the total amount of the loan—the cost of the car plus any taxes and fees.
2. **Interest:** Just like with a credit card, this is an additional cost (or penalty) your lender charges for letting you borrow their money.
3. **Term:** This is the amount of time you have to pay back the loan. Usually, the more time you have, the lower your payment will be—but you'll pay more interest over time.

Listen, the very best way to buy a car is to pay cash for it. Here's why:

> Never spend your money before you have it.
>
> **Thomas Jefferson**
> 3rd U.S. President

Principal: the original amount of a loan; the total amount borrowed before interest

Interest: the additional cost a lender charges for borrowing their money

Term: the amount of time, in months, that you'll be making payments

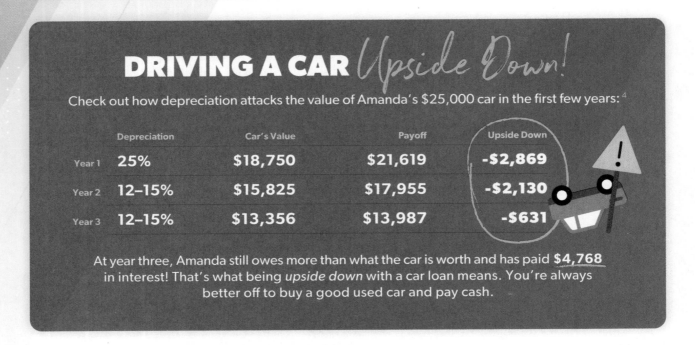

DRIVING A CAR *Upside Down!*

Check out how depreciation attacks the value of Amanda's $25,000 car in the first few years: [4]

	Depreciation	Car's Value	Payoff	Upside Down
Year 1	25%	$18,750	$21,619	-$2,869
Year 2	12–15%	$15,825	$17,955	-$2,130
Year 3	12–15%	$13,356	$13,987	-$631

At year three, Amanda still owes more than what the car is worth and has paid **$4,768** in interest! That's what being *upside down* with a car loan means. You're always better off to buy a good used car and pay cash.

Depreciation: the loss of value of an asset over time

Negative Equity: when the value of an asset falls below what is owed on it

Did You Know?

Over 70% of loans for new cars are for over 60 months—and the average new car loan is 69 months! [5]

Let's say Amanda wants to buy a new car. She got a great job right out of college and wants to upgrade her wheels to match her new title (big mistake). So, she does what most people do—finances the car instead of saving up the cash and paying for it in full (we told you how to save up and pay cash for cars, for life, in Chapter 3).

Amanda got a "good deal" on a new car for $25,000 with no down payment at an 8% interest rate. She promised to pay the loan back over a six-year term (or 72 monthly payments). *Yikes!*

But if Amanda knew how car loans really work, she would have kept her old car. Instead, she ended up with a $438 monthly payment—for the next six years! That will put a huge dent in her budget. Plus, after 72 payments, she will have paid over $31,500 for a $25,000 car—that's over $6,500 in interest payments! Don't pay more for a car (or anything) than it's actually worth.

If that wasn't bad enough, her shiny new car will lose almost 25% of its value in the first year of her loan. That's called **depreciation**, and it will cause her to be upside down with her car loan. That's bad news! Being upside down—also called **negative equity**—means you owe more money on the loan than the car is worth. Check out the chart at the top of this page to see how fast that can happen.

Amanda's "good deal" was a huge financial mistake! If Amanda has a financial emergency and can't make her payments, even if she sells the car, the money from the sale won't cover what she owes.

Leasing

Leasing is the other main way to finance a new car. Leasing is the *most* expensive way to drive a car. But of course, your friendly neighborhood car dealer would never tell you that—that's what this course is for.

A typical lease payment helps cover the depreciation of the vehicle. Your payment also includes a rental charge, taxes, and fees. And, after all that, you don't have a car when the lease is over—typically in three years—unless you decide to *pay even more* to buy the car at the end of the lease.

Leasing a car may sound like a great idea, but in reality, you're paying to drive a glorified rental car. Sure, monthly lease payments are often lower than payments on a car loan. But your hard-earned cash is really just padding the dealer's pockets until the end of the lease term.

Leasing a car is the most expensive way to drive a car.

— Dave Ramsey

Don't forget: Lease agreements come with a mileage cap. If you go over the mileage cap (and most people do), you'll pay a penalty. You're also responsible for maintaining the car and keeping it in great condition—or you'll pay for that later with an excessive wear fee. And there's often a fee just to turn the car back in so the dealer can clean it and sell it.

Pay Cash for Your Car

Don't fall for the myth that car payments are just a normal part of life. Remember, **The Third Foundation** is pay cash for your car. Your first paid-for car may not come with that new car smell (it's overrated) or win any beauty contests, but you can upgrade your car—for cash—and end up with a sweet ride in a few years. Even better, you won't have a huge monthly car payment. It feels great to drive a car when you own it!

Did You Know?

When it comes to money skills, 94% of teens who took a personal financial course feel very confident in saving money.[6]

The Third Foundation: Pay cash for your car.

// *Your* JOURNAL   Why do so many Americans believe that car payments are just a normal way of life?

_____

_____

_____

REMEMBER THIS   Add a ✓ next to each completed learning objective below.

◯ You understand why car loans and leases are horrible ways to purchase a car.

◯ You can explain why paying cash for cars and avoiding car loans is not only possible, but the best way to own a car.

THIS LESSON MAKES ME FEEL   Circle your response to what you learned.

😓 CONFUSED   😗 SURPRISED   🙂 THOUGHTFUL   🤩 CONFIDENT

LESSON VIDEO GUIDE

Going into debt is a huge mistake that seriously steals from your future dreams and goals.

— *Anthony O'Neal*

GUIDED NOTES   While you watch the video, complete the section below.

1. Take _____ off the table.

2. Pay off all debt using the _____.

3. Paying off debt is not a math problem—it is a _____ problem.

4. This is not a theory. It is a _____ process.

5. Why is it important to learn and take advice from people who are successful?

   _____

   _____

ANALYZE AND REFLECT   After you watch the video, respond to the question(s) below.

1. Consider a person who's drowning in debt with credit cards, car payments, and student loans. What advice would you have for them? What can you do now to make sure you don't end up in this situation later in life?

   _____

   _____

   _____

LEARNING OBJECTIVE

Explain strategies to avoid and get out of debt.

MAIN IDEA

Debt causes financial risk and stress. Avoiding debt—of any kind—is the very best way to win with money.

Avoiding Debt Is Important

All right—time for some real talk. Are you on board with the debt-free lifestyle you're learning about? Or are you still asking yourself, *If everyone around me is using credit to buy what they want right now, why should I be different?* Well, here's the deal. With 78% of Americans living paycheck to paycheck, most people only look like they're living the American dream.[7]

The truth is that they're broke and stressed out about how much debt they have. That's not the American dream at all! But by choosing to avoid debt and learning good money habits now, you can give yourself a real chance to build wealth, give outrageously, and live a life of financial security—the real American dream.

The Second Foundation is get out and stay out of debt. That means if you have any debt, you need to pay it off as quickly as possible. And we'll show you how. If you don't owe anyone any money, that's great!

Being debt-free with a small income puts you financially ahead of most Americans already! Keep it that way by avoiding debt throughout your life. Sure, you might not be rolling in cash, but you also aren't up to your eyeballs in debt!

How to Avoid Debt

We get it. Deciding to avoid debt in this culture is like swimming against the current. You'll have to ignore the barrage of credit cards offers, easy financing options, and those annoying "buy now, pay later" promotions. And that's the easy part.

You'll see people just like you—just starting out in life—spending money without a care on fancy vacations and new cars. They'll think you're weird because you're not doing the same thing. At times it won't seem fair. But that's when you need to remember that huge credit card bill they'll get a few weeks after their vacation, or that hefty car payment they'll have to pay *every month*—for five or six years!

> ## Debt doesn't open doors— it closes them. Take debt off the table.
>
> *— Anthony O'Neal*

Your choice to live debt-free starts with your mindset. Just take debt off the table— meaning, aside from a home mortgage, it's *never* an option. Never. Period.

Did You Know?

Americans said the following things are worth going into debt for:[8]

61% Health Care	
47% Housing	
37% Vacation	
16% Clothing	
16% Electronics	
13% Dining	
11% Entertainment	

The Second Foundation: Get out and stay out of debt.

The First Foundation: Save a $500 emergency fund.

Did You Know?

Of Americans who have credit cards, here's how many cards they have:[9]

37
19
16
28

37% 1 credit card
28% 2 credit cards
16% 3 credit cards
19% 4 or more credit cards

How to Get Out of Debt

So, if you do have debt—maybe a car loan, credit card debt, or even a personal loan from a family member or friend—now's the time to tackle it. You don't want debt following you into life after high school!

Remember, **The First Foundation** is save a $500 emergency fund. Once you've done that, it's time to throw as much money as possible at your debt. If you don't have a job, get one. With your parents covering your living expenses, you can throw a lot of your money at debt.

What if you have a car payment? One option: Sell the car. Boom! The debt is gone, and you can save up to pay cash for an affordable used car.

That's a tough choice to make—we understand that. We never said this stuff was easy. But we guarantee it's worth it. If you keep saving to upgrade your car, you can drive paid-for cars for life.

The Debt Snowball Method

You probably know someone who has several debts—credit cards, a car loan, and student loans. It's a tough place to be. But it's possible to get it all paid off.

The debt snowball method is the best way to get all those debts paid off as quickly as possible. Here's what to do:

- List your debts in order from smallest to largest, regardless of interest rates. Pay minimum payments on everything but the little one.
- Attack the smallest debt! When it's gone, add that payment to the next debt—and any extra money you can squeeze out of the budget. Keep paying minimum payments on the other debts.
- Once a debt is gone, take its payment and apply it to the next smallest debt. That creates the snowball. And as the snowball rolls over, it picks up more snow. Get it?

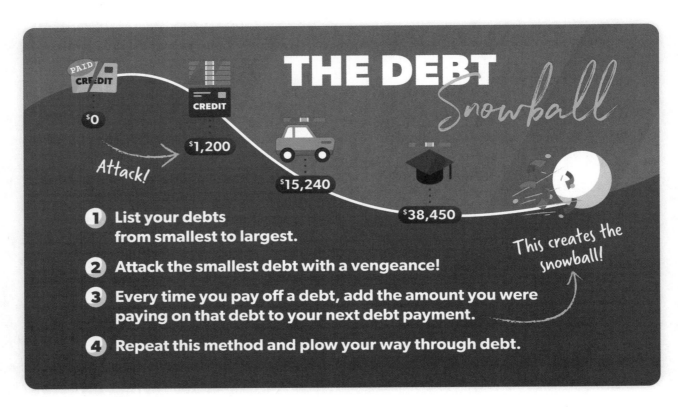

THE DEBT *Snowball*

PAID
CREDIT
$0

CREDIT
$1,200
Attack!

$15,240

$38,450

This creates the snowball!

1. **List your debts from smallest to largest.**
2. **Attack the smallest debt with a vengeance!**
3. **Every time you pay off a debt, add the amount you were paying on that debt to your next debt payment.**
4. **Repeat this method and plow your way through debt.**

Freedom to Give

Giving money away? Really? You might be thinking, *Why should I think about giving when I'm trying to get out of debt?* Simple: Debt steals your ability to be as generous as you want to be. It's true!

Generosity is a lifestyle that changes hearts.

— Rachel Cruze

Like everything else about you, how you spend your money—and give your money—reflects who you are. Giving changes your heart and moves you farther away from money owning you.

If generosity doesn't come naturally to you, you can learn how to be more giving. Giving reminds you that you're part of a larger global community where others have needs that you can help meet. If you feel like you don't have enough money to give, you can start by giving small amounts of money or some of your time. Think about how much money or time you could spare each month. Use that to make a plan for how to practice giving to others.

Life Without Debt

So, really, what's the point of living debt-free? Well, just ask yourself, *What do I have if I don't have debt?* The answer: hope. Hope for your future! Debt is an obstacle that holds you back. Be the generation that sees debt differently—not as a financial tool, but for what it is: a financial trap.

It's up to you!

Steps Out of Debt

- Quit borrowing more money!
- Start saving money.
- Sell something.
- Get a part-time job or work overtime (temporarily).
- Use the debt snowball method.

Your JOURNAL Describe in your own words the benefits of living a debt-free life.

_____

_____

_____

REMEMBER THIS Add a ✓ next to the completed learning objective below.

◯ You can explain strategies for avoiding debt and getting out of debt.

THIS LESSON MAKES ME FEEL Circle your response to what you learned.

😓 CONFUSED   😮 SURPRISED   🙂 THOUGHTFUL   🤩 CONFIDENT

Chapter 4 Review

Fill in the blanks below using the correct key terms from this chapter.

Debt	Appreciating Asset	Depreciating Asset	Principal
Revolving Credit	Equity	Predatory Lender	Term
Collateral	Default	Credit Score	Depreciation
Interest	Installment Credit	Credit Bureau	Negative Equity
Lien			

1. If a loan isn't repaid, the _____ of the borrower—used as security for the debt—could be sold by the lender.

2. A(n) _____ is a number that indicates the likelihood of someone repaying debt.

3. A(n) _____ reports on a person's credit history.

4. The amount of time you have to pay back a loan is called the _____ of the loan.

5. When an item is worth less than what you owe on it, that's called _____ _____.

6. Making fixed payments on a loan over a set period of time is an example of _____.

7. When an asset loses value over time, that's _____.

8. When you fail to repay a loan on time, you're referred to as being in _____.

FINISH THE SENTENCE   Use what you've learned in this chapter to complete these sentences.

1. The first step of the debt snowball method is to list all your debts _____ _____.

2. Checking your credit report regularly can help you spot signs of _____ _____.

1. Which of these is not one of the main credit bureau reporting agencies?

    A. Identifax   C. TransUnion

    B. Equifax   D. Experian

2. With a debit card, you can do everything you can do with a credit card except what?

    A. Rent a car   C. Go into debt

    B. Stay at a hotel   D. Fly on an airplane

3. A clothing store credit card is an example of what type of debt?

    A. Revolving credit   C. Personal loan

    B. Installment credit D. Lien

4. Which of the following is not factored into the loan payment on a new car?

    A. Term   C. Interest

    B. Equity   D. Principal

5. Predatory lenders use all of the following to prey on desperate people except . . .

    A. Unfair practices   C. Truthful logic

    B. Deceptive tactics D. Fraudulent info

6. Which of these isn't a marketing tactic to get you to use credit?

    A. 0% interest   C. 1.5% cash back

    B. Introductory offer D. 50% off sale

Review **QUESTION**   Why is a high credit score not an indication that you're winning with money?

_____

_____

_____

_____

_____

_____

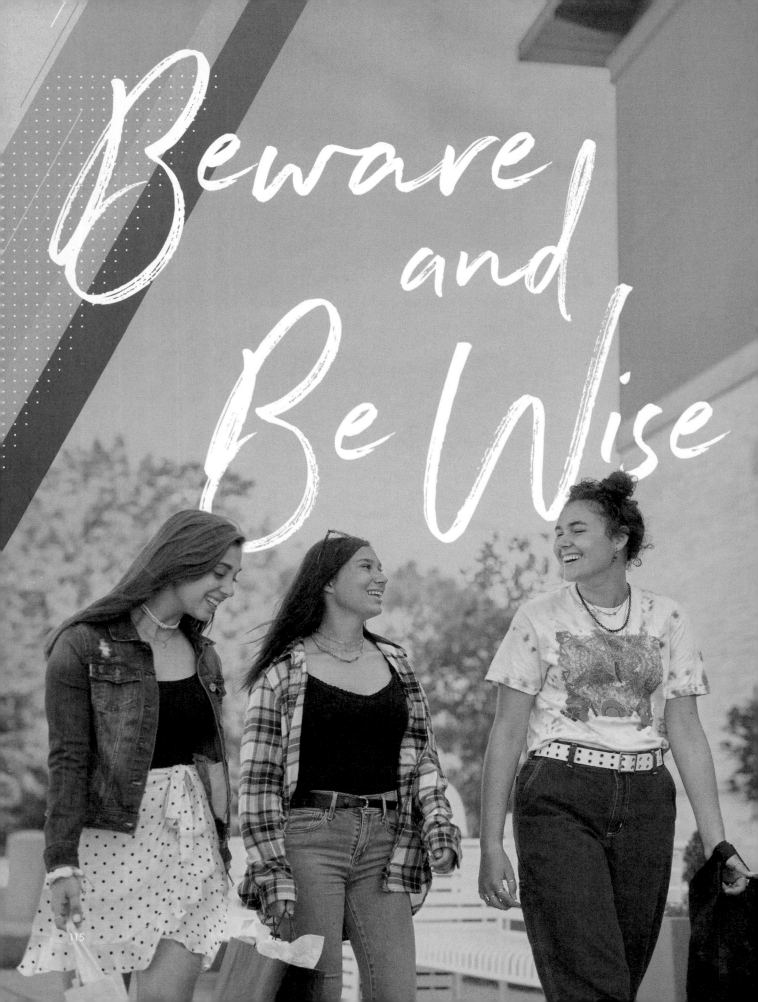

Beware
and
Be Wise

Consumer Awareness

This chapter highlights the importance of being a wise consumer as part of a healthy financial plan, explains strategies to manage spending behavior, exposes common consumer scams, and identifies consumer rights.

LESSON VIDEO GUIDE

I am tempted all the time to buy stuff without really thinking. — Anthony O'Neal

GUIDED NOTES   While you watch the video, complete the section below.

1. Write down a few key takeaways from the discussion on impulse purchases.

   _____

   _____

   _____

   _____

ANALYZE AND REFLECT   After you watch the video, respond to the question(s) below.

1. Think of something you purchased recently on impulse. What made you decide to make the purchase? Would you buy it again, or do you wish you hadn't bought it in the first place?

   _____

   _____

   _____

2. Why do you think buying something on impulse is more likely to cause buyer's remorse?

   _____

   _____

   _____

MAIN IDEA

The temptation to overspend follows us everywhere we go. But to win with money, you'll need to keep your spending in check.

Impulse Buying

No matter where or how you shop, the temptation to overspend on random stuff is everywhere. Yep, we're talking about the checkout lane. Mini hand sanitizers, gum, and a cold drink! How about a candy bar, chips, or a celebrity magazine? It seems they've thought of everything—things you didn't even plan to buy. We've all been there!

Other times, it can feel like shopping finds you! You can't scroll through social media without running smack into an ad for the "perfect" item—that you can buy with one click! **Impulse buying** is so easy it might seem impossible to avoid spending mistakes that bust your budget.

Americans impulsively spend over $600 every month (on average) for things that weren't in their budget—and 76% feel guilty about it.[1] That's money they didn't plan to spend on stuff they didn't plan to buy—and many people use credit cards to pay for all of those extra things.

Consumer spending is a huge part of our economy, and it includes nondiscretionary spending on things we *need* like food and clothes. Then there's discretionary spending, which includes nonessential goods and services. That's right—those would be the *wants*. And most people are just as likely to spend too much on the things they need as they are on things that are just nice to have.

> We buy things we don't need with money we don't have to impress people we don't like.
>
> — Dave Ramsey

The truth is, Americans have made a lifestyle of spending too much money buying things they can't afford. Our obsession with buying and having stuff is *not* the way to win with money.

You Take Control

"Caveat emptor" is an old Latin saying that means "let the buyer beware." In the world of **consumerism** and marketing, "buyer beware" simply means that you'd better

Did You Know?

Consumer awareness refers to a buyer's knowledge of a product or company. It allows the buyer to make informed choices.

Impulse Buying: buying anything without planning to do so in advance

Consumerism: the theory that spending money and consuming goods is good for the economy

He who buys what he does not need steals from himself.

Swedish Proverb

watch out for yourself. It's not someone else's job to make sure you aren't getting duped into buying a bad or over-priced product—or a product you just can't afford. Americans see thousands of advertisements every day—and more than a million marketing messages each year. Each one is designed to separate you from your money. Learning to be a smart consumer—someone who knows how to say no—will save you from some serious financial trouble.

As a consumer, you need to think about what you're buying *and* how it's being sold to you. Americans often make lazy buying decisions—not considering if they really need an item, can afford it, or can get a better deal somewhere else. Millions of marketing dollars are spent every year to prey on that attitude.

It's not just the marketing you see every day. Today's payment methods make it easier than ever to spend. A swipe, click, or wave of your phone (or even watch) and the item is yours—and your money is spent. Digital wallets and mobile payment might be convenient, but if you're not careful, they'll bust your budget!

Power Over Purchase

So, how do you limit your spending and be a wise consumer in a culture that's so focused on consumerism? Let's be honest—going against the norm isn't easy. But there's *hope*: You can control your spending, even when those around you don't. We've said it before, but it's worth repeating: You need a budget!

The point of budgeting is for you to take control of your money and not let your money control you.

— Anthony O'Neal

First, you'll need to have specific money goals *and* be motivated to reach them. We've already talked about the importance of savings goals. Let the *why* behind your goals—and a clear vision of *what* you're trying to accomplish—keep you on track.

That's much easier to do when you remember consumerism and buying things you can't afford won't help you reach your

A Message From **RACHEL**

It doesn't matter how much money you make—it matters how much you keep. What gets me in trouble so often are sales. You might think sales are a good thing, and they can be, but there's something about a sale sign that gets my heart pumping. It's important to know that sales are a marketing gimmick. Marketers know that some people get so distracted by what they could *save* that they lose track of what they could *spend*. In the interest of "saving" money, these shoppers spend money they never planned on spending. And when that happens, marketers and merchandisers make more money.

goals. In fact, the stuff you buy can often make you feel burdened and let down (more about that later). The truth is, you'll never find fulfillment in things you buy. You'll learn that *contentment*—or focusing on what you have rather than what you don't have—is an important part of being a wise consumer.

On a more practical level, you'll also learn how to develop your power over purchase. That simply means slowing down and thinking through your buying motives. You'll start to ask yourself, "Why do I want or think I need this item?" That's really important to understand—especially when you're planning to drop a lot of cash to purchase something. That way, you can avoid impulse spending and the dreaded **buyer's remorse**.

Another important part of being a wise consumer is knowing how to protect yourself from card fraud—and what to do if you're a victim. Card fraud is a real thing, and you need to pay attention to your account to make sure you don't become a victim. That might be a reality of the digital world we live in, but we'll cover the options you have to help make sure your personal info—and your money—stays safe.

That's a lot of ground to cover, and it's all important stuff. But to really be a wise consumer, you'll have to put what you learn into action. Remember, personal finance is 20% head knowledge and *80%* behavior. It's not enough just to *know* the right things to do as a consumer. You actually have to

follow through!

Did You Know?

85% of U.S. teens own a smartphone, which could mean they're doing most of their shopping from a mobile device.[3]

Buyer's Remorse: a feeling of guilt, regret, or uneasiness after making a purchase

---

Your JOURNAL

What are some things that tempt you to spend impulsively or without having planned to spend?

REMEMBER THIS   Add a ✓ next to each completed learning objective below.

◯ You understand the value of consumer awareness as part of a healthy financial plan.

◯ You understand the importance of controlling your spending and avoiding impulse buying in your financial plan.

THIS LESSON MAKES ME FEEL   (Circle) your response to what you learned.

 CONFUSED   SURPRISED   THOUGHTFUL   CONFIDENT

LESSON 2 | The Convenience of Mobile Pay

LESSON VIDEO GUIDE

I don't have a problem with convenient payment methods. It becomes a problem if you overspend. — Anthony O'Neal

GUIDED NOTES   While you watch the video, complete the section below.

1. When you pay for something with _____, you actually feel it more.

2. When you pay with cash, you're less likely to _____.

3. _____ pay and digital payments are becoming more popular.

4. When you set up mobile pay, you are _____ that app to use your debit card.

5. The more convenient the _____ method, the more likely you are to spend more money.

6. Mobile payment apps track your _____ spending habits.

ANALYZE AND REFLECT   After you watch the video, respond to the question(s) below.

1. What are some of the pros and cons of mobile payment methods?

   _____

   _____

   _____

   _____

LEARNING OBJECTIVES

- Understand how cashless payment methods affect your spending behavior.
- Identify strategies for managing your spending in the era of digital convenience.

MAIN IDEA

Today, it's easier than ever to use payment apps and virtual wallets, but you have to think about how that convenience affects your spending behavior.

Mobile Pay Impacts Your Spending Behavior

Treating yourself to an occasional coffee might seem like a small indulgence, but you've probably figured out that the amount you spend on your java habit can add up quickly. And what if you use a payment app instead of cash or your debit card to pay for your favorite coffee? It's simple, quick, and convenient—and you get a 10% discount on every 10th coffee. Who doesn't love that? But have you ever thought about how those customer loyalty perks and the convenience of mobile pay affect how often and how much you spend?

So what exactly is **mobile pay**? It's a type of digital payment you make or receive with a mobile device. While it's probably your go-to form of payment, you need to understand how it impacts the way you spend money.

Of course, mobile pay isn't the only form of **digital payment**. A digital payment happens when you pay by *any* electronic method instead of physically using your debit card or paying with cash. Other examples include online transfers, online bill pay, and direct deposits.

Digital payments are leading us toward a cashless economy, and retailers are joining that shift with their digital apps. Why the change? That's a question a smart consumer would ask! Remember, businesses want to make money—and these payment apps help them do that!

> ## When you and I don't fork over the cash, we're likely to spend more.
>
> — *Chris Hogan*

By developing their own payment apps, stores make it easier *and faster* for you to pay (less time to second-guess that impulse purchase). All you have to do is load your debit card information into their app, and you're ready to spend—without the pain of handing over your cash.

It's no surprise that people are joining in on the shift to cashless payments. These apps come with enticing perks—like rewards programs, discounts, mobile order-ahead—*and* you'll be treated as their loyal customer. Nice!

Did You Know?

From $1.1 trillion in 2019 to over $3.1 trillion in 2024, the growth of mobile pay is exploding![4]

Mobile Pay: a type of digital payment made or received with a mobile device

Digital Payment: a completely electronic transaction between a buyer and seller, replacing the use of cash, checks, or physically swiping/inserting a card

The Perks of Mobile Pay

So, what are some perks of mobile pay for you, the consumer? Let's start with convenience. Paying for things has never been easier. No cash? No problem! And no need to stop at the ATM or pay a fee to get your cash. In fact, many retailers are moving toward not accepting cash at all so they can speed up checkout.

Digital wallets make transferring money quick and easy between family, friends, and even when you're buying or selling with strangers—regardless of distance. That really beats the old method of wire transfer that often took days and came with a high fee. So, that's like two perks. It's fast and it saves you money.

Another perk: Mobile pay and other forms of digital payment give you a real-time record of what you've spent. Remember the importance of tracking your spending throughout the month in order to make sure you're sticking to your budget? Done! Instead of manually doing the math and writing down every transaction in your checkbook ledger (if you're not sure what

Did You Know?

72% of Gen Zs (1997–2012) say they purchased a product online in the last 30 days using a mobile device.[5]

that is, ask you parents), digital pay options use an app or online feature to show you how much you spent and where you shopped. And it shows up right away.

The Downside of Mobile Pay

So with all the benefits of mobile pay, what could possibly be the downside of digital payment options? One word: *convenience.* Yes, that's the first perk, but it's also the first downside. It's way too easy to spend with digital payment methods. You've learned that the most effective way to spend less is to use cash. When you spend cash, you *feel* it. When you hand over cash, you're more likely to think about how much you're spending. And if you don't have a plan for your money, digital wallets make it easy to overspend.

Privacy concerns are another drawback to payment apps. While they make it easier for you to track your spending, you need to be aware that companies are tracking your spending as well—what you buy, how much you typically spend, and how often you shop at their store.

WEAR THIS, *Buy That!*

Younger consumers are more likely to make purchases using a wearable device.[6]

Age 16–24	25–34	35–44	45–54	55–64
58%	57%	48%	37%	20%

Percent who would make a payment using a wearable device

$1.37 TRILLION

PROJECTED SALES MADE THROUGH WEARABLE PAYMENT DEVICES BY 2027

In fact, *all* customer rewards programs—through an app or a store membership—track your spending. Companies use this information to target you with ads based on your spending habits—all with the goal of getting you to spend even more money! Digital pay services are also at risk of data breaches where your information can be hacked and stolen.

While you can't turn back technology and time (and who would want to with all the convenience that comes with it?), you need to be aware of how these changes in payment methods affect your behavior and the way you spend money.

Don't let convenience lead you into reckless spending. Stick to what you've learned about living on a zero-based budget and tracking your spending. Then you can enjoy the convenience of cashless payment without falling into the out-of-control spending trap.

It's okay to have nice stuff. Just don't let your nice stuff have you.

— *Rachel Cruze*

Whether you're using cash, your debit card, or cashless pay options, *you* are responsible for planning and managing your spending. At the end of the day, what matters is how you manage your money—and your spending behavior.

Did You Know?

77% of millennials redeem rewards at least once every four months—Gen Z redeems the least.[7]

Your **JOURNAL**   Which cashless payment methods do you use? What's the best way to control your spending while using cashless payment methods?

_____

_____

_____

REMEMBER THIS   Add a ✓ next to each completed learning objective below.

◯ You're aware of how cashless payment methods can affect your spending behavior.

◯ You can identify strategies for managing your spending behavior in the era of digital convenience.

THIS LESSON MAKES ME FEEL   Circle your response to what you learned.

☹ CONFUSED   😮 SURPRISED   🙂 THOUGHTFUL   🤩 CONFIDENT

LESSON VIDEO GUIDE

We can't let our spending get out of control because we have to buy everything that is advertised to us. — Anthony O'Neal

GUIDED NOTES   While you watch the video, complete the section below.

1. Write down three key takeaways from the discussion about how targeted marketing can influence your spending habits.

   _____

   _____

   _____

2. Marketing _____ are everywhere.

3. _____ get paid to make sure you see their products.

4. Targeted marketing is _____ to bring money into their business.

5. It becomes a problem when we're not _____ of these tactics.

ANALYZE AND REFLECT   After you watch the video, respond to the question(s) below.

1. Think of an ad you recently saw. Do you think the ad was targeting you? Why or why not?

   _____

   _____

   _____

MAIN IDEA

Marketers use time-tested tactics to win your hard-earned dollars. If you know their tactics, you're more likely to hang on to your cash.

Marketing Equals Big Bucks

Whether you're scrolling through social media, searching the web, streaming music, or walking into a mall, you're stepping into a battle—a battle for your money!

We live in the most marketed-to culture in the history of the world! **Marketing** is everything a company does to sell their product to consumers—that's you. The goal is to get you to buy their product or service. Marketers know they're competing for your attention, so they have lots of tricks to use to convince you to buy their product instead of someone else's.

Marketing and Media

Marketing happens everywhere and comes in many different forms. The traditional—or *old-fashioned*—methods include print, radio, television, direct mail, and telephone. More modern marketing channels include email, social media, pay-per-click marketing, search engine marketing, and mobile phone marketing.

To get results—to make money—marketers make it their business to know where their customers spend a lot of time and the marketing methods they respond to most. So, they do a ton of research on specific audiences or demographics.

> ### Sacrifice the latest so you can have the greatest.
> — *Anthony O'Neal*

For example, how often do you watch TV commercials, listen to live radio ads, or flip through a newspaper? Hardly ever, right? Marketers know most people spend a lot of time on their mobile devices. That's why digital ad spending is projected to grow to $526 billion in 2024![8]

Marketers work to build up their brand so that the name or logo becomes easily memorable. That's known as **brand recognition**. Some of your favorite shoe brands and technology brands have done a great job of creating memorable names and logos.

Product placement is also a marketing tool. Seeing actors use or wear an item on TV or in a movie helps sell the item.

Marketing: the process of communicating the value of a product or service to customers

Did You Know? 92% of marketers say video is an important part of their strategy—that's why you see so many video ads on social media.[9]

Brand Recognition: the public's ability to recall and recognize a brand by its logo, jingle, packaging, or name

Sneaky RETAIL TRICKS

You've probably seen all of these, but did you know these marketing tactics are designed to get you to spend more money?

Huge Sales Events
discounts and special shopping events around every holiday

Shopping Carts
located at the entrance to make it easy for you to pick up lots of big and little things

High Profit Items
displayed in the front of the store so they're the first thing you see

Multisensory Marketing
colors, music, and smells that make you spend more time in the store

Essential Items
located in the back of the store so you pick up some nonessential items along the way

Item Specials
buy one item and get a second different item for a discount or free

Impulse Purchase Items
displayed in the checkout line to tempt you with one last item . . . or two

Customer Rewards
earn points and special coupons when you spend more money

Digital Marketing

Picture this: It's Saturday morning, and you're scrolling social media to catch up with friends. Before your feet even hit the floor, you've spent $30 on that new, life-changing thing you didn't even know you needed. All because a well-placed ad found its way to you—their target audience and customer. That's not an accident.

An engaging ad is no reason to buy something you don't need. But how do you guard your budget against these *oh-so-tempting* ads? Great question. First, you need to be aware of when and where you're being marketed to.

Think about what you usually do when you're online. If you're like most people, you're checking out social media and watching videos. What does that mean

to a marketer? To reach larger audiences and get the most out of their ad budget, they include social media and video ad content in their online advertising strategy.

Marketers have a plan to get your money.

— *Dave Ramsey*

In fact, 50% of retailers spend at least half of their annual marketing budget on social media advertising.[10] Here are just a few types of the strategies they'll use:

RETARGETING

Also known as *remarketing*, retargeting is a form of online advertising that keeps a company's product in front of its target audience by following them all over the web, across multiple channels.

CONTENT MARKETING

The goal here is to help customers solve their problems with valuable content in the form of blogs, videos, and podcasts that lead the customer to make a purchase.

INFLUENCER MARKETING

Typically found on social media, influencers are people with a large online audience to whom they market brands and products.

SNACK VIDEOS

These have nothing to do with food. They're just short, entertaining ad videos

(around 10 seconds) on most social media platforms and mobile video games.

NATIVE ADVERTISING

These digital ads look like normal social media posts. Advertisers hope their ads will catch your attention so you'll stop, click, and check it out.

The Bottom Line

Marketing is all around you—and it's a big business! Targeted marketing to your age group, gender, and region are designed to influence your buying choices and habits. Being aware of the marketing going on around you will help you stay in control of what you buy and when. Remember: *You're in control of your money!*

Did You Know?

79% of people say user-generated content highly impacts their buying decisions.[11]

Your JOURNAL   Why is it important as a consumer to recognize and understand marketing techniques and strategies?

_____

_____

_____

REMEMBER THIS   Add a ✓ next to each completed learning objective below.

◯ You recognize the purpose of marketing and the impact it can have on your financial plan.

◯ You can identify various types of media and forms of advertising.

◯ You can identify a variety of common marketing tactics.

THIS LESSON MAKES ME FEEL   (Circle) your response to what you learned.

😓 CONFUSED   😮 SURPRISED   🙂 THOUGHTFUL   🤩 CONFIDENT

LESSON VIDEO GUIDE

 Check your bank statements to make sure there aren't any shady purchases that you don't remember making. — *Anthony O'Neal*

GUIDED NOTES   While you watch the video, complete the section below.

1. Only buy things when your device is connected to a _____ Wi-Fi network.

2. Using an unsecured network can open you up to all kinds of _____.

3. Don't buy things or enter your debit card if you are on a free _____ network.

4. The S in HTTPS stands for _____.

5. Large retailers are huge targets for _____.

6. Make sure your passwords are _____.

ANALYZE AND REFLECT   After you watch the video, respond to the question(s) below.

1. What are some ways you can limit or prevent identity theft or fraudulent charges?

    _____

    _____

    _____

LEARNING OBJECTIVES

- Understand how to recognize signs of debit card fraud.
- Develop strategies to prevent having your bank account information stolen.
- Understand what you should do if you experience card fraud or theft.

MAIN IDEA

There are things you can do to protect yourself from card fraud. In the event your information is lost or stolen, you also have some liability protections.

Card Fraud Is Everywhere

You're driving home after a closing shift at work and roll up to the mom-and-pop gas station. You pull out your debit card, punch in your PIN, fill up your tank, and drive away. Back on the road!

What you didn't notice (blame it on being tired from a long day) was that the card reader looked a bit off. The next day, you get an alert from your bank that your account has been overdrafted. You check your account and see a large transaction you didn't make at a store you've never been to. Yep, you've just experienced **card fraud**.

> **If you 're the victim of fraud, you need to contact your bank immediately!**
> — Dave Ramsey

If you or someone you know has ever been the victim of card fraud or **identity theft,** then you know how scary, violating, and frustrating it can be. How did they

get your information, and what do you do now? When a thief gets access to your card number (debit or credit card), that's card fraud, plain and simple.

As you know, we don't recommend credit cards at all. But if you have one and it's stolen, that's credit card fraud. In our digital world, there are more and more ways for thieves to steal your account information and rip you off. Here are some:

CARD SKIMMERS

Identity thieves attach these tricky devices to card readers at gas stations and ATM machines. When you insert your card to make a transaction, your card information (along with your PIN number, if you used it) goes straight to the thief.

The next time you pull up to the pump, check out the card reader *before* you insert your card. If it looks worn or loose, use cash or opt for a different pump.

INTERCEPTING MAIL

Isn't that illegal? Yep. But identity thieves aren't too concerned about what's right and wrong. They'll shamelessly dig

Card Fraud: the unauthorized use of your debit or credit card number and PIN or the forging of your signature

Identity Theft: the act of fraudulently gaining and using the personal information of someone else, usually for financial gain

Avoid Generosity Rip-Offs

GIVING to charities and good causes is something most people can get behind. Hundreds of billions of dollars are given to charities every year. Unfortunately, while your reason for giving is genuine, not all charitable organizations or fundraising efforts are honest. Phone and email scams prey upon the generous nature of many people. You must beware of what charities you give to and what they do with the money. But being wary doesn't mean being cynical. It just means you need to donate wisely—and only after you've thoroughly checked out a charity.

8 Common Types of Fraud:

Mail **1** fraud

Driver's **2** license fraud

Health care **3** fraud

Debit and credit **4** card fraud

Stolen tax **5** refund fraud

Voter **6** fraud

Internet **7** fraud

Elder **8** fraud

through your mailbox in hopes of finding a bank statement containing *your* personal account numbers.

It's hard to control whether someone searches through your mail. The best way to protect yourself is to look closely at your mail. Does it look like it's been opened? Does it have any sensitive account information in it? If so, contact your bank and the sender to freeze your accounts.

ONLINE PURCHASES

With a click of a button, you can buy a new pair of shoes, cell phone, swimsuit, or even a horse—you can buy *anything* online these days. But with so many online stores at your fingertips, how do you know your payment information is secure? Well, you don't always know. Since that won't make you want to stop buying stuff online, make sure you're keeping your information safe.

For starters, never purchase anything on an unsecured network. That means if you're on public Wi-Fi, wait until you get home to buy those concert tickets. And the same goes for your mobile device. Only make purchases when you're on a password-protected internet connection.

When you do buy online, stick with trusted online stores and brands you've shopped with before. Make sure the web address of the site you're on starts with "HTTPS"—that's a secure site that encrypts your password and financial info.

And remember: Be careful when storing your debit card online. You may want to look into third party services to make online payments more securely.

RESTAURANTS AND STORES

We're all pretty trusting with our debit cards at restaurants. We get the bill, put our card in that fancy leather folder, and don't think twice about the fact that we just gave a stranger in an apron access to our account.

Think about it: When you give your card away, you're trusting that your server is going to swipe the correct amount and return your card to you right away. We're not saying never go out to eat, but we are saying to check your bank account—and check it often.

What to Do if You're a Victim

First of all, remember that any debit card that has a Visa or Mastercard logo has the same fraud protections as a credit card. And it can even be run as credit. You've probably heard people rant about your liability (the risk of something bad happening to you) going up when you use a debit card. Listen: That's only true if you see weird purchases on your account and do nothing about it. If you keep an eye on your bank account (like you *should* when you're budgeting), then you'll spot an unusual purchase pretty quickly.

A debit card is just as safe as a credit card.

— Rachel Cruze

If you're the victim of fraud, contact your bank *immediately*—and that's if they haven't already contacted you. Many banks have special alerts, so when an odd transaction comes through on your debit card, they contact you to see if it was actually you who made the purchase. Some banking apps also allow you to disable your card with a click. Just keep your eyes peeled for purchases from places you've never been before.

Lost or Stolen Card

If you lost your debit or credit card (or if it was stolen), let your bank know you think your card might be comprised—*as soon as possible*. This is even more important when you have a debit card. Thanks to the Electronic Fund Transfer Act, as soon as you report the loss, you're no longer responsible for any fraudulent charges.

Did You Know?

In 2019, almost 34 million breached records exposed sensitive personal identity information.[12]

Your JOURNAL

What are some things you can do to help prevent debit card fraud?

_____

_____

_____

REMEMBER THIS   Add a ✓ next to each completed learning objective below.

◯   You can recognize signs of debit card fraud.

◯   You have strategies for preventing debit card fraud.

◯   You know what to do if you experience card fraud or if your card is lost or stolen.

THIS LESSON MAKES ME FEEL   Circle your response to what you learned.

😥 CONFUSED   😯 SURPRISED   🙂 THOUGHTFUL   🤩 CONFIDENT

LESSON VIDEO GUIDE

*Extended warranties are a
complete mathematical rip-off.* — Dave Ramsey

GUIDED NOTES   While you watch the video, complete the section below.

1. You need to comparison _____ .

2. Consider the opportunity _____ .

3. Don't _____ things you don't understand.

4. _____ overnight.

5. Check your buying _____ .

6. Get some _____ advice.

ANALYZE AND REFLECT   After you watch the video, respond to the question(s) below.

1. What are the reasons you don't need to buy an extended warranty? What role does your emergency fund play with covering the cost of a repair or replacement?

_____

_____

_____

LEARNING OBJECTIVES

- Understand what it means to exercise power over a purchase.
- Evaluate the impact of purchasing decisions on your financial plan as well as the opportunity cost of those decisions.
- Apply strategies for making informed decisions about purchasing consumer goods.

MAIN IDEA

Being a *wise* consumer involves slowing down and making informed decisions before, during, and after the point of purchase.

Being a Wise Consumer

Imagine this: It's a new year and you've decided to start working out. Great! A friend of yours recommends a fitness app, so you check it out. Turns out, they're offering a deal on a year-long subscription. Perfect! Who doesn't love a good deal? You download the app and sign up. Next thing you know, your checking account is overdrawn. Instead of the small monthly fee you thought you'd be paying, they've charged you for a full year up front! *Yikes.*

If it sounds too good to be true, it probably is.

— Rachel Cruze

Needless to say, your budget that month was busted *and* your bank charged you an overdraft fee. Ouch! You tried to cancel the fitness app and get some of your money back, but no luck. Looking back, you were so excited to get that cool app that you forgot to read the fine print! Lesson learned—the hard way.

We've all been there. For most people, shopping is a sport where the score is tallied by how much you buy and how much you save. We've all bought things without much thought or planning. But being a wise consumer means slowing down. It's easy to get caught up in the excitement of buying something you really want and forget to think it through.

To make wise decisions with your money, you'll need to develop power over purchase. Remember that from Lesson 1? That simply means you make it a habit to slow down and think through your motives before you buy something.

After the Purchase

If you find a defect or have any other quality or performance issues with an item, the first thing to do is return it. If that doesn't work, follow up with the manufacturer to work out a solution. You'll generally either get a product replacement or refund of your purchase price. It's your right as a consumer to expect a product to live up to the quality and performance the company promised you before you bought it.

> A budget tells us what we can't afford, but it doesn't keep us from buying it.
>
> **William Feather**
> American publisher and author

Here's a Tip:

Store return policies balance customer service and profits. For store returns:

- Know the store's return policy before you buy.
- Keep your receipts for proof of purchase.
- Keep the labels and price tags.
- Don't miss the return time limit.

HOW TO BE A *Wise Spender*

Comparison Shop

Research prices to know where to get the best deal. Some stores will price match if you can prove the item is selling for less. Tip: Thrift stores and gently used products can save you a ton!

Wait Overnight

Wait overnight—or longer—before making a big purchase. Determine if what you want to buy is a need or a want. Slow down and avoid impulse buying. And make sure it's actually in the budget!

Think About the Opportunity Cost

Opportunity cost means money spent *here* can't be spent *there*. So the money spent on jeans today won't help you save for your laptop. Take your time and make the right decision.

Check Your Buying Motives

No amount of stuff equals contentment. People sometimes get contentment and fun confused. You can buy fun, but you can't buy contentment. Determine *why* you're buying something.

Don't Buy if You Don't Understand

This definitely applies to financial products like insurance or investments. If you don't understand something, research it or find someone who can explain it in a way that makes sense to you.

Get Some Wise Advice

Before you make a big purchase, talk it over with someone you trust. Right now, that could be your parents. Once you're married, talk through those big purchases with your spouse.

Protect YOUR PURCHASE

Part of being a wise spender is knowing what to do after the purchase. Once you've bought an item, especially an expensive one, learn how to protect and maintain it. Try these simple steps:

1 Read the owner's manual and store it someplace safe so you can find it when you need it.

2 Use the product as intended and follow all of the maintenance tips and instructions.

3 Keep the receipt safe. You'll need it if you want to return the item or get it repaired.

4 Register the item online to get any important updates and to verify the item's purchase.

Buying a Warranty

Is it a good idea to spend money on extended warranties? The short answer: No. A manufacturer's warranty promises that a product will be replaced or repaired if it doesn't work the way it's supposed to. That's a good thing. A manufacturer's warranty is usually covered in the price of the product. However, you'll often be asked at checkout if you'd like to buy an extended warranty. This is extra coverage, and it comes with an additional cost. It's best to stay away from extended warranties.

Why? Well, the worst thing about an extended warranty is that it's overpriced. In fact, about half of what you pay goes to the salesperson's commission. There's no reason to pay more "just in case" something goes wrong, for a couple of reasons.

Never buy extended warranties!

— *Dave Ramsey*

First, most retailers or manufacturers will replace or repair a product if it stops working within the first year after you buy it. Second, when you have no debt and you have an emergency fund, you can afford to fix or replace the item on your own if you have to.

Opportunity Cost: the financial opportunity that is lost when you choose to do something else with your money

---

Your JOURNAL

Is it a good idea to buy an extended warranty? Explain your answer.

_____

_____

_____

REMEMBER THIS   Add a ✓ next to each completed learning objective below.

◯ You understand what it means to exercise power over purchase.

◯ You can evaluate the impact of purchasing decisions on your financial plan, and you recognize the opportunity cost of those decisions.

◯ You can apply strategies for making informed decisions about purchasing consumer goods.

THIS LESSON MAKES ME FEEL   (Circle) your response to what you learned.

😥 CONFUSED   😮 SURPRISED   😊 THOUGHTFUL   🤩 CONFIDENT

LESSON VIDEO GUIDE

It's about being satisfied with your life right now and proud of the goals you've set for yourself. — Rachel Cruze

GUIDED NOTES   While you watch the video, complete the section below.

1. Kids give in to their every _____. Adults learn to say no to themselves in order to gain something greater.

2. It takes _____ to block out what everyone else thinks.

3. When you focus on gratitude, it is easier to avoid the _____ of comparison.

ANALYZE AND REFLECT   After you watch the video, respond to the question(s) below.

1. Write down two or three ways you compare yourself to others.

   _____

   _____

   _____

2. Write down two or three things you're grateful for.

   _____

   _____

   _____

LEARNING OBJECTIVES

- Understand how comparison living can have a negative effect on your finances.
- Recognize the benefits of patience and contentment in your money plan.

MAIN IDEA

We've all fallen into the trap of comparing ourselves to others. But to win with money, you'll need to quit comparison living, practice patience, and find contentment.

Thinking Big Picture

Time for a little bit of a hard talk. You've learned a lot about taking control of your money so you can live a debt-free life and reach your money goals. So far, we've focused on how big money decisions can make or break your financial future. That's stuff like:

- Creating and living on a budget
- Being prepared for the unexpected with an emergency fund
- Getting and staying out of debt

Money can buy fun, but it can't buy contentment.
— *Rachel Cruze*

And this stuff—the *big* stuff—matters. It totally matters. But even with all that knowledge and all the good habits you're building, there are some sneaky ways money can still slip through your fingers. You end up with nothing left to save. And that can make you feel like a hamster on a wheel, running as hard and fast as you can but not getting anywhere.

The truth is, if you want to win big when it comes to saving money, you need to think big picture, not just big decisions. So, what's the big picture? Just this: The best way to have more money is to have contentment.

Practice Contentment and Avoid Comparison

First, what is contentment? Contentment is appreciating who you are and what you have instead of wanting what your friends, neighbors, or family members have. But contentment has lots of enemies—and the first one is comparison.

Comparison living is nothing new. That just means you're constantly comparing what you have against what everyone else has—and feeling you need the same things! Our phones have become little windows into the lives of other people. If a friend goes on an awesome vacation, photos of it hit your phone before the plane even leaves the ground!

But we all know that what people post is just a highlight reel of their actual life. Between the photo filters and 56 attempts to get the perfect selfie, all anyone on the outside sees is a vague representation of

> Many a man thinks he is buying pleasure, when he is really selling himself to it.
>
> **Benjamin Franklin**
> Author, inventor and political theorist

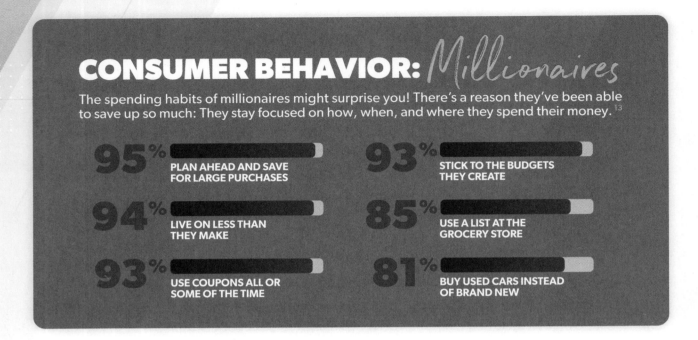

CONSUMER BEHAVIOR: *Millionaires*

The spending habits of millionaires might surprise you! There's a reason they've been able to save up so much: They stay focused on how, when, and where they spend their money.[13]

95% PLAN AHEAD AND SAVE FOR LARGE PURCHASES

94% LIVE ON LESS THAN THEY MAKE

93% USE COUPONS ALL OR SOME OF THE TIME

93% STICK TO THE BUDGETS THEY CREATE

85% USE A LIST AT THE GROCERY STORE

81% BUY USED CARS INSTEAD OF BRAND NEW

reality at its best. You know this—you've *done* this! But the urge to compare your life to what you see is overwhelming.

Here's the point: When you get caught up in those kinds of comparisons, you're comparing yourself to make-believe. Your real life will never seem good enough. Plus, it changes your attitude and your relationships with those people. And it's not just you. It's our entire culture. It's time to break that habit. Here's how:

1. CHANGE YOUR PERSPECTIVE

Stuff doesn't equal wealth. Debt makes people look better off than they actually are. Remember, most Americans are living paycheck to paycheck. On the other hand, wealth doesn't equal stuff. Often, people who have wealth live a lot more simply than you might expect—that's a big reason why they're able to build wealth.

2. CHEER EACH OTHER ON

When you see someone winning, it doesn't mean you're losing. It may take you longer

to save up enough to buy your first car than one of your friends. That's okay. Their success has nothing to do with you, so celebrate *their* success sincerely while you keep working toward *your own*. You can either encourage others or compare yourself to them. You can't really do both at the same time. Be an encourager!

3. BE WILLING TO START SLOW

Many young adults make the mistake of thinking their first apartment needs to have granite countertops and brand-new, trendy furniture. You need to keep your lifestyle affordable. Don't expect to have the same lifestyle right out of school that it took your parents 30 years to achieve.

4. DON'T FALL FOR "I DESERVE IT"

One of the biggest dangers of comparing ourselves to others is the spirit of entitlement, dissatisfaction, and jealousy it can create. The only things you deserve to buy are the things you've planned for and can pay cash for. Period.

Did You Know?

Over 100 million photos and videos are posted to Instagram every day! That's a lot of comparison![14]

5. UNDERSTAND THAT STUFF DOESN'T EQUAL HAPPINESS

Sometimes (a lot of times) people buy stuff for the wrong reasons. They think owning that one thing will make them happy. But after a short-lived rush of pleasure, they're on to wanting the next thing. The reality is that no amount of stuff will make you happy or content.

Delay Gratification

Another common enemy of contentment is immediate gratification. We live in an instant gratification society and say "I want it now!" To win with money, you have to focus on being patient and content. Just because you can't afford something today doesn't mean you'll never have it. And you really need to understand the difference between needs and wants to make wise decisions.

In a heart filled with contentment, there is no room for discontentment.
— Rachel Cruze

Most people don't become billionaires in their 20s. You'll spend a lot of time building wealth, saving money, and investing. That's okay. When you follow the money principles you're learning, you set yourself up for an incredible future. Remember, on your way to discovering financial success, *there are no shortcuts!*

Did You Know?

Finland ranks as the #1 country in the world for happiness and contentment. The United States comes in at 18.[15]

Your **JOURNAL**   Explain how practicing patience and finding contentment are necessary for building wealth.

_____

_____

_____

REMEMBER THIS   Add a ✓ next to each completed learning objective below.

◯   You understand how comparison living can have a negative effect on your finances.

◯   You recognize the benefits of patience and contentment in your money plan.

THIS LESSON MAKES ME FEEL   (Circle) your response to what you learned.

😣 CONFUSED   😯 SURPRISED   🙂 THOUGHTFUL   🤩 CONFIDENT

Chapter 5 Review

REVIEW KEY TERMS   Fill in the blanks below using the correct key terms from this chapter.

Impulse Buying	Mobile Pay	Brand Recognition	Identity Theft
Consumerism	Digital Payment	Card Fraud	Opportunity Cost
Buyer's Remorse	Marketing		

1. _____ will often cause you to overspend or spend more than you've budgeted in a category.

2. You were a victim of _____ _____ if someone used your debit or credit card without your permission.

3. _____ is a type of digital payment made using your phone or watch.

4. Identifying a specific product by its logo, jingle, or name is called _____ _____.

5. If you've ever bought something and then felt guilt or regret later, you've experienced _____.

6. A(n) _____ occurs when you make an online purchase or even send cash using an app on your phone.

7. _____ is all the ways the value of a product or service is communicated.

8. _____ is when someone else uses your personal information to commit fraud.

FINISH THE SENTENCE   Use what you've learned in this chapter to complete these sentences.

1. When you choose to spend your money now instead of invest it so it's worth more in the future, you've experienced _____ _____.

2. The reality is that no amount of purchases will ever make _____ _____.

3. Since it's where most young adults spend their time, 50% of retailers spend at least half of their marketing money on _____ _____.

4. All the discretionary and nondiscretionary spending in our economy is referred to as _____.

1. What's the first thing you need to have so you can develop power over purchase?

   A. Cash

   B. A budget

   C. A credit card

   D. Mobile pay

2. Where's the main place a young adult can find daily examples of targeted marketing?

   A. Social media

   B. Radio

   C. Television

   D. Billboards

3. Short, entertaining ads on social media are called what?

   A. Retargeting

   B. Content marketing

   C. Snack videos

   D. Native advertising

4. When you're buying things online, what should you look for first?

   A. A good price

   B. An HTTPS site

   C. Good reviews

   D. Digital payments

5. What's the main reason why people have trouble being content?

   A. Comparison

   B. Income

   C. Marketing

   D. Patience

6. Impulse buying is a surefire way for you to do what?

   A. Get a deal

   B. Find personal contentment

   C. Spend less

   D. Bust your monthly budget

Review **QUESTION**   What can you do to break the habit of comparison and begin to experience contentment?

_____

_____

_____

_____

_____

_____

_____

Do Work That Matters!

Career Readiness

In this chapter, you'll learn how to find the right career path and create strategies to land a job you love so you can thrive and enjoy your work. You'll also discover tips for building a resumé and presenting yourself well during a job interview.

LESSON VIDEO GUIDE

The size of your dream will always dictate the length of your journey. —Ken Coleman

GUIDED NOTES   While you watch the video, complete the section below.

1. Over their lifetimes, Americans will spend an average of _____ hours at work.

2. What was I _____ to do?

3. Your first job will give you _____.

4. You will _____ a reputation.

5. _____ your role.

6. _____ your role.

7. _____ your role.

ANALYZE AND REFLECT   After you watch the video, respond to the question(s) below.

1. Soft skills are exceptionally important in the work environment. Why are these interpersonal interactions so valuable in the workplace? List at least two reasons.

_____

_____

_____

MAIN IDEA

You're learning skills that will help you handle your money wisely. In the same way, the first few jobs you have can set you up for a career you'll love.

What's Next?

"What are you going to do with the rest of your life?" How many times have you been asked that question lately? It can be a tough one to answer. If you're honest, the answer may be: "I have no idea!" And that's okay. You don't need a complete plan for your life right now. And honestly, even if you have one, it's sure to change!

> **You should never let fear, doubt, or pride hold you back from your potential.**
> — *Anthony O'Neal*

Through the teaching in this course, you're being armed with the truth about handling money and the dangers of debt. But your financial future also depends on the education and career choices you make. You've got so many options, and that's fantastic! But it can also feel like you're traveling to a destination without any road signs. In this lesson, you'll learn how you can create a clearer picture of the right career path for you.

Finding Work You Love

Is it really possible to make a living doing work you love? Do you have to give up on your dream career so you can earn a lot of money? These are common questions people ask about work. Our culture believes this weird myth that work isn't supposed to be meaningful or satisfying. You may hear statements such as:

- "Work isn't supposed to be fun."
- "Working a draining 9-to-5 job is the only way to get by."
- "Finding fulfillment in work is rare—if not impossible."
- "As long as you make a lot of money, it doesn't matter if you like your job."

The good news is, none of that has to be true! You don't have to dread going to work. You were born to fill a unique role. It's up to you to discover what that role is and do it. There's someone out there who needs you to be you.

So, how do you make the contribution you were born to make? That's simple: by doing work you're passionate about. Of course, that means you'll need to discover what that is (more about that in Lesson 4).

Words of Wisdom

In American culture, too many people spend a lifetime chasing wealth in a career that they hate. Or they work an excessive number of hours every week.

"Do not wear yourself out to get rich; have the wisdom to show restraint" (Proverbs 23:4).

Do something you love and that is fun for you! If you make a lot of money, great! But if you don't, at least you will have spent a lifetime doing something that was rewarding. Money should never become your primary motivation.

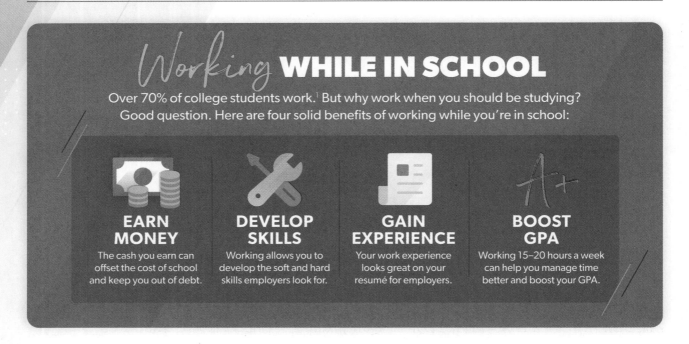

Working WHILE IN SCHOOL

Over 70% of college students work.[1] But why work when you should be studying?
Good question. Here are four solid benefits of working while you're in school:

EARN MONEY
The cash you earn can offset the cost of school and keep you out of debt.

DEVELOP SKILLS
Working allows you to develop the soft and hard skills employers look for.

GAIN EXPERIENCE
Your work experience looks great on your resumé for employers.

BOOST GPA
Working 15–20 hours a week can help you manage time better and boost your GPA.

Your First Job

Before you land your dream job in your unique role, you'll need to get your *first* job. Maybe you already have one. If so, that's awesome! You'll have a small income and build work experience. Win–win! As you enter the workforce, there are a couple of things you'll want to remember.

Hard Skills: technical skills (typically learned) demonstrated with a level of competency requiring IQ (intelligence quotient)

First: When applying for a job—any job—you're a product. Yep, that sounds strange, but when you think about it, a company hires a person to fill a need in the same way you buy a product to fill a need. What does that mean to you? It means you'll want to stand out in a good way from other candidates for the job. You'll learn how to do that when we talk about how to build a resumé and nail your job interview later in this chapter.

Soft Skills: character traits and interpersonal skills requiring EQ (emotional quotient) that guide how you interact with others

Second: Don't take your first job for granted. Whether you start a small business mowing yards or babysitting, get a job at a fast-food restaurant, or sell stuff in a retail store, you'll learn important skills that will transfer to your future career.

Your first job isn't just about what you do. It's also about how you do it and what you learn from it. Don't underestimate the value of the experiences you gain in your first job—whatever those might be.

More Than a Summer Job

It's true that with a lot of first jobs, you may not learn many **hard skills** like writing code or designing houses. Hard skills are the things you learn or receive special training on. But a part-time job in high school is a great way to develop important **soft skills** that will help you advance your career when you're older.

Soft skills are rarely taught in a school classroom. They're often personality traits that are either natural or developed over time—like perseverance, humility, flexibility, communication skills, problem solving, work ethic, respect, and commitment, just to name a few. They're more about *who you are* rather than *what you know*. Soft skills also impact the way you interact and work with a team. That's important!

Believe it or not, employers take these soft skills as seriously as they do hard skills. Why? Because soft skills influence how well you interact with others—team members and customers. Employers know that employees who have good soft skills will:

- Serve customers well
- Act and dress professionally
- Solve problems
- Do more than is expected
- Be team players
- Show up on time
- Have a positive attitude
- Receive feedback gracefully

That's why it's so important to be open to instruction—so you can learn as much as you can. The soft skills you learn will help you now and prepare you for more responsibility in the future.

Learn and Grow

Once you land your first job, appreciate the opportunity as more than just a way to make some money. See it as an opportunity to learn and grow.

> ### Work—meaningful work—is a fantastic thing.
> — Ken Coleman

If you show up and do your best every day, the rewards will go far beyond the dollars you earn on a paycheck. Soak up all the information and experience. Just remember: All the things you learn in your different jobs will equip you to do *work that matters!*

Did You Know?

Over 46% of young adults age 16–24 have jobs.[2]

Your JOURNAL

What are some of the benefits of having a job in high school?

_____

_____

_____

REMEMBER THIS   Add a ✓ next to each completed learning objective below.

◯ You can explain the difference between hard skills and soft skills.

◯ You understand the importance of a first job.

THIS LESSON MAKES ME FEEL   Circle your response to what you learned.

😓 CONFUSED   😮 SURPRISED   🙂 THOUGHTFUL   🤩 CONFIDENT

LESSON VIDEO GUIDE

The interview is your opportunity to stand out and learn what winning looks like. —Ken Coleman

GUIDED NOTES   While you watch the video, complete the section below.

1. Do some _____ about the company you are interviewing with.

2. _____ for the questions you might be asked.

3. Consider questions _____ should ask.

4. Ask: What is the type of person that really _____ in this job?

5. 66% of hiring managers decide if they like a person in the first 30 _____.

ANALYZE AND REFLECT   After you watch the video, respond to the question(s) below.

1. List at least three character traits you think businesses are looking for during the interview process. Explain why businesses want to find these traits in someone they hire.

   _____

   _____

   _____

2. Why should you do research and prepare before an interview?

   _____

   _____

MAIN IDEA

Whether you're trying to land your first job or your dream job, it's important to stand out—in a good way—from your competition.

Landing a Job

It doesn't matter if you're trying to get your first job or your dream job—the process is pretty much the same. It all starts with your application—and most of those are completed online. Whether you're 16 with zero experience or you're a professional, you'll ask yourself the same question when you click Submit on your online application: *Will anyone ever read this?*

Every person was born to fulfill a unique role.
— *Ken Coleman*

Even with a digital application, you can make a great first impression. It's all in how you follow up:

- Apply early. Applications received within the first week of a job posting are more likely to be read.
- A week after submitting, email a copy of your application to the hiring manager.
- Call the hiring manager and ask for a few moments of time to introduce yourself. This is a bold first impression!

- Ask anyone you know who has a good connection to the company to put in a good word on your behalf.
- Finally, send one more email expressing appreciation for being considered and restating your interest in working there.

Resumé and Interview Tips

You'll want a knockout **resumé** to submit along with your job application. There's a lot of old-fashioned advice about resumés out there, so be different! You'll find a lot of templates available online. While you want your resumé to attract attention, you don't want to get too design crazy with it.

Your resumé should include the people you know who are connected to the company you're applying at, why you want to work there, and how you can add value to the company. You'll also want to add your past job experience along with education, training, and certifications.

Now you're ready for the next step—the job interview. Think of it as a performance! Don't just wing it. You need to prepare intentionally so you'll be able to perform exceptionally. The next page provides interview tips in five key areas.

Did You Know?

Out of 250 applications for a job, only four to six people will get an in-person interview.[3]

Resumé: from a French word meaning "to sum up" or a summary

Here's a Tip:

A new resumé template is included with this lesson for you.

HOW TO *Win* THE INTERVIEW

Don't forget to bring your resumé!

WHAT TO EXPECT
Think through your answers for some of the most common interview questions:

> Why do you want to work for us?

> Why should we hire you?

> What are your biggest strengths and weaknesses?

> Why did you leave your previous (or want to leave your current) job?

WHAT YOU NEED TO KNOW
Show the interviewer you care enough about the company to do some research. Before your interview, visit the company's website to learn about:

- The history of the company
- Their vision, values, purpose, and mission statement
- Their products and services
- Their wins and awards in the news

HOW TO DRESS
Here are some Do's and Don'ts for your interview outfit:

 DO dress to the company's dress code.

 DON'T wear old or wrinkled clothing.

 DO dress in classic business attire if you're not sure what to wear.

 DON'T wear a super trendy outfit or color-clashing clothes.

HOW TO ACT
Be aware of the nonverbal messages you could be sending.

- ✔ Smile and make eye contact.
- ✔ Use good posture.
- ✔ Don't cross your arms—it makes you seem closed off.
- ✔ Respect personal space.
- ✔ Don't chew gum.
- ✔ Show enthusiasm and express gratitude for the opportunity.

WHAT TO ASK
Hiring managers want you to ask questions to show your interest in the position. Here are a few good ones:

- **Q** How long have you been with the company?
- **Q** What's the company culture like?
- **Q** What do you enjoy most about your work?
- **Q** How will my performance be measured?

ASK FOR THE JOB
If the interviewer seems interested and you're feeling positive, here are some classy ways to ask for the job:

- **Q** Are there any ways I can help you determine that I'm a good fit?
- **Q** Are there any questions I haven't answered?
- **Q** What's the next step in the hiring process?

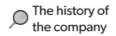

After the Interview

Whew! You survived the interview. Take a breath and relax. Yes, the interview can be a nerve-racking experience. But for a lot of people, it's the waiting to hear back about the job that can create even more anxiety and stress.

> ## A thank-you note is a simple way to set yourself apart from other interviewees.
> — *Ken Coleman*

You can still make a great impression even after the interview. Send a thank-you note to your interviewer within 48 hours—even if you're not interested in the job. Handwritten notes add a personal touch and can really set you apart from the others who applied for the job, but sending an email is also effective.

While you're waiting to hear if you got the job or not, here are a couple of other ways to keep the communication open:

- After one week, send a follow-up email and explain a way you could help the company and add value.
- After three weeks, send one last brief email asking if you're still being considered for the position.

If it's been more than three weeks since your interview, there's a good chance they moved on. Whether you get the job or not, remember that you *do* matter and you *do* have what it takes. Don't give up. *Press on!*

Here's a Tip:

Five traits that many employers look for include:

1. Dependability
2. Integrity
3. Respect
4. Teamwork
5. Initiative

Your JOURNAL

What are some steps you should take to prepare for an interview in advance?

_____

_____

_____

REMEMBER THIS   Add a ✓ next to each completed learning objective below.

○ You can identify best practices for building a resumé.

○ You understand what to do during and after an interview.

THIS LESSON MAKES ME FEEL   Circle your response to what you learned.

😓 CONFUSED   😗 SURPRISED   🙂 THOUGHTFUL   🤩 CONFIDENT

An Entrepreneurial Mindset

LESSON VIDEO GUIDE

Failure is part of the learning process. It is when we fail that we are able to move forward successfully. — Ken Coleman

GUIDED NOTES   While you watch the video, complete the section below.

1. An entrepreneur is a person who sees a problem and starts a business to _____ that problem.

2. The first characteristic of an entrepreneur is they're a _____.

3. The second characteristic is they're _____.

4. The third characteristic is they have _____.

5. Your fear of _____ is never as bad as the fear says it is.

6. Failure doesn't define you—it _____ you.

7. Your personal _____ is what you are known for.

ANALYZE AND REFLECT   After you watch the video, respond to the question(s) below.

1. Why do you need to have an entrepreneurial mindset and understand the value of failure?

_____

_____

_____

MAIN IDEA

Developing an entrepreneurial mindset and building your personal brand will be lifelong tools to help you grow in your career and do work that matters.

What Is an Entrepreneur?

Do you know someone who owns their own business? Maybe you've even thought about starting a business one day. That means you either know or plan to be an **entrepreneur**. That's exciting!

An entrepreneur is a person who starts their own business. And that's a big deal! It takes a unique person to take on the risk of starting a business. No matter how much you've thought through it, you can never be sure that the risk will pay off and you'll be successful.

For entrepreneurs, taking risks and growing a business go hand in hand. It's like a baseball player deciding whether to steal second or keep his foot on first. Does he risk getting thrown out or just play it safe? Sure, he may get thrown out, but he'll never steal a base if he doesn't go for it.

In the business world—as well as in life in general—the willingness to take on risks is one of the ways leaders are different from followers. So, what does that have to do with you? Even if you never start your own business, you can learn to think and act like an entrepreneur.

People with an entrepreneurial mindset are not only risk takers drawn to opportunity, they've also learned—from personal experience—the value of failure and the power of a personal brand.

The Value of Failure

We all know that sinking feeling that hits when you know you've messed up. It might be a failing grade on a test. Or maybe you missed the winning shot. Or you dropped the ball on one of your duties at work. No one enjoys that feeling of failure.

> Often, success happens not *despite* failure but *because* of failure.
>
> *—Ken Coleman*

Accepting failure and constructive feedback can be difficult if you think of failure only as a negative. But every failure is a chance to learn something! That's the value of failure. Yes—you read that right. The *value* of failure.

Entrepreneur: someone who starts and runs their own business

Did You Know?

Almost 70% of American entrepreneurs started a business because they wanted to make a difference.[4]

154

CHARACTERISTICS OF AN *Entrepreneur*

Review this list of entrepreneurial characteristics. Place a ✓ next to the characteristics that come naturally to you and an ✗ next to the ones you need to work on.

- Confident
- Risk Taker
- Adaptive
- Fast Learner
- Strong Work Ethic

- Motivated
- Creative Thinker
- Visionary
- Innovative
- Takes Initiative

- Disciplined
- Courageous
- Passionate
- Independent
- Versatile

Personal Brand: a widely recognized perception or impression of an individual based on conduct, experience, skills, and actions

Bottom line: Don't think about failure as a negative. When it happens, own your part in it and then learn from it. If you failed a test, make plenty of time to study for the next one—or get a tutor! If you mess up at work, first apologize, and then do what you can to fix it. Failure teaches personal responsibility—another soft skill—and helps you grow. So, expect failure and learn from it as you pursue your dreams.

Personal Brand

Most people know what a brand is. You have a favorite shoe brand and a favorite brand of soft drink. Brands are everywhere, but do you know why branding is so important? A brand tells the "story" of a product through creative packaging and advertising so it can stand out from the competition. A brand might focus on the quality or value of a product. Or, a product's brand might make the customer feel a sense of joy, trust, youthfulness, or beauty when they use it.

The price of greatness is responsibility.

Winston Churchill
UK Prime Minister, 1940–1945, 1951–1955

Your **personal brand** has the same purpose. It's a way of identifying your skills, experiences, and strengths—and communicating those to the world. You want to identify what makes you different from everyone else, especially when you apply for a job. Your education, experience, talents, and your personal attributes can help define your personal brand.

For example, if you spend a semester of college studying abroad (learning a new culture and language) or volunteer to help a community after a natural disaster, that sets you apart. Mention those unique experiences on your resumé or in a job interview. What you learned and how you grew as a person through experiences like that is important to an employer.

Believe it or not, your personal brand can also be reflected in how you react and respond to failure. And that ties back to having the mindset of an entrepreneur. This all works together. Because when you take risks, you're going to fail sometimes.

Building Your Brand

You can begin building your personal brand now. Identify what you want others to think about you. That's personal branding in a nutshell. Be authentic to who you are—your passions and values. Get input from friends and family too. What character traits do they see in you?

> ## Every time you work with or for customers, you build up or break down your brand.
>
> — Anthony O'Neal

Building a strong and positive personal brand now, while you're in high school, will impact your ability to land jobs in the future. Really. Employers often check the social media accounts of potential employees. Your social media profiles and posts should line up with the type of personal brand you want to build, so filter what you post. Your friends aren't the only ones looking.

Your personal brand doesn't stop there. The way you present yourself physically should reflect your personal brand. And the way you communicate, along with how and when you show kindness and compassion, also expresses your personal brand. Determine what you want to be known for and do those things. Then your social media, personal style, and the things you say and do will work together to build a personal brand you can be proud of!

Did You Know?

70% of employers use social media to research job candidates.[5]

Your JOURNAL

What are some ways you can improve your personal brand?

_____

_____

_____

REMEMBER THIS   Add a ✓ next to each completed learning objective below.

◯ You can identify common characteristics of an entrepreneur.

◯ You understand the value of failure.

◯ You recognize the importance of developing a positive personal brand.

THIS LESSON MAKES ME FEEL   ⟨Circle⟩ your response to what you learned.

😓 CONFUSED   😮 SURPRISED   😊 THOUGHTFUL   🤩 CONFIDENT

LESSON VIDEO GUIDE

Use your talent to perform work that gets you excited and creates a result that matters to you. — Ken Coleman

GUIDED NOTES   While you watch the video, complete the section below.

1. You need to become a _____.

2. Get confirmation from people who are _____ tellers.

3. Question #1: What do you do _____?

4. Question #2: What do you _____ to do most?

5. Question #3: What are the _____ that matter most to you?

ANALYZE AND REFLECT   After you watch the video, respond to the question(s) below.

1. Why do you need to know where your sweet spot is for your career? What are some consequences of not being in your sweet spot?

    _____

    _____

2. When answering the question "What do I do best?", what are some benefits of asking and listening to the opinion of other people who know you well?

    _____

    _____

LEARNING OBJECTIVES

- Identify your personal talents, your passions, and your values, and use them to find a career you love.
- Develop a strategy to get into the career you love.

MAIN IDEA

Your first job will teach you a lot about yourself, but it likely won't be your dream job. Take some time to figure out what you're good at and what you're passionate about.

Finding Your Dream Job

According to a poll of American workers, 65% are not engaged in their work. And of those, 13% are actively disengaged, meaning they hate their jobs.[6]

Those statistics certainly don't make you look forward to joining the workforce, do they? But you don't have to accept that work reality. The truth is, life's too short to spend so much of your time at a job you don't enjoy.

While you'll learn a lot about yourself with your first job, it's not likely that it'll be your dream job. But with time, perseverance, and patience, you can figure out what you're meant to do and then land your dream job. It's 100% worth the effort to find what you would love to do so you can avoid being stuck in a job you hate.

The first step is **discovery**—identifying your talents, passions, and values. That's finding out what you do best, what you love to do most, and what results you most want to produce. It also means knowing you can combine those three things to do work that really matters to you. When your work matters, you won't hate your job.

Discovery starts with finding your **sweet spot**—the point where your greatest talent and greatest passion intersect. When you're in your sweet spot, you can use your talents (what you do best) to perform your passions (what you love to do most) in a way that lines up with your personal values. Whew! That sounds like a lot. But we're going to break it down for you.

> **Your sweet spot is the point where your greatest talent and your greatest passion intersect.**
>
> — *Ken Coleman*

Find Your Sweet Spot

Ken Coleman describes how you can zero in on your sweet spot by working through a simple process to find clarity. It involves thinking about and writing down your answers to three important questions about yourself. To help get you started on this path to clarity, check out the next page.

Sweet Spot: the spot where what you love to do the most intersects with the things you do the best

Did You Know?

Only 5% of adults say that high school graduates are "very prepared" to be successful in a job.[7]

Discovery: the act of finding something out

IDENTIFYING YOUR *Sweet Spot*

Think about your talents, passions, and values, and list them in the white circles. Then, for each of the blue areas, identify some jobs that match both circles on either side of the blue area. Finally, identify some jobs or careers that all the circles have in common. That's the center, and that's your sweet spot!

Your sweet spot is where these three intersect!

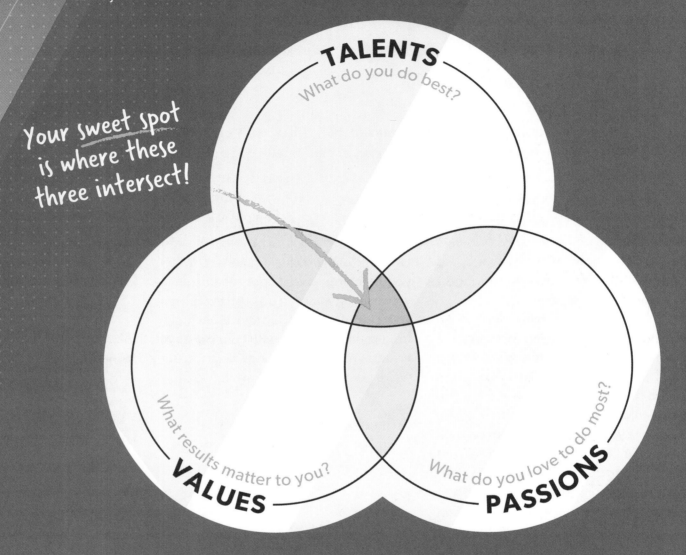

TALENTS
What do you do best?

What results matter to you?
VALUES

What do you love to do most?
PASSIONS

Now that you're getting an idea of what might fall in that sweet spot, use some of the things you identified and create a purpose statement. This entire exercise can help you find a job you'll love.

I will use what I do best—_____—to do
what I love most—_____—so that
I can see these results: _____.

Your Purpose Statement

Now it's time to write your own purpose statement—there's room at the bottom of the previous page. You can keep coming back to this any time you need a reminder of what you're pursuing and why.

To help you get more specific, think about who you most want to help and the problem you most want to solve. Don't overthink it! Your purpose statement is just a simple sentence you can keep editing over time. If it changes, that's okay! Here are a couple of examples:

- *I will use my ability to work with children to be a child psychologist and help kids talk through their problems.*
- *I will use my woodworking and math skills as a carpenter or architect to build homes for people in need.*

Those values you wrote down earlier don't necessarily have to be part of your purpose statement, but they should be the motivating force behind it. Your values help give life to your work.

Every one of us wants to do work that matters.

— Ken Coleman

After you've developed your purpose statement, you can start looking for a role that's in your sweet spot. Work that falls in your sweet spot will help you fulfill your true purpose. How do you find that dream job? Great question. We'll tackle that in the next lesson!

> Happiness lies not in the mere possession of money; it lies in the joy of achievement, in the thrill of creative effort.
>
> **Franklin D. Roosevelt**
> 32nd U.S. President

Did You Know?

25% of Americans say they're currently in their dream job.[8]

Your JOURNAL — How can identifying your sweet spot now help you as you think about a career path?

_____

_____

_____

REMEMBER THIS   Add a ✓ next to each completed learning objective below.

◯ You know how to identify your personal talents, your passions, and your values and use them to find a career you love.

◯ You have a strategy for getting into the career you love.

THIS LESSON MAKES ME FEEL   (Circle) your response to what you learned.

😓 **CONFUSED**   😮 **SURPRISED**   🙂 **THOUGHTFUL**   🤩 **CONFIDENT**

LESSON VIDEO GUIDE

Being around the right people and in the right places is the formula that will bring you great opportunities. —Ken Coleman

GUIDED NOTES   While you watch the video, complete the section below.

1. The secret to opportunities is the _____ Principle.

2. It gives you the opportunity to _____ what you need to learn.

3. It gives you the opportunity to connect with more _____ in the industry.

4. In proximity, you are going to _____ everything involved with that career path.

5. Then you can _____ if you want to do that career.

ANALYZE AND REFLECT   After you watch the video, respond to the question(s) below.

1. List two areas of interest for your career and explain how you can use the Proximity Principle to explore those careers.

_____

_____

_____

_____

LEARNING OBJECTIVES

- Adopt strategies for finding and landing your dream job.
- Connect the realities of today's job market to your career goals.

MAIN IDEA

Once you've identified your talents, passions, values, and purpose statement, it becomes much easier to find career options that fall in your sweet spot.

Research and Explore

Your talents, passions, and values make you who you are—and your work should be an extension of who you are. That's why finding your sweet spot is so important. After you have a good idea about your sweet spot, it's time to research and explore career options. Just a head's up—there will be some homework involved. But it's a super important step in finding the right career for you.

> **That first step toward a dream job is always the scariest.**
>
> — Ken Coleman

Start by brainstorming all the possible careers that will allow you to put your purpose statement into action. Think outside the box and talk to other people who work in a similar field to see how they got to where they are. They'll have a ton of insight on all the different career opportunities in that field—probably some you've never heard of before.

Get Qualified

Once you have an idea of what you want to do and the possible places where you can do that work, you'll need to get qualified to do the job. Stay in research mode and look for the fastest and lowest cost way to get the education and skills you need to get hired for the role you've identified.

Don't assume you need a four-year degree—even if job postings for the role say you need one. There can be plenty of ways to land your dream job without a degree. We'll dive deep into education options in the next chapter. For now, take your time and learn about all your options to get the qualifications you need.

The Key to Opportunities

Once you've taken what you've learned from the research-and-explore phase to help you become qualified for your dream job, it's time to take a huge step forward. That step is to put Ken Coleman's **Proximity Principle** to work for you. The Proximity Principle says: In order to do what you want to do, you need to be around people who are doing it and in places where it's happening.

It's not hard to decide what you want your life to be about. What's hard is figuring out what you're willing to give up in order to do the things you really care about.

Shauna Niequist
Bestselling author

Proximity Principle: the idea that you should connect with people who are doing what you want to do and get in the right places in order to find new opportunities related to your dream job

A Message From KEN

I BET you don't want to grow up and work a boring 9-to-5 J.O.B. Well, guess what? You don't have to. You were created to do work that matters and impact the lives of people around you, which is anything but boring! The world needs you to contribute your unique talents and passions.

It won't be easy. This is your personal Mount Everest. You'll face bigger challenges than you ever thought possible, but the view from the top is worth it. Life is short, and it's never too early to figure out what you were made to do. It's time for you to discover your purpose.

It's not hard to use this principle to help you land your dream job. You just have to be willing to seek out people and experiences that put you in close proximity to your dream job. That will take some effort on your part. So, what does that look like? Here are a few ideas:

> Do more than is required. What is the distance between someone who achieves their goals consistently and those who spend their lives and careers merely following? The extra mile.
>
> Gary Ryan Blair
> Motivational speaker and author

ENTRY-LEVEL POSITIONS

Sometimes, you have to take a role that's in close proximity to your dream job, even if it isn't ideal. This is what people refer to as "getting your foot in the door." You'll gain a bunch of experience while developing hard and soft skills. But if you knock an entry-level position out of the park, it can lead to bigger opportunities!

JOB SHADOWING AND INTERNSHIPS

This is not only a learning opportunity, but also a chance to get in close proximity to lots of people in the industry you want to be in. You'll get paid at some internships, but not all of them. It's important to focus on building relationships that could help you get a personal recommendation and strengthen your chances of getting an interview for your dream job.

> **Did You Know?**
>
> 70% of interns (paid and unpaid) are offered jobs at the company they intern for.[9]

VOLUNTEERING

There's so much value in having an attitude that says, "I don't want anything. I just want to learn." If you have the time and the financial ability, volunteering is a great way to gain experience in your field. When you get around the right people and in the right places, good things can happen.

> **You should never let fear, doubt, or pride hold you back from your potential.**
> — Anthony ONeal

CONVERSATIONS

Take someone to lunch! This is about your dream job. Have a conversation about a career over a meal. It's perfectly okay to ask someone who has a job similar to the one you want to have lunch with you. Ask them how they got where they are, what winning looks like in their role, and what they like and dislike about their work.

Bottom line: Put yourself in places where opportunity can take flight. Your time and effort will pay off.

Today's Job Market

It's difficult to predict the future in anything, particularly in the job market. But let's face it: When you're making big decisions about college and career, predicting the future is exactly what you need to do. Because of globalization (an increasing interdependence among countries) and digital technology, the business world is changing faster than ever right now.

What does all of this mean for you? When you're thinking about your career path, focus on growing industries that align with your purpose statement and avoid industries that are in decline. Your career choice needs to be practical as well as fulfilling. Being a juggler might align with your purpose statement, but it will be challenging to earn a living doing it.

So, what are some things you can do now, while you're still in high school, to help make yourself a valuable employee in the future? Here are a few ideas:

- Develop computer literacy. Technology plays a vital role in most jobs today.
- Improve your communication skills. Verbal (even the ability to speak other languages) and written communication skills can set you apart.
- Become a team player. Chances are you'll work with a team of people, so it's important to be able to work together.

When it comes to finding work in your sweet spot, there are a lot of opportunities. You just have to look and invest some time.

You've got this!

8 Great Emerging Jobs

1. Artificial Intelligence Specialist
2. Robotics Engineer
3. Data Scientist
4. Software Engineer
5. Customer Service Specialist
6. Behavioral Health Tech
7. Cybersecurity Specialist
8. Cloud Engineer[10]

Your **JOURNAL**   What are some career options that match your purpose statement? Which one do you like the most? Why?

_____

_____

_____

REMEMBER THIS   Add a ✓ next to each completed learning objective below.

◯ You've adopted strategies for finding and landing your dream job.

◯ You can connect the realities of today's job market to your career goals.

THIS LESSON MAKES ME FEEL   (Circle) your response to what you learned.

😓 CONFUSED   😮 SURPRISED   🙂 THOUGHTFUL   🤩 CONFIDENT

LESSON VIDEO GUIDE

The idea of always learning will lead to a pattern of always growing. —Ken Coleman

GUIDED NOTES   While you watch the video, complete the section below.

1. The secret to lifelong success: Be a _____.

2. If you're not learning, you're not _____.

3. You are our country's and our world's greatest _____.

4. First, mentors must be _____.

5. Second, mentors must be known for their _____.

6. Third, mentors need to _____ about you.

ANALYZE AND REFLECT   After you watch the video, respond to the question(s) below.

1. Why do you think it's important to continue to learn the rest of your life?

_____

_____

_____

_____

LEARNING OBJECTIVES

- Recognize the correlation between education, training, and potential earnings.
- Understand the value of being a lifelong learner and investing in yourself.
- Explain how income reflects career, education, and skill development choices.

MAIN IDEA

After you graduate and get to work, don't think that learning stops. The more you learn and grow, the more you can advance and earn.

Invest in Yourself

No matter which education path you choose (college, trade school, online study), learning is a necessary, lifelong pursuit. Even after you land your dream job, you'll need to keep up to date with changes in the field and keep your skills current. That's what it means to invest in yourself and become a lifelong learner.

> **Real relationships can't be manufactured or artificially mass-produced.**
> *— Ken Coleman*

It's true that the very best investment you can make in life is in yourself. Charlie "Tremendous" Jones, an author and early leader in the personal and professional development industry, used to say, "You will be the same person in five years as you are today except for the people you meet and the books you read." Reading books written by successful people is a great way to invest in yourself.

Leaders are readers! *The National Study of Millionaires* revealed that millionaires are more likely to read at least one nonfiction book a month.[11] Video streaming, video games, social media, and reality TV are all fun distractions, but they're just entertainment. They don't help you grow professionally or personally. Be smart about how you spend your free time, and look for ways to keep learning. That doesn't mean you can't have fun! Just balance fun time with time spent learning new things.

Investing in yourself, growing in knowledge and experience, and being open to new opportunities are all a part of being a lifelong learner. Investing in yourself will also help you find contentment in what you do rather than in what you have or how much money you make.

The Power of Mentorship

When you read the biography of almost any successful person, you'll find they were supported by a **mentor**. Mentors are people who can guide, encourage, and hold you accountable as you make the climb to your dream job.

Did You Know?

On average, 18- to 25-year-olds play 7.5 hours of video games per week; 11% report playing more than 20 hours per week.[12]

Words of Wisdom

"As iron sharpens iron, so one person sharpens another" (Proverbs 27:17).

Mentor: someone who supports, guides, and advises another person over a period of time

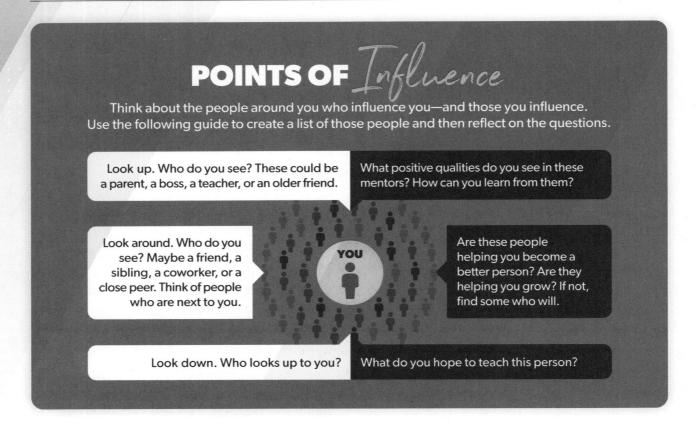

POINTS OF *Influence*

Think about the people around you who influence you—and those you influence.
Use the following guide to create a list of those people and then reflect on the questions.

Look up. Who do you see? These could be a parent, a boss, a teacher, or an older friend.

What positive qualities do you see in these mentors? How can you learn from them?

Look around. Who do you see? Maybe a friend, a sibling, a coworker, or a close peer. Think of people who are next to you.

YOU

Are these people helping you become a better person? Are they helping you grow? If not, find some who will.

Look down. Who looks up to you?

What do you hope to teach this person?

For example, Dr. Martin Luther King Jr. was mentored by Benjamin Mays, who was the president of Morehouse College. Mays made a lasting impact on King's intellectual and spiritual life. The right mentor can make a huge difference in getting you closer to a job you love. Here are three key qualities of a mentor:

- *They're accomplished* in an area of life or work where you would like guidance. That may be career, but it might also be leadership or life in general.
- *They're understanding* because they've faced their share of obstacles and understand the big picture of how to navigate the hardships of life.
- *They're caring* and understand the deep value of the relationship between a mentor and a mentee. That makes them more than willing to help others the way they've been helped.

Did You Know?

Four hours per month is the average amount of time mentors spend with those they are mentoring.[13]

Finding the right mentor to help you grow isn't easy. But taking the time to pursue mentor relationships is an important key to your success.

Once you find someone, be bold in asking them to mentor you. Don't let pride or fear get in the way. Good mentors are usually products of being mentored by someone else, so they understand the importance of your request and will be honored that you asked.

When you find the right person, don't expect them to magically answer all of life's questions. A mentor is just one of many people you need during your career. And like every important relationship, building a strong connection takes time and intention. Once you find someone who agrees to mentor you, be clear about what you're asking them to do and tell them how much you value their time.

A Generous Heart

The great thing about lasting mentor relationships is that you'll eventually see so much personal growth in your life from their guidance and encouragement that you'll be challenged to mentor others. We've talked about giving your time, talents, and money as ways of helping others in need. But have you ever thought about giving of your knowledge and personal experiences? That's valuable too!

Someday, you'll find that you've achieved success in one or more areas of your life—perhaps in your faith, family, career, or a hobby—and mentoring others becomes a natural form of giving. That's right: Mentoring is a form of giving that's just as powerful as giving your time and money to help an organization.

Being a mentor is a job that comes in many forms: coach, teacher, listener, and friend. You just need the desire to share your experiences with someone else.

Mentors see things in you and deposit things in you that will benefit your future.

— Anthony O'Neal

> In order to be a mentor, and an effective one, one must care.
>
> **Maya Angelou**
> American Poet

Mentoring is being generous with your heart and knowledge in order to help others do better. What an amazing gift! When you take hold of the wisdom and knowledge you've received from a mentor and pass it on to the next generation, the mentor relationship has come full circle.

Your JOURNAL

What are some ways you can learn outside of the classroom? Give some examples.

_____

_____

_____

REMEMBER THIS   Add a ✓ next to each completed learning objective below.

○ You understand the value of being a lifelong learner and investing in yourself.

○ You can explain how choices made about jobs, education, careers, and skill development can impact your income.

THIS LESSON MAKES ME FEEL   Circle your response to what you learned.

 CONFUSED   SURPRISED   THOUGHTFUL   CONFIDENT

Chapter 6 Review

REVIEW KEY TERMS   Fill in the blanks below using the correct key terms from this chapter.

Hard Skills	Entrepreneur	Sweet Spot	Proximity Principle
Soft Skills	Personal Brand	Discovery	Mentor
Resumé			

1. A(n) _____ is a person who starts and runs a business.

2. Your _____ is where your talents and passions intersect in a way that allows you to see the results you want.

3. _____ are personality traits that either come naturally to you or are developed over time.

4. The first step in finding your dream job is _____—where you identify all the things that are important to you.

5. Most jobs will want a copy of your _____ before interviewing you.

6. A(n) _____ is someone who will guide you, motivate you, encourage you, and hold you accountable.

7. Your _____ is based on your conduct, actions, and life experiences.

8. _____ are things you learn in school or with special training to help in your career.

FINISH THE SENTENCE   Use what you've learned in this chapter to complete these sentences.

1. Believe it or not, it's actually possible for you to make a living doing work _____ _____.

2. In order to do what you want to do, you need to be around people who are doing it and in _____ _____.

3. After identifying your talents, passions, and values, write _____ _____.

4. A great way to gain valuable experience in a field that interests you, even if you don't get paid for your time, is _____.

KEY QUESTIONS   (Circle) the letter next to the correct answer.

1. Which of these is not considered a characteristic of an entrepreneur?

   A. Risk Taker   C. Passive

   B. Visionary   D. Passionate

2. Your social media posts, your style, and your speech all help to build what?

   A. Hard skills   C. Career

   B. Personal brand   D. Resumé

3. Which of these is considered a soft skill?

   A. Computer coding   C. Cooking hamburgers

   B. Positive attitude   D. GIF creation

4. Which of these is not considered a quality of a good mentor?

   A. Accomplished   C. Wealthy

   B. Caring   D. Understanding

5. Things don't always go right or as planned. Everyone can learn the value of what?

   A. Failure   C. Work

   B. Money   D. Time

6. What should you do to win a job interview?

   A. Dress super trendy C. Avoid eye contact

   B. Chew gum   D. Ask questions

Review QUESTION

How could the Proximity Principle help you find a career that you love?

_____

_____

_____

_____

_____

_____

It's That Serious!

College Planning

This chapter explores the variety of educational options available after high school, highlights the dangers of student loans, and explains how you can pay cash for college and avoid student loan debt.

LESSON VIDEO GUIDE

If you are going to college, I want you to graduate from that college the same way you came in—debt-free!

— Anthony O'Neal

GUIDED NOTES While you watch the video, complete the section below.

1. Take _____ off the table.

2. Have and create a _____.

3. Research and _____.

4. Set a decision _____.

5. Work, _____, and behave.

6. Walk the _____ debt-free.

ANALYZE AND REFLECT After you watch the video, respond to the question(s) below.

1. Why do you think it takes an average of 20 years for people to pay off their student loans?

    _____

    _____

2. Do you believe it's possible to graduate debt-free? Why or why not?

    _____

    _____

LEARNING OBJECTIVES

- Understand the devastating realities of the student loan crisis.
- Explain the steps students can take to avoid student loans.

MAIN IDEA

College is expensive, but you can take a different path—a path that will set you up for real success. You don't have to become another student loan statistic.

Dream or Nightmare?

College: It's an exciting time, for sure. It's an educational time. But let's be honest—it's an *expensive* time. Like, fall-on-the-floor expensive! When you're in high school, it's easy to focus on the exciting parts of college—being on your own, making new friends, awesome tailgate parties—and forget about the rest.

That's where a lot of students get it wrong. They focus on the *experience* instead of looking at how their college choice affects their future. They get caught up in the beautiful campus, team spirit, and school reputation so much that they'll pay anything to go to their "dream school." But when the payments start after graduation, that dream feels more like a nightmare. But that doesn't have to be your story.

The Student Loan Crisis

Let's be real. The student loan crisis in this country is too serious to ignore. Right now, the total amount of student loan debt in the U.S. is over $1.54 trillion. That's enough to buy more than 4.4 million houses at the national median price of $350,000.[1] That's absolutely insane!

Every year, students sign up for tens of thousands of dollars in loans without batting an eye. Why? Because most of the time, they have no idea what they're getting themselves into—that's just how they've been told paying for college works.

> No one tells people that it's actually possible to pay cash for college. It is.
>
> — *Anthony O'Neal*

The stats can be overwhelming. And here's what makes those numbers worse: Almost 70% of high school grads will study at a four-year college, but only two-thirds of them will actually graduate with a degree.[2] That means many students who take out loans leave school with nothing to show for it—except debt. That's not okay!

A Debt-Free Degree

Well-meaning people will tell you that student loans are "good debt." But there's just no such thing. College is great—if you do it the *right way*. That means paying

Did You Know?

In 2019, 62% of public and private nonprofit college graduates had student loan debt.[3]

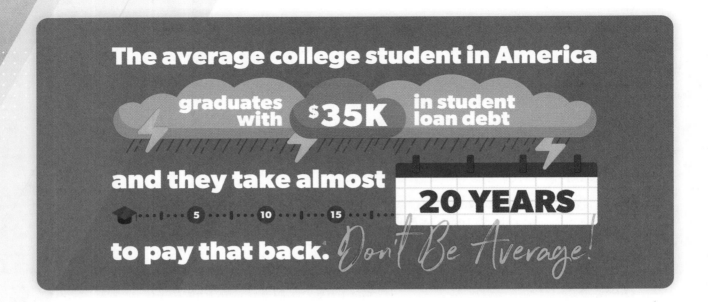

The average college student in America graduates with **$35K** in student loan debt and they take almost **20 YEARS** to pay that back.[4] *Don't Be Average!*

The Five Foundations:

Save a $500 emergency fund.

Get out and stay out of debt.

Pay cash for your car.

Pay cash for college.

Build wealth and give.

for it with cash and walking across that stage with nothing hanging over your head except the tassel from your cap. Check out the graphic above. Too many people can't focus on their future because they're paying for their past. Don't let student debt steal your focus for 20 years!

Start the Right Way

You can decide right now not to become another student loan statistic. It takes a lot of work and a solid plan, but it's absolutely possible. And remember, paying cash for college is part of **The Five Foundations**!

Anthony's been there and made the mistake of taking out student loans. Here are his six steps for avoiding the problems that took him years to overcome.

1. TAKE DEBT OFF THE TABLE

The first and biggest decision you will have to make is to take debt off the table—it's no longer an option. You're not going to fall into the trap of student loan debt, no matter what anyone says or thinks of your decision. Debt is not an option.

Did You Know?

49% of college graduates have student loan debt.[5]

Once that's done—you just need to problem-solve. How will you pay for college without student loans? Apply for scholarships, look for grants, and get a part-time job. And when you're in school, *keep* debt off the table.

If someone offers you a free T-shirt to sign up for their credit card, run the other way. If a broke finance professor tries to teach you how using debt can help you get ahead, ask how much cash is in his wallet. (Okay, not really. But you get the idea!) You *can* make it through college using nothing but cash.

2. CREATE A VISION

College is where you get your education for the field you want to work in one day. That means you need to know what you want to do—or have a good idea—*before* you start. If you aren't sure, stick to community college for a couple of years to knock out your general education courses and figure out your plan. Remember, in Chapter 6 we said you may find that your dream career doesn't require a four-year degree.

3. RESEARCH AND PREP

Make a list of potential schools, then research the costs, tests, coursework, and college visits needed to get you there. Once you realize a local state school is more than $10,000 cheaper—*per year*—than a college across the state line, you might reconsider your shortlist of schools.

Take debt off the table.
— *Anthony ONeal*

4. DECISION DAY

Yep, it's time to select your dream school. Anthony ONeal says your dream school is the one you can afford! A dream school can turn into a nightmare fast if it's out of your budget. Be sure to account for scholarships, grants, savings, and work income when you're identifying an affordable school.

5. WORK, SAVE, AND BEHAVE

Especially in this day and age, everything students do is somehow documented on social media. Be careful with what you post, because most schools keep an eye out for anything that could give them bad press. Make sure you go to class, live on a budget, and stay out of trouble.

6. WALK THE STAGE DEBT-FREE

This is where you realize that your hard work was all worth it. Your whole life is ahead of you, with no shadow of debt in sight to slow you down. What a great feeling. Now, it's time to get after it!

Average Four-Year College Tuition and Fees:

Cost per year at:
- In-state public school: $10,440
- Out-of-state public school: $26,820
- Private school: $36,880[6]

*2019-20 school year

Your **JOURNAL** — How can the six steps for starting college on the right path help you as you make decisions about college?

REMEMBER THIS Add a ✓ next to the completed learning objective below.

- ◯ You understand the serious problem of student loan debt.
- ◯ You can explain how to get a degree without debt.

THIS LESSON MAKES ME FEEL Circle your response to what you learned.

CONFUSED   SURPRISED   THOUGHTFUL   CONFIDENT

LESSON 2 | The Reality of Student Loans

Make the right decisions right now so later in life your income is yours and you're not paying a huge debt. — Anthony O'Neal

GUIDED NOTES   While you watch the video, complete the section below.

1. Student loan debt in America is well over $1.6 _____ and growing.

2. The average person takes _____ years or more to pay off their student loans.

3. The Fourth Foundation: Pay _____ for college.

4. Student loans steal from your _____.

5. There is no such thing as _____ debt.

ANALYZE AND REFLECT   After you watch the video, respond to the question(s) below.

1. After hearing Anthony's example of Ty and Aaron, what is your reaction? Have you considered the opportunity cost of paying off student loans?

   _____

   _____

   _____

2. What is one thing you can do differently today to get your education without debt?

   _____

   _____

LEARNING OBJECTIVES

- Understand the impact student loans can have on your financial future.
- Evaluate multiple viewpoints related to paying for postsecondary education.

MAIN IDEA

Student loans have been called "good debt" and accepted as normal. But the truth is that student loans cost more than just interest—they cost you opportunity.

The Student Loan Myth

As a culture, we've been sold the myth that student loans are "good debt" for far too long. You hear things like: "They're a path to education!" and "You can't go to college without a student loan!" and "They can help you start building your credit score!"

Student loans have become normal, and normal is broke.

— *Dave Ramsey*

Sure, it sounds great. But here's what life with student loans really looks like—in the words of Amy, a college grad: "I regret going to college when and how I did. I didn't know how credit worked when I started college. I was told I would get a fantastic job and wouldn't have to worry about those loans.

"I graduated and got married. While I did find a job in my career field, my income is entry level. So is my husband's. We're both working hard but can't seem to get ahead with such high student loan debt payments each month."

The Fourth Foundation

People may say it's impossible, but you can get your education without becoming a slave to student loan debt. **The Fourth Foundation** is to pay cash for college.

The good news is that you can get a fantastic education and pay cash for it. And you'll save thousands of dollars in interest payments. Is it easy? Nope. It takes a lot more work to pay your way through school than it does to sign up for student loans. But let's take a deeper look at why the "easy" way turns out to be anything but easy in the long run.

The Cost of Student Loans

A student loan payment is based on the total amount borrowed (the principal) and the interest rate. The interest rate depends on the type of loan. **Private student loans** typically come with higher interest rates than **federal student loans**.

Monthly student loan payments can take up to 20% of a graduate's take-home pay.[7] And it can take up to 30 years to pay student loans back![8] Check out the graphic on the next page to see the impact of those loan payments.

The Fourth Foundation: Pay cash for college.

Private Student Loans: loans made by banks, credit unions, or other organizations with terms and conditions set by the lender including higher or variable interest rates

Federal Student Loans: loans made by the government with terms and conditions set by law; often have a lower fixed interest rate

The Story of AARON & TY
AND THE COST OF STUDENT LOAN PAYMENTS

The typical monthly student loan payment is between $200 and $300. But what would happen if those payments didn't exist? What could that money do? Check out what happened to Aaron and Ty.

 AARON

Aaron graduated from college with $35,000 in student loans at a 4.5% interest rate. He made monthly payments of $222 for 20 years. When he completed his payments, he had paid back $18,280 more than he borrowed. That stinks!

TY

Ty graduated from college without any student loan debt because of scholarships, grants, and a job. He started investing $222 per month with an average annual return of around 11%. After 20 years, Ty ended up with about $189,000. That's amazing!

AARON PAID $53,280 in total over 20 years

TY EARNED $189,000 in total over 20 years

 Ty invested $222 per month toward his future for 20 years.

Years 0   5   10   15   20

 Aaron paid $222 per month toward his student loan debt for 20 years.

That's about a $240,000 difference!

179

Opportunity Cost of Loans

Aaron took $35,000 in loans, but it's not uncommon for students to have $100,000 or more in loans. And many of those students become teachers or social workers making $30,000–40,000 per year. Their student loan payments hold them back from pursuing other life goals. Graduates with large amounts of student loans report putting off major life events like getting married, buying a house, investing for the future, and having children because of their debt.[9]

Dropping Out of College

It's not just graduates who struggle under the weight of student loans—so do those who drop out. They may leave school but their student loans go with them.

Dropouts still owe, on average, over $7,000 in student loans.[10] Without that degree, they'll earn less per year than college grads, making monthly payments even more of a burden.

Student debt messed up my financial life for *years.*
— *Anthony O'Neal*

A lot of people turn to bankruptcy to escape their debts. But student loans, in most circumstances, are *not* bankruptable. There's no easy way out of student loans. Borrowing money for college is like stealing from your future—and the true cost of those loans is more than meets the eye!

Did You Know?

After seven years, 49% of college dropouts actually owe more on their federal student loans than they originally borrowed due to a lack of repayment.[11]

Your **JOURNAL**   What is one financial opportunity you could enjoy if you didn't have to worry about making a monthly student loan payment?

_____

_____

_____

REMEMBER THIS   Add a ✓ next to the completed learning objective below.

◯ You understand the impact student loans can have on your financial future.

◯ You can describe different ways to pay for postsecondary education.

THIS LESSON MAKES ME FEEL   Circle your response to what you learned.

😥 CONFUSED   😮 SURPRISED   🙂 THOUGHTFUL   🤩 CONFIDENT

LESSON VIDEO GUIDE

Your dream school is an affordable school, which is a school you can graduate from 100% debt-free.

— Anthony O'Neal

GUIDED NOTES   While you watch the video, complete the section below.

1. Write down your key takeaways from the discussion panel. Include the different ways each of them were able to pay for college without student loans.

   _____

   _____

   _____

   _____

2. _____ around and do your research.

3. _____ for scholarships and grants.

4. You want to _____ income share agreements.

ANALYZE AND REFLECT   After you watch the video, respond to the question(s) below.

1. After hearing several different ways the panel paid for college, which way do you think best fits your situation? Why?

   _____

   _____

   _____

LEARNING OBJECTIVES

- Identify strategies for reducing the overall cost of postsecondary education.
- Develop a plan for cash flowing postsecondary education.

MAIN IDEA

You don't need debt to get a degree—you *can* pay cash for your education.

Planning for College

A lot of people believe it's impossible to pay for college with cash. They'll say things like, "Tuition is just too expensive," or "I don't have any other options," or "Everyone takes out loans, so it's no big deal, right?" We hear it all the time—and they're wrong!

Listen, it's absolutely possible for you to cash flow your education after high school. What does that mean? It just means you pay for any education with cash (including scholarships and grants) instead of using credit or debt. That's how you achieve **The Fourth Foundation**!

Treat college like a big purchase and shop around!

— Rachel Cruze

The first step is to make a plan. Start now! Planning for college involves more than just getting a good test score and completing an application for admission. You need to understand how much it's going to cost—tuition, fees, books, and living expenses—and then figure out how you're going to pay for it without debt.

Get help from your parents and school counselors along the way. Discuss what kind of financial help you'll get, if any, from family. Ask your parents about scholarships their employers might offer. Find out how much scholarship money your school of choice will offer based on your academic achievements and financial need. Then see where you stand. How much will you be short? Now it's time to start applying for as many scholarships as you can find, get a part-time job, and start saving!

Paying for Your Education

Any form of education after high school is called **postsecondary education.** For a lot of students, that means college. Here are some of the things you can do to cash flow your education:

GET GOOD GRADES

Great grades will do more than just get you into the school and career you want. They also help you get free money. Really! Academic scholarships go to those who *earn* them. They're kind of like getting a paycheck for your hard work in high school. The better you do at this "job," the more money you'll make!

Paying for It

Here's how the typical family pays for college (2019–2020).[12]

44% parent income and savings

25% scholarships and grants

13% student loans

9% parent loans

8% student income and savings

1% relatives and friends

The Fourth Foundation: Pay cash for college.

Postsecondary Education: all education that takes place after high school, including university, college, community college, certification, or trade school

ACE THE COLLEGE ENTRANCE EXAMS

The COVID-19 pandemic changed the ways some colleges are handling admissions. Still, for a majority of colleges, you'll need to take one of the standardized tests—the ACT or the SAT. Your scores on these tests are important when it comes to admission. But that's not all those test scores are good for. Schools use your scores to award scholarships too. That means it's important to do well! You can take the tests multiple times to raise your score. Increasing your score by just a few points could result in a lot of extra scholarship money.

Check with the colleges you're really interested in to determine what they're requiring, the deadlines, and available scholarships. Most students start taking the SAT and ACT in the fall of their junior year. But if you're a sophomore, it's a great idea to take the PSAT or PreACT to practice and prepare for the real deal. Check out the graphic below for a plan that will set you up for your best score on these standardized tests—and the most scholarship money!

Did You Know?

The average ACT score is a 21, and the average SAT score is a 1070. But to be considered for more scholarships, you'll want to score near the top 10%—a 29 or 1340.[13]

SHOP AROUND

Narrow your school choices down to five. Look at each school's degree programs and how well they match your career interests, budget, and scholarship eligibility. Your test scores may earn more scholarship money at one school than another.

Consider going to community college for your first two years to knock out required courses at a low cost—or even no cost in some states. And living at home can drastically reduce your living expenses.

Another great way to save a ton of money is to attend a state school instead of a private or out-of-state school. Don't be sold on prestige, where your friends are going, or a cool location. The focus here is to get the best deal on your education and graduate debt-free!

APPLY FOR FINANCIAL AID

One of the most basic things you can do to help cash flow college is fill out your financial aid paperwork. Every year you'll be in college, you'll need to complete

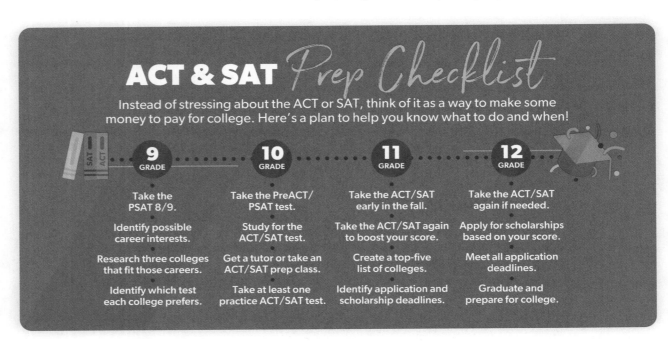

ACT & SAT *Prep Checklist*

Instead of stressing about the ACT or SAT, think of it as a way to make some money to pay for college. Here's a plan to help you know what to do and when!

9 GRADE
- Take the PSAT 8/9.
- Identify possible career interests.
- Research three colleges that fit those careers.
- Identify which test each college prefers.

10 GRADE
- Take the PreACT/ PSAT test.
- Study for the ACT/SAT test.
- Get a tutor or take an ACT/SAT prep class.
- Take at least one practice ACT/SAT test.

11 GRADE
- Take the ACT/SAT early in the fall.
- Take the ACT/SAT again to boost your score.
- Create a top-five list of colleges.
- Identify application and scholarship deadlines.

12 GRADE
- Take the ACT/SAT again if needed.
- Apply for scholarships based on your score.
- Meet all application deadlines.
- Graduate and prepare for college.

the **FAFSA** (Free Application for Federal Student Aid) as the first step to receiving any kind of financial aid for college—we'll go into more detail in Lesson 4. But don't stop yet, because there are thousands of scholarships and grants out there just waiting to be found. The more you apply for, the more money you can rack up.

The caliber of your future will be determined by the choices you make today.

— Anthony O'Neal

FIND PART-TIME WORK

Students who work while going to school learn time-management skills and often earn better grades. You can find on- and off-campus jobs that offer flexible schedules for students. Off-campus roles usually pay more. Many schools offer hourly positions that pay minimum wage—but you can often study while you work.

Determination Will Pay Off

We get it—we just laid out a lot of work. That's why you should get started right away. Whether you're a freshman or senior, you have what it takes to cash flow your education. Don't believe anyone who says otherwise! It's your choice.

It'll take focus, a plan, hard work, and some sacrifice. But when you're out of college and you actually get to keep your paycheck instead of sending it all to student loan debt, you'll be so glad you did.

FAFSA: the federal application required to receive any financial aid, including scholarships, grants, or loans offered through a college or university

Getting Funding

High school students who have taken a personal finance class say that their top college funding sources include:[14]

86%
Scholarships

61%
Help from parents

60%
Paying own way

Your JOURNAL

What are some money-saving options that can help you cash flow your education after high school?

_____

_____

_____

REMEMBER THIS   Add a ✓ next to the completed learning objective below.

◯ You can explain options for reducing the cost of postsecondary education.

◯ You understand ways to cash flow your postsecondary education.

THIS LESSON MAKES ME FEEL   Circle your response to what you learned.

😓 CONFUSED   😯 SURPRISED   🙂 THOUGHTFUL   🤩 CONFIDENT

LESSON VIDEO GUIDE

 I recommend spending just one hour per day applying for scholarships so you can live your dream for your life. — Anthony O'Neal

GUIDED NOTES   While you watch the video, complete the section below.

1. Nearly $2.9 _____ for scholarships goes unused each year.

2. Teens spend an average of _____ hours on social media, video games, and other technology each day.

3. FAFSA stands for _____ Application for Federal Student Aid.

4. Fill out the _____ no matter what.

5. It's never too _____ to apply for scholarships and grants.

ANALYZE AND REFLECT   After you watch the video, respond to the question(s) below.

1. If you spent one hour each day researching and applying for scholarships, do you believe you could pay cash for college? Why?

    _____

    _____

    _____

2. Which scholarships did Anthony say you should apply for?

    _____

- Understand how, why, and when to complete grant and scholarship applications.
- Explain how, why, and when to complete the FAFSA.

MAIN IDEA

A major part of your plan to cash flow college is to find the right mix of grants, scholarships, and work to fund your education.

Finding Money for School

In Lesson 3, you learned how to cash flow college. One of the big steps on that list is applying for financial aid. Aid comes in a lot of forms, but it's a key step in cutting down that pricey tuition bill. (Sometimes down to a big, fat zero!) Get excited, because this is where the hunt for free money begins! And for the record, we aren't even talking about student loans, because you've already taken debt off the table.

The only dream school is the one that you can graduate from debt-free!

— Anthony ONeal

Financial Aid: The First Step

As mentioned in Lesson 3, the FAFSA (Free Application for Federal Student Aid) is your starting point in your search for financial aid. You'll fill out the FAFSA before *every year* of college so you can be considered for need-based aid like grants, work-study, and certain scholarships.

Essentially, the FAFSA looks at your family's income (for you and your parents) through tax information and calculates your level of financial need. While it's not technically required for admission, it's the only way to qualify for any sort of federal financial aid and some private aid.

You can complete the FAFSA online starting October 1 for the following school year. Submissions stay open through the academic year, but don't put it off. The sooner you submit your FAFSA, the more likely you are to get financial help. That's because some federal funding is awarded on a first-come, first-served basis.

Once it's been submitted and reviewed, you'll receive a Student Aid Report to look over and respond to. It's important to understand that in order to actually *receive* your aid, you have to complete the entire process. So, don't forget! Also, keep in mind: The FAFSA will automatically qualify you for federal student loans, so ask that these be removed from your funding options. Remember, your goal is to graduate debt-free, so avoid student loans every chance you get. Just know that student loans will be pushed hard.

Education is the most powerful weapon which you can use to change the world.

Nelson Mandela
Revolutionary and politician

Financial Aid Facts

43% of families skipped filling out the FAFSA and missed out on financial aid.

30% of the families who didn't file the FAFSA say they didn't know about it or missed the deadline.[15]

*2019–20 school year

Scholarships

Scholarship: financial aid that does not need to be repaid; usually awarded based on achievements

A **scholarship** is money for education that's awarded to students by schools, foundations, or businesses based on achievement. The best part? You don't have to pay them back! Scholarships are *free money*! Anyone can earn one—or a bunch—if they just put in a little effort.

That's right, you don't have to be a straight-A student or a professional athlete to win money for school. (So, no excuses!) You just have to research scholarships that you're a fit for, fill out the application, and (typically) write an essay. So many students skip this step and miss out on hundreds or thousands of dollars because they didn't want to write an essay. That's crazy! Even if it's a smaller scholarship, like $500, if you spend two or three hours on the essay and win, you just got paid $500 for a few hours' worth of work. Not too shabby!

Grant: financial aid that does not need to be repaid; usually awarded based on financial need

And there are so many scholarships out there. You can find them by exploring scholarship websites and filling out your college's general scholarship application. A lot of schools and foundations also award scholarships based on involvement in the community, hobbies, after-school work, and financial need. Of course, you'll also find academic, athletic, and diversity scholarships. There's pretty much something for every student's interests.

Here's a Tip:

If you're not a strong writer, ask for a teacher's input on your scholarship essays. Since most applications will require a similar essay, once you've got a good one, you can just tweak it to meet the needs of different scholarships.

Don't believe us? Try spending an hour a day researching and applying for scholarships and just see what you find— and what you get. You'll be amazed at both the variety and availability!

Grants

Similar to scholarships, **grants** are another type of financial aid that you don't have to pay back. They're funded through schools, organizations, or federal programs. Grants are a little harder to find, and they're almost fully based on financial need and full-time or part-time school status.

The best way to find out if you qualify for government grants like the Pell Grant or the Federal Supplemental Educational Opportunity Grant is to fill out your FAFSA. Then research any outside options and fill out those applications.

KRISTINA'S *Story*

THE FIRST DAY of my freshman year of high school, my mom said, "I love you and I believe in you, but you've got to figure out your own way to pay for college." I was shocked. She told me I could start applying for scholarships. I worked hard through high school to build up my resumé and build a strong scholarship application. I treated my scholarship search as a part-time job and applied, applied, and applied for scholarships. If I spent two hours applying for, and getting, a $1,000 scholarship, I made $500 per hour! When it was all said and done, I was awarded over $500,000 in scholarships. I was able to go to my dream school and graduate school completely debt-free.

You *could* be required to repay a grant if you drop out, if you change from full-time to part-time enrollment, or if you receive scholarships or other grants that reduce your need for federal aid. Be sure you know the specifics before accepting grant money.

Scholarships and grants are free money to help you pay for college.
— Rachel Cruze

Work-Study Programs

A lesser known type of financial aid, the federal **Work-Study** program lets students earn federal funding by working part time while in school. Pretty self-explanatory! Like grants, work-study opportunities are also awarded based on need.

If you're interested, you'll need to check the option on the FAFSA that says you want to be considered for work-study. If you qualify, it'll come as one of your offerings in your financial aid package from the school, then you'll need to apply for a work-study position.

Work-study alone likely won't cover *all* your education expenses—after all, most of those are minimum wage positions. But you can think of scholarships, grants, and work-study like single pieces to your college puzzle. Alone, they may not look like much, but when you start putting them all together, you'll get the full picture of how they really can add up!

Here's a Tip:
Scholarships aren't just for incoming college freshmen! Some scholarships are open to sophomores, juniors, and even seniors—so keep applying and building that school fund as you go.

Work-Study:
a program that allows students to work part time while continuing their studies

Your JOURNAL

What are your next steps to finding money for school? Why is completing the FAFSA an important step in this process?

REMEMBER THIS Add a ✓ next to each completed learning objective below.

◯ You recognize how grants and scholarships can help you pay college costs.

◯ You understand the importance of completing the FAFSA.

THIS LESSON MAKES ME FEEL Circle your response to what you learned.

CONFUSED   SURPRISED   THOUGHTFUL   CONFIDENT

LESSON VIDEO GUIDE

If you're a person with character and you're intentional, hard working, and willing to learn, you'll be successful. — Anthony ONeal

GUIDED NOTES   While you watch the video, complete the section below.

1. Community college is a _____ way to start your postsecondary education.

2. The college you go to does not determine your _____.

3. No matter where you go, be a good _____ of where you are.

4. _____ is not for everyone.

ANALYZE AND REFLECT   After you watch the video, respond to the question(s) below.

1. What are some alternative ways to get an education other than attending a four-year university? List at least two.

   _____

   _____

2. What will bring you success in life: The name of the college you attend? Or your own personal character, intentionality, work ethic, and willingness to learn? Why?

   _____

   _____

   _____

LEARNING OBJECTIVES

- Understand the different options for a college education.
- Identify the types of costs associated with attending college.

MAIN IDEA

It's important to know which college path makes the most sense for you based on your career goals.

Is College Really Worth It?

College is expensive, so it's not uncommon to ask: Is a college degree worth it? The short answer is, typically, *yes*. Any post-secondary education can make a difference in the amount of money you earn in your career. And there's a lower **unemployment rate** for people who invest in education after high school. So, it's no surprise that so many students begin their journey toward a college degree each year. But you have options for how to get to that degree.

A useless degree or field of study is just that—useless.

— Rachel Cruze

Now, before you start applying to schools, ask yourself: Do I *need* this degree for my career? If you want to become a doctor or lawyer, obviously the answer to that question is *yes*. If you want to become a teacher, you'll need at least a **bachelor's degree**. But there are plenty of careers out there that don't require a college degree. (We'll dig into that in Lesson 6.)

COMMUNITY COLLEGE

These used to be called junior colleges, but today's community colleges offer academic courses like history, English, and math that will transfer to a four-year school, as well as associate degree programs and some professional certification courses.

ASSOCIATE DEGREE

An **associate degree** is typically a two-year degree (sometimes three) that can lower educational costs, offer specialized training, and provide a flexible schedule so you can work while you earn your degree. Fields like fashion design, nursing, medical technology, and criminal justice are offered at the associate level. Sometimes, you may need to earn certain licenses and certifications in addition to your associate degree for your career.

Community College: A Great Starting Point

For students who are looking at careers that require a bachelor's degree, community college could be the best first step in their college journey. Why? Because most university students don't start their

Unemployment Rate: the percentage of the labor force, or a specific demographic, who are jobless and who are looking for work

Bachelor's Degree: an under-graduate degree from a college or university, usually after completing four or five years of study

Associate Degree: a two- or three-year, postsecondary, undergraduate degree

Did You Know?

In America, adults with an advanced degree (master's, professional, or doctorate) earn 3.7 times as much as a high school dropout.[16]

A Message From ANTHONY

WHEN you're thinking about college, you probably picture a traditional, four-year school. You might've even been dreaming of going to a certain college for years—and there's no shame in that! But when you're college-hunting, here's one huge thing to remember: Don't get caught up in the hype of name-brand schools. I mean, let's be honest. Have you ever asked a doctor where they went to school before they gave you a checkup? Nope! And employers don't usually care either, as long as you're educated in your field. So before you buy that college logo sweatshirt, be sure the school actually makes sense for your career path—and for your budget.

degree-related classes until the end of their sophomore or beginning of their junior years. They have to knock out their general education courses and prerequisites first.

You can save thousands of dollars in tuition and living expenses—and *save up* for future college costs—if you opt to spend those first two years at a local community college, live at home, and then transfer your credits to your school of choice. Just be sure that you understand exactly which classes you need to fulfill your prerequisites and that all the courses directly transfer.

And here's a great deal: Some states offer free or reduced tuition for community college, so research your options. One example would be the Tennessee Promise program, which allows high school graduates to attend two years at a community college or technical school free of cost.

College and University

When it comes to four-year schools, you've probably heard the terms *college* and *university* used interchangeably, but they're technically different. It comes down to school size in most cases. Universities offer undergraduate and graduate programs and have multiple schools within their system (like a school of business or a school of engineering). Colleges typically have more limited options and often only offer undergraduate programs.

Don't let people talk you into making a decision you can't afford.

— Anthony O'Neal

When you're researching schools, here's a great tip: Don't get sucked into the name-brand school hype. The Ivy League has a nice ring to it, but unfortunately, that ring will cost you tens of thousands of dollars more than state schools. And the reality is that most employers don't usually care about where you got your degree—they just want to know that you're educated in your field. So be sure you choose a school that has a good program for your career goals and fits your budget.

Education Levels of Adults Over Age 25:

39% High school education or less

16% Some college but no degree

10% Associate degree

22% Bachelor's degree

13% Advanced degree (master's, professional, or doctorate)[17]

Campus Living Costs

Yes, tuition is expensive, but don't forget to include these costs in your college budget.

HOUSING

Living on campus often has a higher price tag than getting an apartment off campus and splitting the rent with roommates. Check your options before deciding where you'll relax at the end of the day.

MEAL PLANS

Get ready, because it's not uncommon for meal plans to run $1,000 per semester. Go for the least expensive plan you can and supplement it by making your own meals. Even dorm rooms usually allow mini fridges and microwaves, so this is where you can embrace a little culinary creativity.

PARKING

Parking fees vary by school. Those in big cities will likely come with higher price tags for parking. If that's your situation, consider leaving your car at home. Can you walk, bike, or use public transportation to get where you need to go? If so, you might be able to save big!

Is College for Me?

Education is fantastic, but you want to make sure you get the right education for you. It all comes down to research and planning. You've got to figure out what you want to do, research the education you need, and then make a plan to get that education without going into debt. It's not easy, but *it's definitely worth it!*

Did You Know?

The average cost per year for room and board (for everything beyond tuition and fees) at a four-year college is $11,500.[18]

Your **JOURNAL**   How could community college help you save money, even if you plan to pursue a bachelor's degree?

_____

_____

_____

REMEMBER THIS   Add a ✓ next to the completed learning objective below.

◯   You can explain the different college options.

◯   You understand the variety of costs associated with going to college.

THIS LESSON MAKES ME FEEL   (Circle) your response to what you learned.

😓 CONFUSED   😮 SURPRISED   🙂 THOUGHTFUL   🤩 CONFIDENT

LESSON VIDEO GUIDE

Get a clear vision for your future, and that vision is going to tell you the path you need to take. — Anthony ONeal

GUIDED NOTES While you watch the video, complete the section below.

1. Write down two key takeaways from the conversation about other education options.

   _____

   _____

2. A traditional _____ college isn't for everyone.

3. Trade schools allow you to study and _____ for a specific career.

4. Trade schools usually take less than _____ years to complete.

5. Joining the _____ can help cover education expenses through the GI Bill.

6. Another option is to become a business _____.

ANALYZE AND REFLECT After you watch the video, respond to the question(s) below.

1. What alternative education options have you considered, or what options are you willing to consider?

   _____

   _____

   _____

LEARNING OBJECTIVES

- Understand non-college options for postsecondary education.
- Identify types of costs associated with postsecondary education and training.

MAIN IDEA

From trade and vocational schools to on-the-job training, there are plenty of options for education if college isn't the right path for you.

What if College Isn't for Me?

Whether you're a freshman or a senior, there's one question that seems to follow you through the halls of high school: Where are you going to college?

But the real question is: What do you want to do? Because the truth is, college isn't for everyone. And that's okay. In fact, it's a good thing! Don't force yourself into an education that you don't need. If your career interests take you on a path that doesn't include four years of college, you'll save a ton of money and stress—and you'll get to start doing what you love a lot sooner.

> **When you love what you do, you will work like crazy—but it will never feel like work.**
>
> — Dave Ramsey

And there's plenty of opportunity. There are more than 6 million jobs available each year that don't require a college degree.[19] Now, getting one of those jobs *will* require education. Just because you don't need a college degree doesn't mean you don't need to be educated. Today, the most promising jobs for workers without four-year degrees are in skilled industries like health care and financial services, as well as service industries including auto repair, plumbing, and electrical work. To compete, you'll need some training.

Find Your Path

Remember, postsecondary education isn't a one-size-fits-all situation. With so many options for jobs, you have the opportunity to find a plan for education that fits your passions and meets your goals.

So take a deep breath and relax. These are big decisions, but they're also big opportunities for you to chase what you want to do. And you can start now! Start thinking about what your goals are and researching what you need to do—college, trade school, or something else—to reach those goals. Your future is up to you!

On the next page, you'll find some information about the most common postsecondary options. These include trade and vocational schools, licenses and certifications, the military, on-the-job training, and starting your own business.

> I have never let my schooling interfere with my education.
>
> **Mark Twain**
> American author

Did You Know?

31% of Gen Z students have considered taking a gap year between high school and college.[20]

OTHER *Education* OPTIONS

Trade and Vocational Schools

Students who want to work in a specific trade—like a dental hygienist, plumber, electrician, or auto mechanic—can attend a vocational or trade school to learn those skills. These schools take less than two years and their costs are a lot lower. Also, trade schools are generally tied into the employment needs of a region or state, so employers look to hire trade school graduates.

Start a Business

What if you want to start your own business? That's fantastic! While there's always risk involved, if you have passion and an entrepreneurial spirit, this path might be right for you. You'll need a solid business plan and a stockpile of cash for a start-up fund first. Whatever you do, stick with a debt-free plan. Remember, debt will only add more risk to your venture.

Enlist in the Military

The military isn't for everyone, but it has helped a lot of people get through college debt-free while giving them the honor of serving their country. You can commit to full-time or part-time service to fit your career needs. And even if school isn't in your plan, military service offers plenty of training to help you build technical and leadership skills that will carry through to future roles.

Licenses and Certifications

Students who are looking to get licensed in a particular trade—like an insurance or real estate agent—need to study for and take their state's certification test. You can prepare on your own or through an online course. Once you've earned the basic certification and get some experience, you'll want to keep up with professional development opportunities to advance your career.

On-the-Job Training

On-the-job training happens while you're doing the actual job. A professional trainer serves as the course instructor and uses a combination of hands-on activities and formal classroom training. For instance, to be a police officer, you need a high school diploma and then you must pass background, polygraph, and drug tests. Then you'll attend a police academy for your training.

Find Your Strengths by Giving of Your Time

Figuring out what you want to do after you graduate from high school can feel like an all-consuming task. But you can still find ways to help others by giving of your time! And when you give your time, it helps others just like when you give money.

Never pursue something as a career that you're not passionate about.

— Anthony ONeal

One of the best ways to find what you want to do—what you're really passionate about—is by getting out there and doing it.

Do you think you might want to be a nurse? Volunteer at a hospital or nursing home where you can make a difference while observing the day-to-day work.

Interested in teaching? Offer to tutor younger students for free or donate your time as a counselor at a day camp where you'll get the chance to work with kids.

Volunteering is a hands-on approach that not only gives you an idea of how well you might like a future profession, but it also softens your heart as you give of your time and talents.

But what if you end up *not* loving the work? Well, you just saved yourself a lot of money and frustration from going to school for something and realizing late that it's not where your passion lies. That's what we call a win-win!

Did You Know?

Over 30% of the adults in America volunteer their time.[21]

Here's a Tip:

The easiest way to find volunteer opportunities is just to ask. Call a business you're interested in and ask if they'd like some volunteer help. You may even get school credit.

Your **JOURNAL** What kind of education or training will you need in order to pursue your chosen career path?

_____

_____

_____

REMEMBER THIS Add a ✓ next to the completed learning objective below.

◯ You can explain the different non-college options for postsecondary education.

◯ You can identify costs associated with education and training opportunities.

THIS LESSON MAKES ME FEEL Circle your response to what you learned.

😓 CONFUSED   😮 SURPRISED   🙂 THOUGHTFUL   🤩 CONFIDENT

Chapter 7 Review

Fill in the blanks below using the correct key terms from this chapter.

Private Student Loans	Scholarship	Unemployment Rate	Bachelor's Degree
Federal Student Loans	Grant	Postsecondary Education	Associate Degree
FAFSA	Work-Study		

1. In order to qualify for student aid, a student and his or her parent(s) must complete the _____ every year the student is in college.

2. A(n) _____ is also referred to as a four-year college degree or an undergraduate degree.

3. A(n) _____ is financial aid that's based on a student's financial need and doesn't need to be paid back.

4. Any formal education after you graduate from high school is referred to as _____.

5. On average across the country, the _____ is lower for those with a college degree.

6. _____ typically have lower interest rates than those offered by private lenders.

FINISH THE SENTENCE Use what you've learned in this chapter to complete these sentences.

1. The first and biggest decision you'll have to make about going to college the right way financially is to _____ _____.

2. A great alternative to a four-year college—and one that could save you a bunch of money—would be to go _____ _____.

3. When it comes to financial aid, you definitely want to avoid any and all loans, but you can accept _____ _____.

4. The student loan crisis in our country is too serious to ignore because, right now, the total student loan debt is _____ _____.

1. If you receive financial aid that's based on your achievements, that's called:

   A. A grant

   B. Work-study

   C. A scholarship

   D. An award

2. What will students who drop out of college have to do with their student loans?

   A. Pay them off

   B. Forget them

   C. Bankrupt them

   D. Forgive them

3. Student loans you take out to pay for college are almost impossible to . . .

   A. Enjoy

   B. Bankrupt

   C. Pay off

   D. Sign up for

4. Someone who wants to be a hygienist or electrician should go to . . .

   A. A university

   B. The military

   C. The internet

   D. A trade school

5. When it comes to picking a college, look for one that is . . .

   A. Affordable

   B. Well known

   C. A big name

   D. Out of state

6. On average, how many years does it take someone to pay back student loan debt?

   A. 5 years

   B. 10 years

   C. 15 years

   D. 20 years

Review **QUESTION**   Many people say student loans are "good debt." How would you respond?

_____

_____

_____

_____

_____

Keep Your Money Safe

Financial Services

This chapter explores the services provided by banks and credit unions, including the different options and features. You'll learn about responsible banking, how to manage your accounts, and the importance of keeping records.

LESSON VIDEO GUIDE

You want to partner with a good bank in your community that you can trust. — Anthony O'Neal

GUIDED NOTES   While you watch the video, complete the section below.

1. _____ is when someone doesn't have a bank account.

2. Underbanked means they have a bank account but still rely on _____ financial services.

3. When you use a bank, your money is _____.

4. Banks are _____ expensive than predatory financial services.

5. Banks and credit unions are safe and _____.

6. The FDIC and NCUA insure your money up to _____ per account.

ANALYZE AND REFLECT   After you watch the video, respond to the question(s) below.

1. Do you generally consider banks to be trustworthy? Why or why not?

_____

_____

_____

_____

LEARNING OBJECTIVES

- Evaluate the purpose of financial institutions and their role in personal finance.
- Describe some financial struggles that unbanked or underbanked people might face.

MAIN IDEA

Earning, budgeting, and saving money are all a part of personal finance, but so are managing and protecting your money. Financial institutions help you do all of that.

Keep Your Money Safe

So you've got a small income and you're creating a budget every month. But where's the best place to *keep* the money you're earning and saving? That's where financial service providers, like banks, come in.

A **bank** may seem a little intimidating at first, especially if you've never dealt with one. But most banks are all about helping you protect, access, and manage your money. Some of them can even help put your money to work through accounts that earn compound interest like we talked about in Chapter 3.

The number in your bank account matters more than the one on your credit report.

— Anthony ONeal

Your bank can be a valuable partner as you work toward your money goals. When you open an account, the bank will offer you a lot of services. Some of those services will help you manage your money and keep it safe. But other services, like credit cards and personal loans, will *not* help you get ahead. You'll learn about these bank services later in this chapter.

Your Money Is Insured

As long as your bank is insured by the **Federal Deposit Insurance Corporation (FDIC)** or the **National Credit Union Administration (NCUA),** your money is safe. Just look for the FDIC or NCUA logos. These federal agencies insure deposits in your accounts up to $250,000. That means if something were to happen to the bank—if it was shut down, robbed, or hacked—your money would be safe. Well, unless you had more than a quarter of a million dollars in one bank!

Living Unbanked

Is your money safer in a shoe box under your bed or in a bank? "In a bank" is the easy answer, of course, but do you know why? First, your money is much more secure (and insured) in a bank. Second, a bank account is the most basic way to manage your money. Without one, you're at a serious disadvantage when it comes to spending and saving your money.

Bank: a financial institution licensed to receive deposits and provide financial services

FDIC

Federal Deposit Insurance Corporation: independent federal agency that insures deposits in bank accounts up to $250,000

NCUA

National Credit Union Administration: independent federal agency that insures deposits in credit unions up to $250,000

Unbanked: people who don't have bank accounts

Underbanked: people who have savings or checking accounts but still use alternative financial products and services

Did You Know?

Over 14 million Americans are unbanked, meaning they don't have bank accounts.[2]

Still, one out of every four American households are **unbanked** (they have no bank accounts) or **underbanked** (they have a bank account but depend on other financial products and services).[1] Neither of these is a good thing. Here are some of the most common reasons people give for not having a savings or checking account:

1. *Distrust.* Some unbanked and underbanked people have had bad customer service at banks, so they avoid them. But remember, you can find another bank if you're unhappy with the service you're getting.

2. *Lack of financial literacy.* Some people are intimidated by traditional financial services because they never learned about them. That's why it's great that you're learning this stuff now!

3. *Unemployment.* Although you don't need to have a job to open an account, unemployment and job loss can cause people to abandon their bank accounts.

And some banks charge higher and more frequent fees to customers who have lower account balances.

4. *Bank fees.* Some banks charge high, unexplained, and even unexpected fees. A good bank will outline all their fees when you open your account. But it's your responsibility to understand what you're paying for.

5. *Blacklisted.* Some people can't pass the background check required to open a bank account because they have a negative financial history. This might include bounced checks or too many overdrafts. You won't have to deal with this if you do the stuff we teach in this course.

6. *Lack of services.* People in some areas (lower income or rural) may find fewer and more expensive bank options. But there's a bank and an account out there for everyone. Again, you just need to know what to look for.

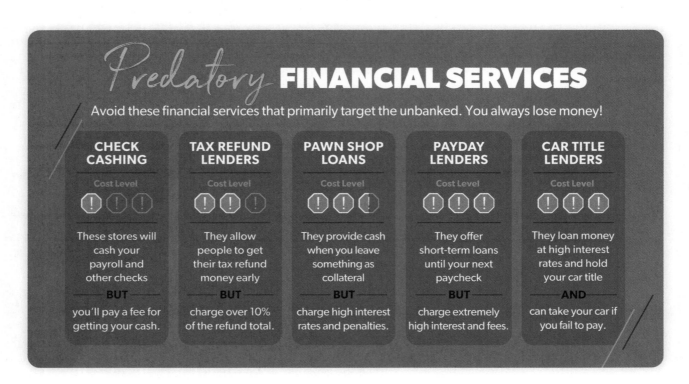

Predatory FINANCIAL SERVICES

Avoid these financial services that primarily target the unbanked. You always lose money!

CHECK CASHING	**TAX REFUND LENDERS**	**PAWN SHOP LOANS**	**PAYDAY LENDERS**	**CAR TITLE LENDERS**
Cost Level	Cost Level	Cost Level	Cost Level	Cost Level
! ! !	! ! !	! ! !	! ! !	! ! !
These stores will cash your payroll and other checks	They allow people to get their tax refund money early	They provide cash when you leave something as collateral	They offer short-term loans until your next paycheck	They loan money at high interest rates and hold your car title
—BUT—	—BUT—	—BUT—	—BUT—	—AND—
you'll pay a fee for getting your cash.	charge over 10% of the refund total.	charge high interest rates and penalties.	charge extremely high interest and fees.	can take your car if you fail to pay.

Do Your Research

What's the worst part of being unbanked or underbanked? People with few or no legitimate banking options often end up using alternative financial products or services that don't meet their needs or that take advantage of their situation. Both of these are terrible options. You don't want that for your personal finances!

Predatory financial services are pretty smart. Their ads for services like title loans and payday loans sound like the perfect solution for someone struggling with money. Don't fall for it! The chart on the previous page gives the lowdown on some of these predatory lenders and why you never want to do business with them.

While not having a bank account and using alternative, shady financial providers are terrible ideas, so is having an account or using services you don't completely understand. Not every bank is created equal, and some financial services are great for the bank's profits—but not for you.

> **You have to become intentional with your money.**
>
> — *Chris Hogan*

You'll need to do your homework to find the bank that's right for you. It's the only way to avoid paying ridiculous fees and other costs that drain money out of your account. We'll talk more about how to choose the right place and the right accounts in the next two lessons.

Did You Know?

70% of borrowers use the cash from a payday lender for regular monthly expenses like rent or utilities.[3]

Man must cease attributing his problems to his environment and learn again to exercise his will—his personal responsibility.

Albert Einstein
Physicist

Your **JOURNAL**   How can a financial service provider—like a bank or credit union—help you manage and protect your money?

_____

_____

_____

REMEMBER THIS   Add a ✓ next to each completed learning objective below.

◯ You can explain the purpose of financial institutions and the role they can play in personal finance.

◯ You can describe some financial struggles that un- or underbanked people might face.

THIS LESSON MAKES ME FEEL   (Circle) your response to what you learned.

😓 CONFUSED   😮 SURPRISED   🙂 THOUGHTFUL   🤩 CONFIDENT

LESSON VIDEO GUIDE

Sticking to your budget will help you avoid overspending and overdraft fees.

— Anthony O'Neal

GUIDED NOTES   While you watch the video, complete the section below.

1. There are _____ banks (or traditional banks).

2. There are _____ unions.

3. There are _____ banks.

4. Avoid _____ products.

5. Avoid _____ protection.

ANALYZE AND REFLECT   After you watch the video, respond to the question(s) below.

1. What are three ways banks make money?

_____

_____

_____

2. Why do you think banks will try to sell you credit cards or personal loans?

_____

_____

LEARNING OBJECTIVES

- Identify the various types of financial institutions and the services they provide.
- Understand how banks and credit unions are able to make money.

MAIN IDEA

Finding the right type of financial institution will help you reach your money goals as well as help you manage and protect your money.

Banking Options

Beginning with your first piggy bank, you learned that an important part of having money is keeping it safe. That's how people see banks—as a safe place to keep money in checking and savings accounts. And they are. But banks provide many types of financial services to people and businesses, including loans, mortgages, and check writing, along with debit and credit cards. You may not realize it, but there are also different types of banks.

RETAIL BANKS

Retail banks, or traditional banks, are the most common and most familiar. They provide a variety of banking services and have multiple locations in cities and towns. They have physical buildings (also called brick-and-mortar locations) where your checking and savings accounts are held.

These banks can be large, nationally branded banks or small regional banks. Honestly, there's no upside to the massive name-brand bank unless you like higher fees and enjoy being treated like a nameless, faceless account number.

On the other hand, a small community bank will often give you great, personalized customer service. What a concept!

> **I prefer the customer service relationship in small, local banks or credit unions.**
> — *Dave Ramsey*

CREDIT UNIONS

Credit unions are like traditional banks but with a few differences. They usually have fewer branches and ATMs but typically have fewer fees and higher interest rates on your money (and that's good for your account balance). Credit unions often require membership based on specific criteria, like being a teacher, serving in the military, or working for a certain company.

ONLINE BANKS

Online banks are the new kid on the block. With an online bank, *everything* happens digitally—deposits, transfers, bill payments, and savings. Everything is done online.

Retail Banks: for-profit financial institutions that accept deposits and offer a variety of deposit accounts and financial services

Credit Unions: nonprofit financial institutions that are owned and operated by their members; offer deposit accounts and lending services similar to a retail bank but at a lower cost

Online Banks: also known as internet banking; all transactions done online; no physical location

Weigh YOUR BANKING OPTIONS

You have to decide what banking features are the most important to you.
Here's a general list of features, but you may find exceptions based on where you go.

	Bank	Credit Union	Online Bank
No Membership Requirements	✓		✓
Walk-In Convenience	✓	✓	
Check Cashing and Cash Deposits	✓	✓	
Higher Interest on Savings Accounts		✓	✓
Better Rates and Lower Fees		✓	✓
In-Person Service Available	✓	✓	
Earned Account Dividends		✓	
More Physical Locations	✓		

However, with an online bank, you can't walk in and talk to the branch manager if you have a problem or special need, because there isn't a branch manager. Be ready to spend time on the phone or virtual chat if you have a problem.

So, which type of bank is right for you? That's a personal choice that really depends on what options are the most important to you. Check out the chart at the top of this page for a quick comparison.

Other Financial Services

While not as common as banks, there are plenty of other financial services that offer money-management services like investing, insurance, lending, and real estate. These places also offer advising services for individuals, businesses, and the government.

In addition to banks, credit unions, and online banks, here are some other financial services you may use:

Here's a Tip

There's no such thing as a one-type-fits-everyone bank. Before signing up for any type of bank account, do your research and make sure you're getting the features that matter to you.

- **Investment banks** provide market advice, explain regulations, and help businesses price and sell stocks or bonds to their investors.
- **Investment service institutions** help people who want to invest their money in stocks or mutual funds.
- **Financial advisement companies** provide investment advice, income tax preparation, and estate planning.
- **Wealth management firms** help people with specific advice related to comprehensive investing strategies.
- **Insurance brokers or agents** will find affordable and appropriate insurance plans for their clients.
- **Credit card companies** provide lines of credit to consumers.

Whew! That's a lot. The good news is, you won't need all of these services right from the start—and some of them, like credit card companies, you won't need at all.

How Do Banks Make Money?

Obviously, banks are businesses, and they exist to make money. So how does that work? The ways you're probably most familiar with are through interest on loans, ATM fees, overdraft fees, and account fees.

Avoid any bank services that have to do with debt.

— Anthony ONeal

Banks also make money by investing their customers' deposited money. Banks earn interest on their investments and then pay their customers a small amount of interest on their savings and checking accounts. It's a win-win for both parties.

Bank Services to Avoid

You know that having debt is no way to get ahead. It's a huge financial risk that stands in the way of building wealth. Avoid any bank service that leads to debt—credit cards, personal loans, and car loans.

Many banks also offer **overdraft protection** and make it sound like a really good idea. But let's be clear: Overdraft protection isn't a safeguard—it's an unhealthy money lifeline. Basically, the bank automatically deposits money into your checking account any time you overdraft your account (spend more than you have). You avoid the **overdraft fee** but have to pay the money back with interest.

If you live on a budget and monitor your account regularly, you shouldn't have to worry about overdraft fees!

Did You Know?

The average overdraft fee is $33.36. That's for each one![4]

Overdraft Protection: an option offered by banks to cover overspending an account and then charge a fee for it

Overdraft Fee: a penalty charged if the account holder spends more than their account balance, causing the available balance to go below zero

---

Your JOURNAL

What are some things you can do to reduce or avoid bank service charges and fees?

_____

_____

_____

REMEMBER THIS   Add a ✓ next to each completed learning objective below.

◯ You can identify the various types of financial institutions and the services they provide.

◯ You understand how banks and credit unions make money.

THIS LESSON MAKES ME FEEL   Circle your response to what you learned.

☹ CONFUSED   😮 SURPRISED   😊 THOUGHTFUL   🤩 CONFIDENT

LESSON VIDEO GUIDE

A savings account is for long-term savings goals, while a checking account is for regular spending. — Anthony O'Neal

<u>**GUIDED NOTES**</u>   While you watch the video, complete the section below.

1. A _____ account is the best option for your emergency fund and saving for large purchases.

2. A _____ account is used for your regular spending.

3. The most common way people use their checking account is through a _____ card.

4. It's more difficult to _____ with a debit card.

5. What are some of the things you should look for when selecting the right bank?

   _____

   _____

<u>**ANALYZE AND REFLECT**</u>   After you watch the video, respond to the question(s) below.

1. Think of the bank you or your family uses. What are some things that are positive or negative about the bank? What are some questions you have that you would like to know?

   _____

   _____

   _____

LEARNING OBJECTIVE

Evaluate the features, benefits, and costs of various financial services and accounts.

MAIN IDEA

It's important to research the cost, convenience, and customer service options when you're choosing a bank and account type.

Choosing the Right Bank

With all the options out there, how do you choose a bank? Maybe you flip a coin. Or play rock, paper, scissors. All banks offer pretty much the same stuff, so it doesn't matter which one you choose, right?

Hang on! Not every bank is created equal. You'll need to do your homework to find the one that's right for you. It's the only way you'll avoid paying fees, charges, and other costs that will eat up your money.

> ### You want to make sure your money is insured.
>
> *— Dave Ramsey*

You can narrow down your choices by identifying: 1) what kind of accounts you want, 2) what type of bank you want, and 3) the features that matter the most to you.

Account Types Offered

You'll need a checking account for your regular spending (of course). Plus, you'll need a savings account for your emergency fund (remember **The First Foundation**) and large purchase savings.

CHECKING ACCOUNTS

Checking accounts make spending and managing your money safe as well as convenient. Most checking accounts offer similar basic features, including checks, debit card, ATM access, payroll direct deposit, online banking with bill pay, and account transfers.

SAVINGS ACCOUNTS

Savings accounts make storing your cash safe and easy. Savings accounts are usually interest-bearing accounts. That means your bank will pay you a small amount of interest on your money. Most banks offer three types of savings accounts:

Basic (or regular) savings account: Basic savings accounts earn a small amount of interest and give you quick access to your money when you need it. They typically have online and mobile banking access.

Money market account: These are similar to basic savings accounts. They may offer a higher interest rate based on your balance. They may offer check writing or debit card capabilities but may limit the number of withdrawals you can make each month. Money market accounts are a great option for your emergency fund.

Here's a Tip:

Many banks offer free checking accounts. Do your research and find a bank that doesn't charge extra for basic services.

The First Foundation: Save a $500 emergency fund.

Choosing THE RIGHT BANK

With so many different banks to choose from, how do you know which one is going to be the best for you? Here are some good things to look for:

Interest Rates

This is interest you earn on your checking, savings, CDs (certificates of deposit), and money market accounts. Online banks can offer better rates since they don't have brick-and-mortar locations.

Fees

ATM fees, foreign transaction fees, and card replacement fees can take a lot of your money. Many banks and credit unions offer free checking, which means you won't have to pay minimum balance charges or monthly maintenance fees.

ATMs and Branches

Make sure the bank you choose has plenty of ATM locations (including in the town where you may attend college) so you won't have to pay fees for using the ATMs at other banks.

Mobile and Online Banking

A bank with a strong website and mobile banking app will simplify your life. You should be able to transfer money, view your accounts, make payments, and make mobile deposits.

Ease of Use

Choose a bank or credit union that you actually enjoy doing business with and that has good customer service. Check online reviews and ask friends and family who they recommend.

Security

In today's hack-happy world, you can't be too careful about protecting your money and personal information. Make sure you know how your bank handles information breaches.

FDIC and NCUA

Always choose a bank or credit union that's insured by the Federal Deposit Insurance Corporation (FDIC) or the National Credit Union Administration (NCUA). Both will protect your accounts up to $250,000.

Certificates of deposit (CDs): CDs offer higher interest rates, but you'll have to "lock" your money for a specified amount of time (18 months for example). You can withdraw your money early, but you'll have to pay a penalty.

The biggest difference between the types of savings accounts is **liquidity**—which refers to how quickly and easily you can access your money. Money in a basic savings or money market account is very liquid—you can get it quickly. Money saved in a CD is less liquid. It's still accessible, but you'll be hit with fees if you want your money quickly.

The Right Features

We talked about the different types of banks in Lesson 2—retail banks, credit unions, and online banks. The bank you choose is often the one that offers the kind of features and services that make sense for you. You'll find a list of some of the most common features to look for on the previous page.

Keep your emergency fund in a money market account.

— Chris Hogan

Protect and stack your cash by doing your research and finding a bank you can trust. It should be a bank that has the features you want and need. And don't forget to shop around for the best rates and offers. It's your money—and you've worked hard for it—so work with a bank or credit union that's right for you!

Liquidity: how quickly you can access the money in an account or the value of an asset without a penalty or fee

When to Open a Bank Account:

- When you have income
- Between the ages of 13–17 (may need to be a co-owned account)
- When you understand how to manage an account

Your JOURNAL

What are the most important features you want to consider when shopping for a bank?

_____

_____

_____

REMEMBER THIS Add a ✓ next to the completed learning objective below.

◯ You understand how to evaluate the features, benefits, and costs of various financial services and accounts.

THIS LESSON MAKES ME FEEL (Circle) your response to what you learned.

 CONFUSED   SURPRISED   THOUGHTFUL   CONFIDENT

LESSON VIDEO GUIDE

***You have to know what's going on
with your checking account.*** — *Dave Ramsey*

GUIDED NOTES While you watch the video, complete the section below.

1. What are two key takeaways from using auto-drafting to pay your bills?

   _____

   _____

   _____

2. As the owner of your account, you need to know _____ going on.

3. Monitor your account at least _____ times per week.

4. _____ is when you validate that all transactions from your bank statement match your records.

5. _____ is when you include transactions that haven't posted to your bank account yet.

ANALYZE AND REFLECT After you watch the video, respond to the question(s) below.

1. Why is it important to track your expenses? What would happen if you didn't monitor your bank account on a regular basis?

   _____

   _____

LEARNING OBJECTIVES

- Develop a basic understanding of how to manage your bank accounts.
- Recognize things to look for when reviewing a bank statement.

MAIN IDEA

Your money is *your* responsibility. Knowing how to balance your checking account and catch any bank errors or fraudulent charges will help you manage your account.

Money Management

Imagine yourself in line at your favorite store getting ready to check out. You insert your debit card and enter your PIN. Beep! A message pops up on the screen saying your card has been declined. Instantly, you feel like everyone is looking at you.

Maybe that's never happened to you. Maybe if it did, it was a card reader error. Great! Keep it that way by being responsible with your checking account. Knowing the actual balance of your account will help you avoid that sweaty scenario as well as the most frequent and costly banking mistake—the overdraft.

Your Checking Account

Many people end up with errors in their checking account just because they don't pay attention to their money. And opening up your bank app to take a quick peek at your account balance while you're standing in the checkout line doesn't qualify as paying attention to your account!

There are several ways to track your spending, deposits, and transfers. Find out what works best for you to track the activity in your checking account. That might even mean using the old-fashioned pencil-and-paper method with a **checking account register**. That's how most people did it before there were digital options.

Overdrawing your account indicates laziness or a lack of responsibility.

— *Rachel Cruze*

But now that we have digital choices, a budgeting app may be the easiest and most natural option for you. Finish a transaction, punch it into your app, and—*Boom!*—you have an immediate record. The point is to have your own record of the running balance in your account.

Track Your Spending

It's super important to track your spending to make sure you don't overdraw your checking account. You need to track everything that involves spending money: debit card purchases, written checks, third-party app transactions, and money you get from an ATM. It's important to understand that

Checking Account Register: also called a ledger; a lined and divided journal to record checking account activity

Words of Wisdom

Have you ever wanted to know what was really important to someone?

Look at their checkbook entries. Are they spending a lot on "stuff" like entertainment, clothes, friends, etc.? People spend their money on things most meaningful to their heart.

"For where your treasure is"—the money you spend or save—"there your heart will be also" (Matthew 6:21).

some types of transactions take longer to hit your account, which is why you have to keep track of things. What your bank app or ATM receipt shows as a balance may not reflect some of your transactions. For example:

Transaction Type	Time
Debit Card	Immediate (when you use your PIN)
Debit Card (as credit)	2–3 days (when you don't use your PIN)
Tips	Not shown on immediate transaction balance
Digital Wallet	2–3 days (when processed as a credit)
Checks	May be run as an immediate debit or may take several business days

You'll usually have some transactions, as show in the graphic below, that aren't yet reflected in your account balance. Automated payments for music or video subscriptions that hit your account each month can catch you off guard too!

Direct Deposit: option to allow automatic electronic deposit of your payroll checks

Reconciling: the process of making sure you and the bank agree on how much money is in your checking account

Did You Know?

ACH (Automated Clearing House) electronic payments are used to pay bills online and make bank-to-bank transfers. They're fast, reliable, and cost less to process. *Note:* They're also called EFT (electronic funds transfer) payments.

Track Your Deposits

Make sure to track every deposit you make into your checking account. Just beware that some deposits can take up to three business days to show up in your account. If you have your paycheck set up with your employer for **direct deposit** (and you absolutely *should* if it's offered), those funds are available on your payday.

Since you're already monitoring your checking account transactions, then verifying your bank's online account statements for accuracy—often referred to as balancing or **reconciling** your account—is an easy step to add to the process.

The Balancing Act

Reconciling your bank accounts is *your* responsibility. You'll need your personal transaction record (or register) and your monthly bank account statement. Your statement is available both on your bank's mobile app and their online banking site (most people have moved away from paper statements sent by mail).

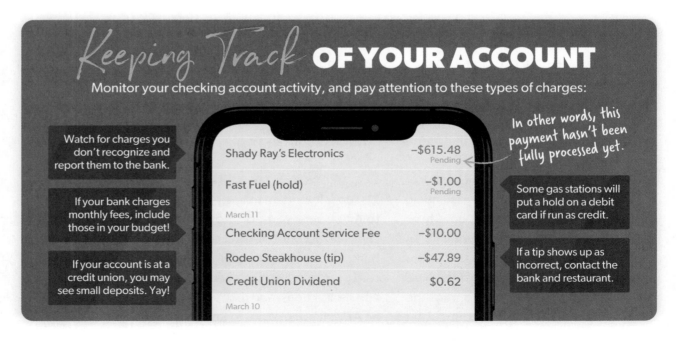

Keeping Track **OF YOUR ACCOUNT**

Monitor your checking account activity, and pay attention to these types of charges:

Watch for charges you don't recognize and report them to the bank.

If your bank charges monthly fees, include those in your budget!

If your account is at a credit union, you may see small deposits. Yay!

Shady Ray's Electronics	−$615.48 Pending
Fast Fuel (hold)	−$1.00 Pending
March 11	
Checking Account Service Fee	−$10.00
Rodeo Steakhouse (tip)	−$47.89
Credit Union Dividend	$0.62
March 10	

In other words, this payment hasn't been fully processed yet.

Some gas stations will put a hold on a debit card if run as credit.

If a tip shows up as incorrect, contact the bank and restaurant.

Regardless of where you access your statement, you'll want to reconcile, or balance, your account. First, make sure your records match what your bank shows. Match up all the transactions and make sure to record any bank fees or service charges.

Then, if you've been keeping good records, you may notice transactions in your record that aren't included on your bank statement. That's okay. To check that your balance is accurate and matches what your bank shows, add any outstanding deposits and subtract any outstanding withdrawals. The new total should match the running balance on your record.

If the numbers don't match up, you've probably forgotten to record a transaction. It happens. Look over your statement and try again. You'll also want to check for any fraudulent transactions or a mistake made by the bank. If you find any of those, report them to your bank right away.

> ## Live below your means. That's how you stack money.
> — Anthony ONeal

Banking in the U.S.

71% of customers regularly use online banking

43% of customers regularly use mobile banking[5]

Balancing your checking account is a lot like working on your budget. It can be difficult when you first start, but it gets easier the more you do it. Good bank account management will help you stick to your budget. Managing your bank account regularly will help you *handle money confidently!*

Your JOURNAL

How can monitoring your bank account transactions help you stick to your budget?

_____

_____

_____

REMEMBER THIS   Add a ✓ next to the completed learning objective below.

○ You have a basic understanding of how to manage your bank accounts.

○ You understand the importance of monitoring your bank statements.

THIS LESSON MAKES ME FEEL   (Circle) your response to what you learned.

 CONFUSED   SURPRISED   THOUGHTFUL   CONFIDENT

Chapter 8 Review

REVIEW KEY TERMS   Fill in the blanks below using the correct key terms from this chapter.

FDIC	Underbanked	Overdraft Protection	Liquidity
NCUA	Retail Banks	Overdraft Fee	Direct Deposit
Bank	Credit Unions	Checking Account Register	Reconciling
Unbanked	Online Banks		

1. Two federal agencies insure the money you deposit (up to $250,000); the _____ insures money in credit unions.

2. When you compare your spending records with the records from the bank, you are _____ your account.

3. Banks often promote _____ as a financial safeguard, but it's actually an unhealthy money lifeline.

4. _____ don't have a physical building or a branch manager.

5. Using a(n) _____ _____ is one way you can track your spending, deposits, and transfers.

6. It's not uncommon to be charged a $35 _____ if you spend more money than you have in your account.

7. Setting up _____ is the best way to make sure your paycheck makes it to your bank account safely.

8. _____ refers to how easy it is to convert an asset (such as a house) into cash.

FINISH THE SENTENCE   Use what you've learned in this chapter to complete these sentences.

1. No matter how you choose to track your transactions (income and spending), it's your responsibility to _____ _____.

2. While a basic savings account is a great option for short-term savings goals, you should keep your emergency fund money in _____.

1. Rachel Cruze describes overdrafting your checking account as a sign of . . .

   A. Responsibility

   B. Boredom

   C. Laziness

   D. Debt

2. Many Americans are _____, meaning they don't have a bank account.

   A. Unbanked

   B. Underbanked

   C. Banked

   D. Overbanked

3. Which bank service would typically offer the highest interest rate?

   A. Checking account

   B. Basic savings account

   C. Money market account

   D. Certificate of deposit

4. A traditional brick-and-mortar bank is what kind of bank?

   A. Retail bank

   B. Credit bank

   C. Credit union

   D. Online bank

5. Which of the following is not an example of a predatory lender?

   A. Pawn shop

   B. Payday lender

   C. Credit union

   D. Car title lender

6. Which of the following is not a way that banks make money?

   A. Interest on savings balance

   B. Account overdraft charges

   C. Interest on personal loans

   D. ATM withdrawal fees

Review **QUESTION** What are the differences between each of the three types of banks—retail banks, credit unions, and online banks?

_____

_____

_____

_____

_____

_____

Coverage You Need

The Role of Insurance

This chapter breaks down the purpose of insurance, explains how insurance works, shows how insurance protects your assets, and highlights the seven basic types of insurance everyone needs to have in place.

Insurance Is Important

LESSON VIDEO GUIDE

You have to have good financial defense, and insurance is absolutely necessary. —Dave Ramsey

GUIDED NOTES   While you watch the video, complete the section below.

1. Insurance does not make you _____.

2. The purpose of insurance is to transfer _____ that we can't handle ourselves.

3. We want to transfer the _____ things we can't handle.

4. Insurance _____ you from losing money if something bad were to happen.

5. Insurance doesn't _____ money for you—it just protects you from getting into financial trouble.

ANALYZE AND REFLECT   After you watch the video, respond to the question(s) below.

1. Dave mentions that insurance is the defense for managing your money. Why is this true?

_____

_____

_____

2. In what way is your emergency fund a form of insurance?

_____

_____

LEARNING OBJECTIVES

- Understand why insurance is an essential part of a healthy financial plan.
- Identify ways to lower the cost of insurance premiums.
- Recognize risk as the potential loss of assets or earning potential.

MAIN IDEA

Insurance is a key defensive part of any financial plan because it transfers risk from your bank account to the insurance company.

The Importance of Insurance

One of those big moments in high school is getting your driver's license. Sitting behind the wheel without your mom or dad in the front seat is that first taste of real independence. It's great! You can get yourself to and from school and drive your friends to the movies. Going to work and even running to the grocery store for your parents seems more fun when you drive.

But nothing can burst that bubble of independence quite like accidentally rear-ending someone's car on your way home. Ouch!

That's the moment you learn to love insurance. Without it, you'd be covering repairs for the damage on your own. Yes, you'll still have to cough up some cash—that's what your emergency fund is for—but once you hit a certain amount, the insurance company will cover it from there. Let's take a look at how this works.

What Is Insurance?

Basically, your **insurance** is an agreement between you and an insurance company. You'll pay them a fee, and in return, they'll pay for certain expenses or damages. How? Well, insurance companies work with lots of people—and (usually) only some of them request payment or reimbursement at any one time. The insurance company uses the money from everyone's monthly payment to cover the cost of those claims.

The purpose of insurance is to transfer risk.

— Dave Ramsey

Policies and Premiums

There are a few terms that people get mixed up—and that makes insurance seem confusing. Don't worry! It's pretty simple if you keep a few things straight.

First things first, an insurance **policy** is the financial contract between the insurance company and the person being insured. It spells out all the details of what the insurance will and will not cover, as well as the costs associated. It's important that you understand any contract you agree to,

Here's a Tip:

You can save on insurance by:

- Raising your deductible.
- Paying premiums once or twice a year instead of monthly.
- Removing any unnecessary coverage.

Insurance: an arrangement in which an individual will receive financial protection or reimbursement of losses from an insurer

Policy: the contract between an insurance company and the insured individual

222

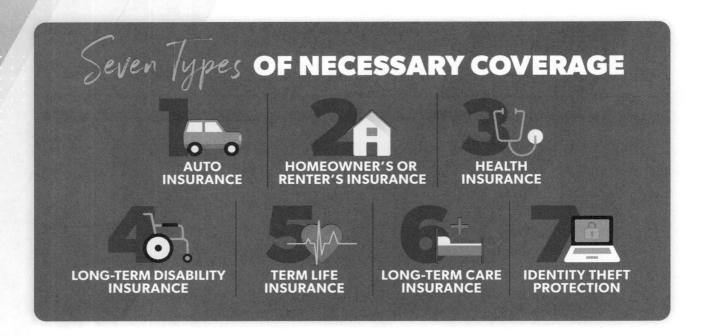

Seven Types OF NECESSARY COVERAGE

1 AUTO INSURANCE

2 HOMEOWNER'S OR RENTER'S INSURANCE

3 HEALTH INSURANCE

4 LONG-TERM DISABILITY INSURANCE

5 TERM LIFE INSURANCE

6 LONG-TERM CARE INSURANCE

7 IDENTITY THEFT PROTECTION

Coverage: the amount of liability protection offered to an individual through an insurance policy

Premium: the amount of money paid for an insurance policy

Grace Period: the amount of time after the premium is due in which a policyholder can make a premium payment without suffering a lapse (break) in coverage

Deductible: the amount of money you will pay out of pocket before the insurance company will make a payment

Definitions continued on next page

so don't be afraid to ask questions if the fine print of a policy makes your head spin. The most important details to check are the coverage, premium costs, deductible amounts, copay costs, and out-of-pocket maximum costs you will pay.

Your **coverage** is the amount of money the insurance company agrees to pay for an incident according to your policy. A **premium** is the amount of money you pay for an insurance policy. Premiums can be billed monthly, quarterly, biannually, or annually and are due on a set date.

You won't lose your coverage unless you pay later than the **grace period** allows. Grace periods can be as short as 24 hours or as long as 30 days, so be sure to check your policy to know yours—and always make those premium payments on time.

The cost of your insurance premium is based on lots of things, including your age, your marital status, your deductible, and the type of insurance. Different types of insurance will have different amounts of deductibles and coverage.

The **deductible** is the amount you'll have to pay out of your pocket before the insurance company will make a payment. For example, with auto insurance there's typically a set deductible amount every time you file a **claim**—when you report an accident or incident and ask to be compensated for the cost.

Let's go back to the fender bender at the start of this lesson. The cost to fix your car is $1,500, and your deductible is $500. You file a claim for the damage, but you're on the hook for the first $500 before your insurance company will cover the other $1,000.

You've also probably heard of **copays** or coinsurance. These are typically part of health insurance. They're the payments you make—typically a percentage of the total cost—each time you go to the doctor or pick up a prescription. These start *after* you've reached your deductible and *before* you reach your **out-of-pocket maximum**. That's the most money you have to spend for covered services in a year.

Do I *Really* Need Insurance?

Chances are that something major and unexpected will happen at some point during your lifetime. It's not a question of *if* but *when*. Insurance helps cover the big costs when those things happen. Think about it: If you were at fault in a really bad car accident and didn't have insurance, you would personally be on the hook for tens of thousands of dollars to fix or replace both vehicles and cover any health costs. Yikes!

And even though you hope you never have to file a claim, insurance is a key part of a solid financial plan. Why? Because insurance transfers the financial risk of life's major catastrophes from you to your insurance provider. You pay the premiums (that you can afford), and the insurance company pays the full cost (which you probably can't afford). This is helpful if you experience a major loss like losing a home or suffering a major health issue.

Something as simple as getting insurance will give you true peace of mind.
— Rachel Cruze

Look at it like this: Your budgeting, saving, and investing are the offense in your financial plan. Your emergency fund and various forms of insurance are the defense. It's up to you to make sure both teams are firing on all cylinders!

Claim: a formal request by a policyholder to their insurance company for compensation for a covered loss

Copays: (also copayments or coinsurance) the payments an individual makes each time they get medical service

Out-of-Pocket Maximum: the most a policyholder has to spend for covered services in a year

---

Your JOURNAL

Why is insurance an essential part of a healthy financial plan?

_____

_____

_____

REMEMBER THIS Add a ✓ next to each completed learning objective below.

◯ You can explain why insurance is an important part of a healthy financial plan.

◯ You can describe ways to lower the cost of insurance premiums.

◯ You understand that risk is the potential loss of assets or earning potential.

THIS LESSON MAKES ME FEEL Circle your response to what you learned.

😓 CONFUSED   😮 SURPRISED   🙂 THOUGHTFUL   🤩 CONFIDENT

LESSON VIDEO GUIDE

You always want to have auto insurance and also an emergency fund that can cover your deductible.

— Anthony O'Neal

GUIDED NOTES   While you watch the video, complete the section below.

1. Write down two key takeaways from the discussion about auto insurance.

    _____

    _____

    _____

2. If you have a full emergency fund in place, choose _____ deductibles.

3. For _____ coverage on your auto insurance, you want three things: collision, comprehensive, and liability.

4. Collision covers the cost of repairs to _____ car after a collision.

ANALYZE AND REFLECT   After you watch the video, respond to the question(s) below.

1. In your own words, describe why it is critical to always have auto insurance. Provide at least two examples of situations where you might need insurance.

    _____

    _____

    _____

LEARNING OBJECTIVES

- Explain the importance of liability protection.
- Understand basic auto insurance coverage options and liability limits.

MAIN IDEA

Auto insurance is not only required by law, but it's also necessary to protect your financial assets whenever accidents happen.

Auto Insurance Is Important

In Lesson 1, you read about a scenario when you'd be really thankful for insurance: a fender bender. Auto insurance is probably the insurance you're most familiar with. Now, you may be thinking, *I'm a great driver. If I'm careful, why do I need to pay for auto insurance?*

First, it's required by law in most states. If you don't want to get fined or lose your license and registration, you have to carry the minimum amount of **liability insurance** required by your state. Second, even if you're a perfect driver, there are plenty of people on the road with you who aren't—so you never know when an accident will happen. Insurance is there to protect your finances and keep you moving when things go wrong. Insurance covers you if you're at fault, or liable, for an accident by paying up to the limits you purchased.

Basic Components

Most basic car policies include six types of coverage: collision, comprehensive, uninsured/underinsured motorist, personal injury protection, property damage liability, and bodily injury liability. What on earth do all those do? Well, some cover you and some cover other people—so be sure you pay attention to the details!

Don't ever drive without having auto insurance.

— *Dave Ramsey*

COVERING YOUR CAR AND YOURSELF

When you're looking through insurance policy options, you'll notice that each type of coverage is pretty specific on what it covers. These are the types of coverage that protect you and your vehicle:

- **Collision insurance** covers damage to your car after a collision with another car or object—like if you hit a tree—and will pay you the market value (pre-wreck) for your car if it's totaled in an accident. If you owe money on your car, the lender will require collision coverage.
- **Comprehensive coverage** pays for loss or damage to your vehicle caused by something other than a collision—think theft, vandalism, a falling tree, hail, or accidentally hitting a deer.

Liability Insurance: protection against claims resulting from personal injury or property damage as the result of an auto accident

Collision Insurance: protection for damage to your car resulting from a collision with another car or object

Comprehensive Insurance: protection for loss or damage to your vehicle caused by something other than a collision (such as vandalism)

BUY THE RIGHT *Coverage*

When shopping for auto insurance, avoid the temptation to get just the state minimum liability policy to save money. This one decision could be costly in the long run. To understand why, you first need to know what your insurance agent means when you hear the three main numbers quoted on the policy.

STATE MINIMUM COVERAGE LIMITS

$25k / $50k / $15k

Pay attention to these three important numbers!

GOOD COVERAGE LIMITS

$100k / $300k / $100k

That's a BIG difference!

Covers Injuries to Individuals: the maximum amount (in thousands of dollars) that will be covered per person

Covers the Total of All Injuries to People: the maximum amount (in thousands of dollars) that will be covered per accident

Covers Damage to Property: the maximum amount (in thousands of dollars) that will be covered per accident

IMAGINE THIS. While you're driving to work, a text distracts you, and you crash into another car. You're at fault. The driver and passenger are both taken to the hospital. The driver ends up with $30,000 in hospital bills. The passenger, who was more seriously hurt, ends up with $75,000 in medical costs. The new $40,000 car was totaled. Which insurance would you rather have?

	25 / 50 / 15			100 / 300 / 100		
	Driver	Passenger	Driver's Car	Driver	Passenger	Driver's Car
Total Cost of Accident	$ 30,000	$ 75,000	$ 40,000	$ 30,000	$ 75,000	$ 40,000
Insurance Pays	−$ 25,000	−$ 25,000	−$ 15,000	−$ 30,000	−$ 75,000	−$ 40,000
You Have to Pay	=$ 5,000	=$ 50,000	=$ 25,000	=$ 0	=$ 0	=$ 0

YOU PAY $80,000   **YOU PAY** $0

State minimum insurance can be costly!
And this doesn't include the cost to fix your car.

- **Uninsured/underinsured motorist protection** covers you and any other passengers if you're hit by an uninsured or underinsured driver. Underinsured just means that their coverage isn't enough to pay for your expenses.
- **Personal injury protection (PIP)**—or medical payments coverage—pays for the treatment of injuries to the driver and passengers of the policyholder's car (see the "Buy the Right Coverage" graphic). It can cover medical expenses, lost wages, and other financial losses suffered by the injured person.

Proof of Insurance

Your insurance card is your proof of insurance—you'll need it if you're ever in an accident. Your insurance card has all the information you'd need in case of an accident: name and policy number, vehicle description, expiration date, and the phone number you'd need to call to get started on the claims process.

Keep a copy of your insurance card in your vehicle. Most insurance companies also have apps where you can store your cards digitally. But be careful! Not all states accept digital proof of insurance.

How to Get a Good Deal

Auto insurance can be expensive. Here are some things you can do to lower your cost on auto insurance:

- Get good grades.
- Take a driver education class.
- Drive an older car.
- Shop around for the best rate.
- Stay on your parents' policy, if you can.
- Be a safe driver.

Uninsured/ Underinsured Motorist Protection: protection for you and passengers if you're hit by an uninsured or underinsured motorist, or if you are the victim of a hit-and-run

Personal Injury Protection (PIP): a component of auto insurance that pays for medical expenses, lost wages, and other financial losses of the driver and passengers of the policyholder's vehicle

---

Your JOURNAL Besides the fact that it's the law, why is it important to have car insurance even if you're a really good driver?

REMEMBER THIS Add a ✓ next to each completed learning objective below.

◯ You can explain the importance of liability protection.

◯ You understand the basic aspects of automobile insurance coverage and liability limits.

THIS LESSON MAKES ME FEEL (Circle) your response to what you learned.

😓 CONFUSED   😮 SURPRISED   🙂 THOUGHTFUL   🤩 CONFIDENT

LESSON VIDEO GUIDE

When you get renter's insurance, you will need to take inventory of your belongings to know what is covered. — Anthony O'Neal

GUIDED NOTES   While you watch the video, complete the section below.

1. Homeowner's insurance is for people who _____ their home.

2. Homeowner's insurance includes _____ coverage.

3. Renter's insurance covers damage or _____ of your belongings.

4. Check with your insurance agent every one to two _____ to make sure you have the proper amount of coverage.

5. _____ insurance is not very expensive.

6. An _____ policy extends liability coverage over your car and your home.

ANALYZE AND REFLECT   After you watch the video, respond to the question(s) below.

1. What is the primary difference between homeowner's insurance and renter's insurance?

_____

_____

2. When should you consider getting umbrella insurance?

_____

MAIN IDEA

Whether you own or rent, it's crucial to have the right insurance coverage in place to protect your home and possessions from the unknowns in life.

Homeowner's Insurance

A home is one of the largest purchases you will ever make. We're talking hundreds of thousands of dollars here! So, you need to make sure your house is protected with a **homeowner's insurance** policy.

Insurance protects the things that will make you wealthy.

— *Dave Ramsey*

One of the worst risks you could take with homeowner's insurance is not buying enough. You want to be sure your policy covers the costs of repairing or replacing your home, as well as all of your personal possessions inside the house.

Imagine your home burned down and you didn't have enough coverage to replace the house and your stuff. That's called being underinsured—having the right insurance but not enough to cover all the costs to repair or replace. The reality is—due to the increased cost of materials to rebuild—many Americans are underinsured on their home. That's not okay!

It's crucial to make sure that you have the right types and amounts of coverage when you insure your home. Home insurance policies include these basic categories:

- **Dwelling coverage:** This covers the structure of your home, including the roof, walls, floors, and any other part of the structure. Make sure your policy covers replacement costs—that means enough to cover the cost of rebuilding your home from the ground up at current prices, not how much you paid for it or market value.
- **Liability coverage:** This protects you from legal liability of property damage or bodily injury. For example, if a guest falls on your property and you're sued for medical expenses, your homeowner's policy will cover the cost of any liability expenses up to your policy limit.
- **Personal property coverage:** Your policy covers your personal belongings if they are damaged, destroyed, or stolen. It's important to regularly estimate the value of your belongings so you know if your coverage is enough to replace those things.

Homeowner's Insurance: protection for losses to a private residence and the possessions within it, as well as liability coverage against accidents in the home or on the property

Did You Know?

Most mortgage companies require you to buy a homeowner's insurance policy before they'll approve a mortgage loan on a home.

Renter's Insurance: protection for destroyed or stolen personal property for a renter

- **Loss of use coverage:** This covers additional living expenses—like the cost of a hotel—if you're unable to live in your home while it's being repaired.

Remember to check every year or two to make sure your coverage amount is high enough. Why? Construction and material costs are always increasing.

BUYING HOMEOWNER'S INSURANCE

The average annual cost of homeowner's insurance is about $1,211 a year.[1] That rate varies depending on what state your home is located in. It could be around $833 per year in Delaware but about $1,885 per year in Oklahoma.[2] As you might guess, states that are most susceptible to natural disasters like hurricanes, floods, or tornadoes have the highest homeowner's insurance rates.

Similar to auto insurance, you'll also be responsible for a deductible for each claim. If you've got a fully funded emergency fund, you can push that $500 deductible up to $1,000–2,500 or more and save on your annual premium costs.

Did You Know?

The top three causes of homeowner's insurance claims:[4]

Fire and lightning ➊
Wind and hail ➋
Water damage ➌ and freezing

Here's a Tip:

You can often save money by bundling your homeowner's and auto insurance policies with the same company.

Renter's Insurance

Renter's insurance is basically the same as homeowner's but provides coverage for a person who does not own their home. The big difference is that the policy doesn't cover the structure of the home—that's up to the owner. A renter's insurance policy provides coverage for personal possessions lost to fire, theft, or vandalism. It also provides liability protection and living expenses if you can't live in your rented home because of a covered incident.

If you go to college and live in a dorm on campus, your personal stuff may be covered under your parents' homeowner's insurance. Just make sure to check the policy! If you decide to rent an apartment or other space off campus, you'll need to get renter's insurance.

BUYING RENTER'S INSURANCE

Renter's insurance is very affordable. The national average is $180 a year ($15 per month).[3] That gives you coverage for your stuff as well as liability protection. But you'll have to pay a deductible (the average is about $1,000) if you make a claim.

WHAT'S *Covered?* WHAT'S NOT?

Here are some commonly covered and not covered homeowner's insurance situations:

USUALLY COVERED

FIRE   STORMS

HAIL   INJURIES   THEFT

NOT USUALLY COVERED

SEWER BACKUPS   EARTHQUAKES

FLOODING   MOLD   PEST CONTROL

There's really no excuse for not having renter's insurance. But it's completely on you to set it up. It's not your landlord's responsibility to insure your belongings. A lot of leasing companies require their tenants to show proof of renter's insurance before they'll hand over the keys.

> **Renter's insurance is not expensive, and it gives you peace of mind.**
>
> — Anthony O'Neal

Umbrella Insurance

As you get older and continue to work your financial plan to build wealth, you'll want to make sure it's all protected. You'll want to have your major insurance coverages in place. But what about the things that fall outside those policies? That's what **umbrella insurance** is for. This is extended liability coverage that you can add to auto and homeowner's policies.

Picture it like an umbrella over your other insurance policies, catching all the things like big claims and lawsuits—"raindrops"—that they might not cover.

You can get $1 million in coverage for $150–300 a year.[5] And there's no deductible since you'd have already paid it on your home or auto policy first.

Remember, building wealth takes decades of consistent work. Don't let that work go to waste because you didn't have the coverage you needed! Work these policies into your plan so you can stay on track no matter what life throws at you.

Umbrella Insurance: optional extended liability coverage that can be added to auto and homeowner's policies

Did You Know?

Only 37% of renters have renter's insurance.[6]

Your JOURNAL

What is the main reason someone would want to have—and need to have—renter's insurance?

_____

_____

_____

REMEMBER THIS   Add a ✓ next to each completed learning objective below.

◯ You can explain the difference between homeowner's and renter's insurance.

◯ You understand the concept of umbrella insurance.

THIS LESSON MAKES ME FEEL   Circle your response to what you learned.

😓 CONFUSED   😮 SURPRISED   🙂 THOUGHTFUL   🤩 CONFIDENT

LESSON VIDEO GUIDE

You have to plan to protect yourself and your loved ones. Health insurance helps you do that. — Anthony ONeal

GUIDED NOTES While you watch the video, complete the section below.

1. _____ emergencies can happen to anyone at any time.

2. You can stay on your parents' health insurance plan until you turn _____.

3. _____ expenses are the number one cause of bankruptcy in America.

4. A Health Savings Account (HSA) can pay for _____ expenses tax-free.

5. A _____ deductible means lower premiums.

6. An _____ account can only be used for qualified medical expenses.

ANALYZE AND REFLECT After you watch the video, respond to the question(s) below.

1. List at least two benefits of a Health Savings Account (HSA).

_____

_____

2. Why does having a higher deductible lower your insurance premiums?

_____

_____

MAIN IDEA

Health insurance is the insurance everyone needs. It's important to understand the basics so you'll be able to pick the plan that's right for you.

You Need Health Insurance

Health insurance may be the most widely discussed type of insurance. Politicians debate about it constantly. Employers use it to attract good job candidates. You probably even hear your parents talk about it. Why? Because everyone needs it. But what exactly is it?

Health insurance helps cover your medical expenses—which can add up really fast. You may think that because you're young and healthy, health insurance isn't necessary, but you'd be wrong. Medical emergencies can happen to anyone at any time. And with the ever-rising cost of health care, you need to be prepared.

> It's financial suicide not to have health and disability insurance.
>
> — Dave Ramsey

Health insurance helps pay for those major medical costs and can save you tens of thousands of dollars (or more). Plus, you can get a discount for many medical services and prescription medications through your health insurance.

Getting Health Insurance

As a student, you're most likely covered by your parents' insurance—so you don't have to stress about getting your own policy just yet. Under the **Affordable Care Act (ACA)**, you can even stay on a parent's health insurance plan until you're 26 years old. If your parents are cool with you staying on their plan, it's your best—and least expensive—option. But after age 26, you'll have to figure out the best plan for you. So, where do you start?

First things first, health insurance is expensive, but you've got to have it. Next, understand that there are two types of health insurance: private health insurance and public health insurance. Public health insurance includes government programs such as Medicare and Medicaid. About 67% of all Americans who have health insurance have private insurance, so we'll focus on that type.[7]

The most affordable place to get private health insurance is through your employer because they usually split the

Health Insurance: coverage for an individual's (or family's) medical expenses from illness or injury

Affordable Care Act (ACA): also known as Obamacare; the health care reform law enacted in 2010, intended to make affordable health insurance more available

Did You Know?

8.5% of Americans (over 27 million people) have no form of health insurance.[8]

It is unwise to hope for the best without preparing for the worst.

Anonymous

Subsidizing: the practice of employers paying for a portion of their employees' insurance premiums

Health Insurance Marketplace: a platform where individuals, families, and small businesses can compare health insurance plans

Did You Know?

Medical bills are a leading cause of money problems (consumer debt, bankruptcy, and foreclosure) and personal problems (divorce, anxiety, and work stress).

High-Deductible Health Plan (HDHP): a health plan with a high minimum deductible for medical expenses

premium costs with you. That's known as **subsidizing**, and it can cut your monthly costs down to a more manageable amount.

If getting health insurance through your employer isn't an option, you'll need to shop for a provider and a plan on the **health insurance marketplace**—or the exchange. The marketplace is federally operated, but some states also run their own marketplaces for health insurance. Unless your income qualifies you for a subsidy (or financial aid) from the government to help pay your premiums, you'll have to foot the bill for your entire premium amount.

Different Insurance Plans

All private health insurance plans partner with networks of health care providers (doctors, hospitals, etc.) to provide care at agreed-upon rates. There are four different network types—also known as managed care plans. Each uses a specific network of providers who agree to charge lower fees in exchange for access to the network's plan members. Let's compare the two most popular types:

HEALTH MAINTENANCE ORGANIZATION

Also known as HMO, these plans will typically have lower premiums—and you get what you pay for. They are the most restrictive about access to your network's health care providers. Your primary care physician (PCP) coordinates all your care. To see a specialist, for instance, you would first need a referral from your PCP. HMOs don't cover any of your medical costs that are provided outside of their network.

PREFERRED PROVIDER ORGANIZATION

Also known as PPO, these plans offer more provider access and cover care outside the plan's network. But that flexibility comes at a price—PPOs are typically more expensive than other types of plans. And while you can get out-of-network care without a referral from your primary care physician, it will still cost you more.

High-Deductible Plans

For young, healthy people who don't go to the doctor often, a **high-deductible health plan (HDHP)** can be a good option to save money on your health care costs.

A Message From CHRIS

LEARNING about health insurance might feel pretty boring. But you know what isn't boring? Having extra money to spend! And that's exactly what a Health Savings Account (HSA) gives you. It's a savings account where you set aside money to pay for medical costs, which can rack up pretty fast. And here's the best part: Not a single penny in your HSA ends up in the government's pocket! In fact, you get a triple tax benefit. You contribute pretax money, you can invest inside the account for tax-free growth, and when you use the money for approved medical expenses, it comes out tax-free! Now that's a win-win-win situation!

These plans offer lower monthly premiums. Of course, there's a catch: As the name suggests, you'll have to pay more of your medical costs before insurance starts to chip in. The good news is that having an HDHP qualifies you to take advantage of tax-free savings for health care expenses with a **Health Savings Account (HSA)**.

Health Insurance Limits

We covered some of the insurance basics like premiums, deductibles, copays, and coinsurance back in Lesson 1, so let's take a closer look at two other important costs of your health insurance policy: your out-of-pocket maximum and lifetime limit.

The out-of-pocket maximum is the most money you have to spend for covered services in a year. Once you reach this amount, your insurance plan covers 100%

of covered services, protecting you from a financial crisis if those bills add up!

You have to plan to protect yourself and your loved ones.
— Anthony O'Neal

Your **lifetime limit** is the cap on the total amount of benefits you're allowed to get from your insurance company. After you hit this number, the insurance plan no longer pays. The insurance company can put a lifetime limit on the total amount of benefits (like a $1 million lifetime cap), on specific benefits (a $200,000 lifetime cap on organ transplants), or both.

Bottom line: Health insurance can be expensive, but you need to have it.

Health Savings Account (HSA): a tax-exempt savings account dedicated to health care costs; only available for individuals on a high-deductible health plan (HDHP)

Lifetime Limit: the maximum amount of lifetime benefits a person can receive from their insurance company

---

Your **JOURNAL**   Why is health insurance important even if you are young and healthy?

_____

_____

_____

REMEMBER THIS   Add a ✓ next to each completed learning objective below.

◯ You understand the costs and benefits of health insurance.

◯ You can explain the differences between types of health insurance.

THIS LESSON MAKES ME FEEL   (Circle) your response to what you learned.

😓 CONFUSED   😮 SURPRISED   🙂 THOUGHTFUL   🤩 CONFIDENT

Understanding Life Insurance

LESSON VIDEO GUIDE

Life insurance is really death insurance, and you don't even get to collect the money—someone else does. —Dave Ramsey

GUIDED NOTES   While you watch the video, complete the section below.

1. Life insurance replaces lost income due to _____.

2. _____ life insurance is very inexpensive.

3. _____ value life insurance is much more expensive.

4. Myth: The need for life insurance is a _____ need.

5. _____ life insurance is the only life insurance you should buy.

6. Never use life insurance as an _____.

ANALYZE AND REFLECT   After you watch the video, respond to the question(s) below.

1. If you are 18 years old with no debt or dependents, do you need life insurance? Why?

    _____

    _____

2. If you are married with young children and make $75,000 per year, how much term life insurance should you have?

    _____

LEARNING OBJECTIVES

- Understand the differences between term and whole life insurance.
- Explain how one becomes self-insured.

MAIN IDEA

Nobody likes to consider when life insurance would be needed, but having life insurance is important for anyone who has loved ones to support.

Life Insurance Is Important

What does it mean to have insurance on your life? Well, like other types of insurance, life insurance is a contract between you and an insurance company to transfer financial risk. But instead of paying you if something goes wrong, it guarantees your loved ones (or **beneficiaries**) get a certain amount of money (called a **death benefit**) when you pass away.

The purpose of life insurance is to replace your income when you die.

— Dave Ramsey

So technically, it's *death* insurance—but who would want to buy that? It's not a fun topic, but life insurance is important. It will help take care of your family if something awful happens to you. The idea is to cover your lost income, funeral expenses, and other financial needs. For a parent raising children, this is a way to make sure their spouse and kids are provided for financially if they die.

Types of Life Insurance

Your two main options for life insurance are based on how long the policy is designed to last: term life and whole life.

TERM LIFE INSURANCE

Term life insurance provides coverage for a certain amount of time—often 20, 25, or 30 years. If you pass away at any time during your term, your beneficiaries will receive the death benefit from the policy.

Term life insurance plans are very affordable because the term life policy is only focused on providing the death benefit. There are no other add-ons—such as cash value investments—to inflate your premiums. Of course, the hope is that you'll never have to use your term life insurance policy at all. But if something does happen and you have a spouse and children, at least you know they'll be taken care of.

WHOLE LIFE INSURANCE

As you can imagine, **whole life insurance** is called "whole" because it lasts your entire lifetime. Variations of this are *universal, variable,* or *permanent life insurance*—each is a little different.

Beneficiaries: people who are designated by the policyholder to receive the death benefit of a life insurance policy

Death Benefit: benefit paid to the beneficiaries after the policyholder dies

Term Life Insurance: life insurance for a specified amount of time; at the death of the policyholder, the insurance company pays the death benefit to the beneficiaries

Whole Life Insurance (or Cash Value): life insurance that lasts for the life of the policyholder and uses a portion of the premium as an investment

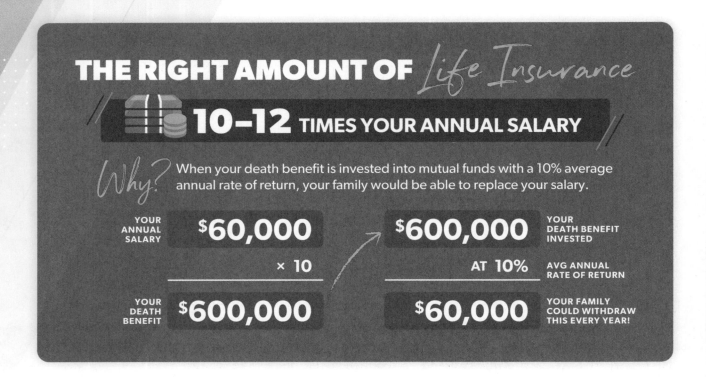

THE RIGHT AMOUNT OF *Life Insurance*

10–12 TIMES YOUR ANNUAL SALARY

Why? When your death benefit is invested into mutual funds with a 10% average annual rate of return, your family would be able to replace your salary.

YOUR ANNUAL SALARY: **$60,000**

× 10

YOUR DEATH BENEFIT: **$600,000**

$600,000 YOUR DEATH BENEFIT INVESTED

AT **10%** AVG ANNUAL RATE OF RETURN

$60,000 YOUR FAMILY COULD WITHDRAW THIS EVERY YEAR!

Besides the insuring-your-life part, whole life insurance (or permanent insurance) adds an investing-your-money piece to your policy called "cash value." The insurance company takes a chunk of your premium to start an investment account. This sounds like a good idea until you dig into the details.

First, fees often eat up the returns on those investments, so never mix investing with insurance. Then—and this is the kicker—when you die, your family only gets the death benefit amount stated in the policy. The insurance company keeps any cash value you've managed to build. Bottom line: Whole life insurance is one of the worst deals you can get sucked into.

If you practice the principles we teach, you won't need life insurance forever. Ultimately, you'll be **self-insured**. How? You'll have zero debt, a full emergency fund, and a hefty amount of money in your own investments. If you pass away when your

children are in their 20s and your spouse is 55 with a paid-for home and $1 million in investments, do you think they'll be okay? Yes! Of course they will.

Who Needs Life Insurance?

While you're a student, you don't need life insurance. As a young professional with no debt and no **dependents** (people who rely on you financially), all you *really* need to worry about is having enough to cover burial costs.

Once you get married and have kids, however, be sure both you and your spouse have life insurance—even if one of you doesn't work outside of the home. Why? The absence of a stay-at-home parent would have a huge impact on the childcare budget! And when you're retired? Like we mentioned before, you could be self-insured by that point. But if your spouse couldn't live off of your retirement savings, you'll still need a life insurance policy.

Self-Insured: having enough money saved and invested so a spouse or loved one could live off of it when you die, eliminating the need for life insurance

Dependent: a person who relies on someone for financial support

The Cost of Life Insurance

Several factors affect the cost of any kind of life insurance: your age, your gender, your weight, your personal and family medical history, whether you smoke or not, if you have any dangerous hobbies (like skydiving or shark wrestling), and if you travel to risky places. They'll also request you get a physical exam including blood work to make sure you're in good health before they agree to insure your life.

Insurance companies look at all this information and use **actuarial life tables**—life expectancy charts—to figure out the rate for your premiums. The younger and healthier you are, the cheaper your premiums will be. If you're older or have ongoing health issues, it's going to cost significantly more. In addition, the term (or number of years) for your policy can impact the cost. Your agent and insurance company will come up with your "rating classification" to determine the cost of your life insurance premiums.

> ## Keep your insurances and your investments separate.
>
> — *Chris Hogan*

If you're young and healthy, a longer term life policy may only be about $20 per month. That's nothing compared to the peace of mind you'll have knowing your family will be taken care of should something happen. Hopefully, you'll never need to use your life insurance policy. But *is it worth the risk?*

Did You Know?

In 2018, only 59% of Americans had some form of life insurance in place.[9]

Actuarial Life Table: life expectancy chart used by insurance agents to figure out life insurance premiums for an individual based on a variety of factors

---

Your **JOURNAL**

Which type of life insurance is the better option, term or whole life? Explain your answer.

_____

_____

_____

REMEMBER THIS   Add a ✓ next to each completed learning objective below.

◯ You understand the differences between term and whole life insurance.

◯ You can identify what it means to be self-insured.

THIS LESSON MAKES ME FEEL   (Circle) your response to what you learned.

 CONFUSED   SURPRISED   THOUGHTFUL   CONFIDENT

LESSON VIDEO GUIDE

There are 74 robberies every hour in the U.S., but there are nearly 2,000 identity theft incidents every hour. —Chris Hogan

GUIDED NOTES   While you watch the video, complete the section below.

1. Disability insurance replaces _____ due to short-term or long-term disability.

2. Long-term disability insurance is an absolute _____.

3. With disability insurance, the deductible is called the elimination _____.

4. Make sure your long-term disability coverage is at least _____ of your income.

5. Do not buy ID theft protection with _____ monitoring only.

6. You want ID theft protection that provides _____ services.

ANALYZE AND REFLECT   After you watch the video, respond to the question(s) below.

1. Why does Chris mention you don't need short-term disability insurance?

   _____

   _____

2. Why is it so important to have restoration services with your ID theft protection?

   _____

   _____

> **LEARNING OBJECTIVES**
>
> - Distinguish between necessary and unnecessary types of insurance.
> - Understand why long-term disability insurance, identity theft protection, and long-term care insurance are important to have in place.

> **MAIN IDEA**
>
> Some types of insurance are important to your financial plan, while others just aren't worth it. That's why it's important to know the difference.

Other Types of Insurance

So far, we've covered four major types of insurance that you'll need to have: auto, homeowner's/renter's, health, and life insurance. But there are three more you'll need to work into your financial plan to have all your bases covered—and a handful you'll want to avoid.

Disability Insurance

Have you ever known someone who had to leave their job because of a health issue? Imagine if you were in an accident and lost your ability to walk. If you were a writer, you would still be able to do your job, right? But what if your career was doing manual labor on a construction site? You may have just lost the ability to do your job.

According to the Social Security Administration, one in four of today's 20-year-olds will become disabled for 90 days or more before they turn 67.[10] So, how can you prepare? You'll want to have the right kind of disability insurance in place.

Disability insurance replaces part of your income if you become disabled. That means if you're injured or develop a health condition that prevents you from working, you'll still have an income. There are two types:

- **Short-term disability** is exactly that—short-term. Payments only last a few months to a year. But this type of coverage is unnecessary if you've saved a full emergency fund, are out of debt, and are living on a budget.

The goal of disability insurance is to pay your bills and keep food on the table, not to make you rich!

— *Dave Ramsey*

- **Long-term disability**, on the other hand, will provide money to replace lost income for years—even up to retirement age—depending on your policy. This type of disability insurance is an absolute must-have. The best place to get it is through your employer, but if they don't offer it, check with your insurance agent to find the best deal.

Disability Insurance: a type of insurance that will replace a portion of the policyholder's income in the event that the policyholder becomes disabled and is unable to work

Elimination Period: the period of time between when a doctor confirms a disability and when the policyholder receives a disability payment

Identity Theft: the act of fraudulently gaining and using the personal information of someone else, usually for financial gain

Long-Term Care Insurance: a type of insurance that covers some or all of the costs of nursing home care, assisted living, in-home care, and other end-of-life care

Did You Know?

In 2018, 14.4 million people were victims of identity theft or identity fraud.[12]

Out of Work

When you're shopping for long-term disability insurance, you want to buy own occupation (or own occ) disability, which will pay you if you can't do the job you were educated to do. The other option, any occupation, will only pay if you can't do *any* type of work.

Keep in mind, if you became disabled, you wouldn't receive payments right away. (That's why you need an emergency fund!) The time between when a doctor confirms that you're disabled and when the payments from disability insurance kick in is called the **elimination period**. For long-term disability, that's typically 90 days, while short-term disability is around two weeks. Note: A longer elimination period usually means lower premiums.

WHO NEEDS DISABILITY INSURANCE?

Everyone. You need to get long-term disability insurance to cover 60–70% of your income. That's about how much you bring home after taxes. This is really important if you have a high-risk job. Just remember, this isn't intended to make you rich but to pay your bills when you need it.

Identity Theft Protection

These days, thieves can steal more than just money and possessions—that's why **identity theft** protection is a necessity. Technically, it isn't insurance. But it serves a similar purpose: to cover you if someone steals your personal information and uses it to make a royal mess.

You need to protect your information and your finances, so don't wait to get this coverage. And don't pay for a plan that just offers credit monitoring. That's about as helpful as a bystander yelling, "Look, a thief!" while a bank gets robbed. You need a team that will catch the thief, help put a stop to it (even before it starts), and clean up the mess—that's restoration coverage.

Long-Term Care Insurance

The last type of insurance you need is **long-term care insurance**. Now, you won't need this until you're 60. But a whopping 52% of people turning 65 these days will need some sort of long-term care, and that care isn't cheap.[11] It can run from $1,500–8,500 (or more) per month! Very few health or disability policies cover these costs, so this can eat up your nest egg quickly. And

---

Insurance **Meets the Needs of Others**

THE RIGHT insurances protect you as well as your loved ones. The truth of the matter is that when you have the right types of insurance in place, you're being generous to others. Obviously, life insurance can provide income for your family in the event of your death. Disability insurance and long-term care insurance can provide the financial resources your family would need to care for you—without your care becoming a financial hardship for them. That means they can continue to care for you without impacting their budgets or how they demonstrate generosity to others. With the right insurances in place, you're demonstrating your love and care for your family as well as others. That's a win-win!

it puts that financial burden on your family. Long-term care insurance is a way for you to guarantee that you'll be taken care of later.

Typically, most people end up needing some long-term care assistance.

— *Chris Hogan*

Coverage You Don't Need

Now you know about the seven types of insurance you need. But what about the insurance plans you don't need? Some **supplemental insurance** plans like vision, dental, and cancer aren't necessary if you have health insurance, a Health Savings

Account, and a fully funded emergency fund. Why? Because you can cover those things.

Think about it. The point of insurance is to transfer risk you can't afford to take. That's why some supplemental plans like long-term disability and long-term care are worth having. But while it may sound like a good idea to have extra coverage for eye exams, dental work, or in case you get cancer—those policies are really just a waste of money. You've got your HSA to cover vision and dental expenses. And if you do get cancer, your health insurance will cover your treatment. There's no need to pay twice.

Insurance works as your defensive line protecting your wealth from the major risks in life. Make sure you've got the right insurance players on your team!

When to Buy Insurance
- Auto: when you get a car
- Home/rent: when you're on your own
- Health: when you're not on your parents' plan
- Life: when you're on your own (increase when married and start a family)
- ID theft: when you're on your own
- LTD: when you're on your own
- LTC: age 60

Supplemental Insurance: plans to cover expenses and services not on typical policies

---

Your JOURNAL

Why is it important to have identity theft protection?

_____

_____

_____

REMEMBER THIS   Add a ✓ next to each completed learning objective below.

○ You can identify necessary and unnecessary types of insurance.

○ You can understand why long-term disability, identity theft protection, and long-term care insurance are important.

THIS LESSON MAKES ME FEEL   (Circle) your response to what you learned.

😓 CONFUSED   😮 SURPRISED   🙂 THOUGHTFUL   🤩 CONFIDENT

Chapter 9 Review

Fill in the blanks below using the correct key terms from this chapter.

Insurance	Out-of-Pocket Maximum	Subsidizing	Self-Insured
Policy	Liability Insurance	Health Insurance	Dependent
Coverage	Collision Insurance	Health Savings Account	Actuarial Life Table
Premium	Personal Injury Protection	Lifetime Limit	Disability Insurance
Grace Period	Homeowner's Insurance	Death Benefit	Elimination Period
Deductible	Renter's Insurance	Beneficiaries	Identity Theft
Claim	Umbrella Insurance	Term Life Insurance	Long-Term Care Insurance
Copays	Affordable Care Act	Whole Life Insurance	Supplemental Insurance
High-Deductible Health Plan	Comprehensive Insurance	Health Insurance Marketplace	Uninsured/Underinsured Motorist Protection

1. A(n) _____ is someone (typically a child) who relies on you financially.

2. The money you pay each month for health insurance is your _____.

3. Extra liability coverage on top of your homeowner's and auto insurance is called _____.

4. Collision insurance is a type of coverage with _____.

5. The _____ _____ indicates the most you would pay for health insurance in a year.

6. Your _____ is the amount you have to pay before insurance pays.

7. _____ covers loss to your personal items but not the building.

8. You can save money on life insurance (and invest that money) by getting a(n) _____ policy.

9. The purpose of _____ is to transfer financial risk.

10. _____ _____ protects you if you're the victim of a hit-and-run accident.

1. You should buy a life insurance policy that's
    _____ times your annual salary.

    A. 6–8   C. 10–12

    B. 8–10   D. 12–15

2. What's the payment you make each time
    you visit the doctor?

    A. Claim   C. Premium

    B. Copay   D. Liability

3. HDHP insurance with a health savings
    account can save you money on what?

    A. Premiums   C. Claims

    B. Deductibles   D. Copays

4. You can remain on your parents' health
    insurance plan until you're:

    A. 21 years old   C. 26 years old

    B. 25 years old   D. 29 years old

5. Which insurance covers you if you're injured
    and can't work for a period of time?

    A. Long-term care   C. Term life

    B. Renter's   D. Disability

6. Whole life insurance is also called each of
    the following terms except:

    A. Universal   C. Variable

    B. Beneficial   D. Permanent

Review **QUESTION**   Explain why saving money with a state minimum auto
liability insurance policy generally isn't the best idea.

_____

_____

_____

_____

_____

_____

The Truth About Taxes

Income and Taxes

This chapter digs into a huge reality in life: If you earn an income, you're going to pay taxes. This chapter also breaks down the basics of different types of taxes—like sales, excise, and federal taxes—including how they impact your income and spending.

LESSON

1 | What Happened to My Money?

The expenses that are taken out of your paycheck are called withholdings or deductions.

— Anthony O'Neal

GUIDED NOTES   While you watch the video, complete the section below.

1. _____ income is the total amount of money you earn.

2. _____ income is the amount of money you have left after taxes and other expenses are taken out of your paycheck.

3. The amount of money that you get to keep is called your _____ pay.

ANALYZE AND REFLECT   After you watch the video, respond to the question(s) below.

1. If you make $9.00 per hour and worked 36 hours over the past two weeks, what would your gross income be on your paycheck?

   _____

2. If 10% of your paycheck was withheld for federal income taxes and another 6% for state income taxes, how much would your net (or take-home) pay be?

   _____

3. Why is it important to pay attention to the amount of taxes withheld from each paycheck?

   _____

   _____

   _____

MAIN IDEA

Nobody likes having to pay taxes, but taxes are a reality for everyone. Tax dollars are used to fund government services and projects.

Where's My Money?

You landed an awesome part-time job that works with your school schedule, activities, and family responsibilities. Yes! You're only going to be working 15 hours per week—which is super manageable—and you're making $10 an hour! That comes out to $150 at the end of the week with direct deposit into your bank account. That means you'll be set for the weekend!

After your first week of work, you check your bank app . . . and see that your payroll deposit was only $120. *Wait,* you think. *What happened to my money? I'm missing $30!* After five weeks at this rate, you'll be missing $150. That's a whole week's pay. Now you *really* want to know what happened to your money!

> ### I couldn't believe how much was taken out in taxes.
> — Anthony ONeal

In 1789, Benjamin Franklin wrote the following words in a letter: "In this world nothing can be said to be certain, except death and taxes." Taxes are fees charged by the government to fund government expenses. Taxes have been around for a long time, and they impact your personal finances in a big way.

The Reality of Taxes

You might as well face it: If you're earning an income, you're paying taxes. That's just a part of life in the United States. Everyone who works has to pay taxes. And you'll likely end up paying more in taxes as you get older. Sure, having $30 taken out of your $150 paycheck as a student stinks, but think about how adults feel! An adult's $2,000 every-other-week paycheck typically ends up being $1,600 by the time it hits their bank account. That's $400 in taxes taken out every two weeks, or $800 per month. Ouch!

Taxes Everywhere You Turn

If taxes are a part of working and living in the United States, then it's important for you to understand how that works. There are two ways you'll personally feel the impact of taxes: taxes on the money you *earn* and taxes on the money you *spend*.

Government Revenue Sources:

51% Income taxes

35% Payroll taxes (FICA)

8% Excise, estate, and gift taxes

6% Corporate taxes[1]

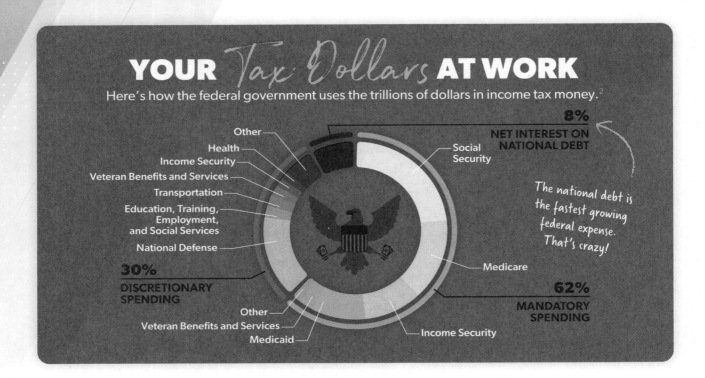

YOUR *Tax Dollars* AT WORK

Here's how the federal government uses the trillions of dollars in income tax money.[2]

8%
NET INTEREST ON NATIONAL DEBT

The national debt is the fastest growing federal expense. That's crazy!

Other
Health
Income Security
Veteran Benefits and Services
Transportation
Education, Training, Employment, and Social Services
National Defense

Social Security

Medicare

30%
DISCRETIONARY SPENDING

62%
MANDATORY SPENDING

Other
Veteran Benefits and Services
Medicaid
Income Security

MONEY YOU EARN

In Chapter 2, we explained that money you earn is called *income*. When you get a job, you'll find that the salary you agreed to and the actual amount of money you get to take home are different—that's the difference between gross income and net income.

Gross income is the total amount of money you earn in a given pay period. That could be every week, every other week, or every month. If you're paid a salary, divide your annual salary by the number of pay periods in a year to determine your gross income. Hourly workers can find their gross income by multiplying the number of hours they work by their hourly rate of pay ($10 an hour x 15 hours a week = $150). You pay income tax based on your gross income.

Net income refers to the amount of money left in your paycheck after all **withholdings** or deductions are taken out of your gross income. This is the first place you feel the personal impact of taxes.

(We'll break down everything that comes out of your pay in Lesson 3.) You'll also hear net income called your "take-home pay." Remember the $120 paycheck from our example? That's your net income.

It used to be common for employers to actually give people a physical paycheck. Today, most people are paid by direct deposit so their pay goes directly to a bank account on the day it's scheduled to be paid. You don't have to deal with a physical paycheck—or worry about losing it—and your employer doesn't have to process physical checks every pay period.

MONEY YOU SPEND

Whenever you buy something, you're a consumer. We're all consumers! And, of course, there's a tax for that. This is the second way you feel taxes. Consumption taxes are applied to the goods and services we buy. We'll break this type of tax down more in Lesson 2.

Gross Income:
the amount you earn before taxes and other payroll deductions

Net Income:
what a person earns after payroll taxes and other deductions are taken out; often referred to as take-home pay

Withholdings:
the portion of an employee's pay held back to cover taxes and other deductions

Why Do We Pay Taxes?

So, if you're out there working hard and earning money, it's natural to ask why the government gets to pocket so much of the money you earn. Good question. The short answer is that you're basically paying to be a citizen of the good ol' USA.

As citizens of this country, we all have access to a variety of government services and resources like roads, public education, social services, and law enforcement. The money that's collected in taxes—referred to as tax revenue—is how the government pays for all of those services.

So, how does that work? The proposed federal budget for **fiscal year** 2020 was $4.8 trillion.[3] Of that total, an estimated $3.8 trillion was funded through taxes. So what about the remaining $1 trillion? That's the **deficit spending** amount planned for

2020, and it was added to the **national debt**—which is why the national debt is so huge! By the way, that's not how we're teaching you to budget. You can only spend what you bring in. What a concept!

You can't borrow your way out of debt.

— Dave Ramsey

Clearly, it's not any smarter for the government to rely on debt than it is for you to use debt. But for now, we're focusing on taxes and how they impact you. You've already seen how big of a bite income taxes can take out of your paycheck. In the next lesson, we're going to dig into how taxes affect your spending.

Fiscal Year: a one-year period that governments or companies use for financial reporting

Deficit Spending: spending more than you earn; an economic policy in which the government spends public funds raised by borrowing rather than by taxation

National Debt: the total amount of debt a country owes to companies and other countries as a result of deficit spending

---

Your **JOURNAL** Why is there a difference (sometimes a big difference) between your gross income and your net income?

_____

_____

_____

REMEMBER THIS Add a ✓ next to each completed learning objective below.

◯ You understand why we have to pay taxes and how the money is used.

◯ You can explain the difference between gross and net income.

THIS LESSON MAKES ME FEEL (Circle) your response to what you learned.

 CONFUSED   SURPRISED   THOUGHTFUL   CONFIDENT

Taxes on Things You Buy

LESSON VIDEO GUIDE

Consumption taxes pay for things you get to use and enjoy, like a park, library, and fire department.

— *Anthony O'Neal*

GUIDED NOTES   While you watch the video, complete the section below.

1. _____ tax is money we have to pay on things we buy.

2. _____ tax is what you pay on things you buy.

3. Sales tax is a _____ of the total sale price.

4. Excise tax is also called a _____ tax.

5. Excise taxes are usually factored into the _____ of the item you are buying.

6. Sales tax usually goes to the state, city, and _____.

ANALYZE AND REFLECT   After you watch the video, respond to the question(s) below.

1. List at least five public services that sales tax pays for.

   _____

   _____

   _____

   _____

   _____

LEARNING OBJECTIVES

- Explain the different types of consumption taxes—sales tax and excise tax.
- Understand how consumption taxes are used.

MAIN IDEA

When you buy almost any good or service, you'll have to pay extra money called a consumption tax.

Everything Costs More

Do you remember the first time you realized sales tax existed? Maybe you were a kid and had saved up for a new game, only to realize that $19.99 game was ringing up a total of $21.98.

What? The sales ad said $19.99! You didn't know you'd need more than the ticket price. So, unless you had a few extra dollars or a willing parent, you'd have to save a little longer before you could buy it. That's the effect of **consumption taxes**. And the more expensive an item is, the higher the taxes are going to be.

While you may not have a job or have to worry about tax on your income just yet, we all buy things, so we all deal with consumption tax in one way or another. This is a tax on the purchase of goods or services. When you buy something, the tax is added to the price (usually at checkout), collected by the vendor, and sent to the local, state, and federal governments.

It's easy to remember the difference between income tax and consumption tax if you think of it like this: You pay income tax when you *earn* money; you pay consumption tax when you *spend* money on certain items. And it's rarely one-size-fits-all. There are typically different rates charged based on circumstances like the city you're in or whether the thing you're buying is categorized as a luxury or a necessity. Consumption tax is one of the few taxes where you can control how much tax you pay each year by controlling how many things you buy.

> **Live below your means and you'll have a great life.**
>
> — *Anthony O'Neal*

Sales Tax

When it comes to taxes on the things we buy, there are two types that usually affect you: sales tax and excise tax. Of course, the one we're most familiar with is **sales tax**. You pay this tax on retail purchases—like when you buy clothes, shop at the grocery store, or check out online.

These taxes are a percentage of the purchase price that's added to the overall total. So if your state has a 9% sales tax,

Did You Know?

Supporters of consumption taxes appreciate that everyone is taxed equally. Critics argue that consumption taxes discourage buyers and hurt those with low incomes.

Consumption Tax: a tax on the purchase of goods or services in the form of sales tax, excise tax, and other special taxes

Sales Tax: a tax on goods and services that goes to a state or local government

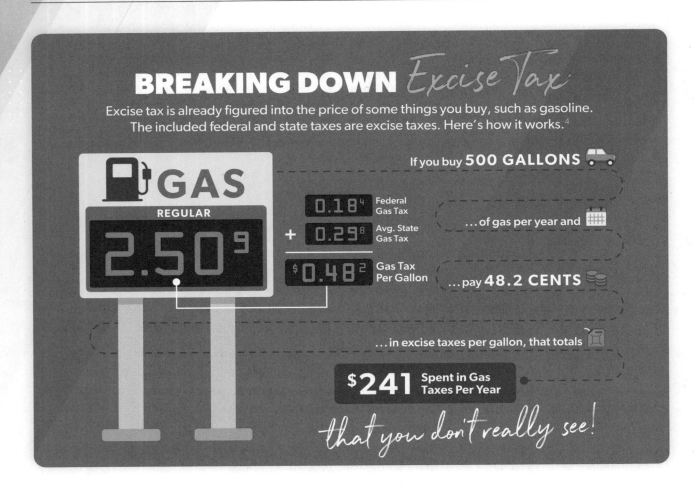

BREAKING DOWN *Excise Tax*

Excise tax is already figured into the price of some things you buy, such as gasoline.
The included federal and state taxes are excise taxes. Here's how it works.[4]

GAS
REGULAR
2.50⁹

0.18⁴ Federal Gas Tax
+ 0.29⁸ Avg. State Gas Tax

$0.48² Gas Tax Per Gallon

If you buy **500 GALLONS**
...of gas per year and
...pay **48.2 CENTS**
...in excise taxes per gallon, that totals

$**241** Spent in Gas Taxes Per Year

that you don't really see!

Excise Tax:
a tax on a certain goods that aren't typically considered a necessity; sometimes called a luxury tax

Did You Know?

In 2019, over 44% of the total federal excise tax revenue came from the tax on fuel and other highway-related taxes.[6]

you'd pay $1.09 for a $1 candy bar. On small purchases, you won't always notice it that much, but you'll definitely feel it when you buy something big like, say, a $350 TV that totals $381.50 at checkout.

Sale Price	Sales Tax	Total Tax	Total Price
$350.00	9%	$31.50	$381.50

Okay, so how much tax do *you* have to pay? Your sales tax rate depends on where you live and is usually a combination of city, county, and state rates. If you lived in Nashville, Tennessee, for instance, you'd pay a 9.25% sales tax that includes the 7% Tennessee rate and the 2.25% Davidson County rate. A few states don't have a state sales tax at all!

Excise Tax

While you pay sales tax on pretty much everything you buy, you'll only pay **excise tax** on specific items like gasoline, airline tickets, cigarettes, and alcohol. These are sometimes called luxury taxes because many of the items they apply to aren't considered necessities.

A big difference between sales and excise taxes is that excise tax is typically already included in the purchase price of an item, so you don't really see it. For example, gasoline prices (as illustrated in the graphic above) include excise tax at the federal and state levels. The federal excise rate is 18.4 cents per gallon of gasoline while the average state excise tax is 29.8 cents per gallon.[5] That's on every gallon of gas.

So, let's say the listed price for a gallon of gas is $2.50 at your local station. Of that price, 48.2 cents is the total of the excise taxes. The rest of the price includes the cost of the crude oil, the refining, and the transportation of the fuel.[7] When you add up all the gallons of gas you put into your car every year, that's a lot of excise tax.

Consumption Taxes at Work

Remember, just because the price you pay at the register bumps up when taxes are added, it doesn't mean that the seller is making any extra money. The business owner is responsible for turning in the appropriate amount of tax to the local and state governments based on the total of all their sales.

Federal, state, and local governments all have the ability to set consumption tax rates. So when you buy something and pay sales tax or excise tax on the item, that money is distributed between the different governing authorities according to tax rates that were set. That money helps federal, state, and local governments fund their budgets.

If you're feeling annoyed about the extra costs that these taxes add to the items you buy, you're not alone. But remember, taxes help pay for roads, public schools, police and fire departments, jails, hospitals, public employees, libraries, zoos, parks, museums, and local civic centers. These are places and services we all benefit from. Consumption taxes help provide the necessary funding for all of those things. So, those few extra pennies per dollar can *make a real difference!*

Did You Know?

Federal excise tax revenues totaled nearly $100 billion in 2019.[8]

Your JOURNAL

What's the difference between sales tax and excise tax?

_____

_____

_____

REMEMBER THIS   Add a ✓ next to each completed learning objective below.

◯ You can explain the difference between sales tax and excise tax.

◯ You understand how consumption taxes are used.

THIS LESSON MAKES ME FEEL   (Circle) your response to what you learned.

😓 CONFUSED   😯 SURPRISED   🙂 THOUGHTFUL   🤩 CONFIDENT

LESSON VIDEO GUIDE

You should never get a big tax refund. It is your money.
You just stored it with the IRS at 0% interest all year. —Dave Ramsey

GUIDED NOTES   While you watch the video, complete the section below.

1. Two types of income tax: _____ income tax and state income tax.

2. Federal income tax is based on your _____ form and your tax rates.

3. FICA stands for Federal _____ Contributions Act.

4. FICA includes social security and _____ taxes.

5. If you are employed by a company, you will pay about _____ in FICA taxes.

ANALYZE AND REFLECT   After you watch the video, respond to the question(s) below.

1. What's the purpose of the W-4 form?

_____

_____

2. Why is it so important to have the proper amount of taxes withheld from your paycheck?

_____

_____

_____

LEARNING OBJECTIVES

- Explain different types of income.
- Identify the taxes (including FICA), withholdings, and benefits that impact the amount of take-home pay an employee receives.

MAIN IDEA

While there are three basic types of income, most people live off of—and pay taxes on—their earned income.

Types of Income

If you earn money in the United States, you'll owe income taxes. It's a fact of life—but it's not always a simple process. Why? Well, you may think of income as your salary or hourly pay. That's true—but that only covers *part* of it.

Income is any money you get that comes from work or from investments. There are three kinds of income: earned income, passive income, and portfolio/investment income. And guess what—all three are taxed. Uncle Sam needs to keep the lights on, you know!

EARNED INCOME

Earned income is any money you make by working. It's where the majority of people feel the impact of taxes. You can see the impact of taxes and withholdings on your paycheck on the next page. Your **wages** are the money you earn for your time and effort at work and are paid hourly. The United States has a federal **minimum wage** (in addition to some states setting their own), which is the lowest amount per hour an employee can be paid to work.

Some people are paid a **salary**—a fixed, annual rate of pay that doesn't change by working more or fewer hours. Employees paid a salary know what their paycheck will be each pay period.

Whether you're salaried, hourly, full time, or part time, the downside of earned income is that if you stop working, you stop earning money.

> ## There's a great place to go when you're broke. To work.
> — *Dave Ramsey*

PASSIVE INCOME

While earned income is from actually working, **passive income** is just that—passive. It's money you earn on a regular basis that requires little to no effort to keep it going. That sounds great, right? Passive income can come from renting out property, creating and selling content on a blog or YouTube channel (and generating ad revenue), or owning a business where you don't have an active role.

Earned Income: any income (wages/salary) that is generated by the work someone performs

Wage: money paid by the hour and for an agreed number of hours per week; especially for unskilled or manual labor

Minimum Wage: the smallest amount that employers can legally pay their employees per hour of work

Salary: a fixed annual amount earned by an employee, typically paid weekly, biweekly, or monthly

Definitions continued on next page

WITHHOLDING *Basics*

Your employer is required by law to withhold federal taxes from your gross pay and send them to the government. In addition, here are some of the most common withholdings you'll see on your paystub.

FEDERAL INCOME TAX (FITWH)

The amount of federal income tax taken out is based on your income and on your Form W-4.

STATE INCOME TAX

This tax goes to your state's government. Not all states have an income tax.

RETIREMENT PLANS

Choosing to invest for retirement with a company plan like a 401(k) reduces your taxable income. We'll go into more detail on this in Chapter 12.

HEALTH SAVINGS ACCOUNT (HSA) OR FLEXIBLE SPENDING ACCOUNT (FSA)

This deduction allows you to set aside pre-tax dollars to pay for medical expenses.

FEDERAL INSURANCE CONTRIBUTIONS ACT (FICA)

This pays into Social Security (SOC), a federal supplemental retirement program, and Medicare (MED), a federal insurance plan that provides benefits for citizens over age 65 and those with disabilities.

LOCAL INCOME TAX

Your city or county may also have an income tax to pay for local public services.

HEALTH INSURANCE

This deduction is for employer-provided health insurance premiums. The annual cost is divided among pay periods.

ACME supplies corp | Earnings Statement

123 SUNSHINE AVE
ANYTOWN, STATE 10401

Period Ending: May 1, 2021
Pay Date: May 6, 2021

JANE SMITH
101 MAIN ST
ANYTOWN, STATE 10401

Taxable Marital Status: Married
Exemptions/Allowances:
Federal: 3   State: 2   Local: 2

Gross Earnings

EARNINGS	Rate	Hours	This Period
Regular	15	80	1200.00
		Gross Pay	$1,200.00

Withholdings

STATUTORY	This Period
Federal Income Tax	-78.46
Social Security Tax	-62.31
Medicare Tax	-14.57
State Income Tax	-35.75
Local Tax	-19.94
OTHER	
*401(k)	-75.00
*Health Insurance	-70.00
*HSA	-50.00

*Excluded from federal taxable wages

Total Withholdings	$406.03
Net Pay	**$793.97**

Tax Deductions

While you can't control which taxes you have to pay, you can lower your taxable income (the amount of income you pay taxes on) by contributing to benefits such as health insurance, HSA/FSAs, and retirement plans. After all these deductions are taken out of your gross pay, taxes are calculated. That leaves your net income. Your pay stub details how much money went to each category. Make sure to check for errors each pay period!

PORTFOLIO INCOME

Portfolio income is money you receive from your investments as they grow. It also includes any extra money or interest you earn on investments and savings. You produce portfolio income by buying and selling stocks, bonds, mutual funds, other **paper assets**, real estate, and any other assets that have increased in value.

> ## You don't need a big income to have a large net worth.
> — *Chris Hogan*

All three forms of income get taxed. Earned income is taxed at the employer level. And you typically pay taxes on your passive and portfolio income when you fill out your taxes each year. It's best to talk to a tax professional about these.

Form W-4 and Taxes

When you start a job, you have to fill out Form W-4 to let your employer know how much tax to withhold from your pay. It's your responsibility to fill out the form correctly. But don't worry, instructions are available with the form, and online, to help you fill it out.

If too much is withheld, you'll end up getting a refund—which means you've given the government an interest-free loan. If too little is withheld, you'll end up owing the government money. You want to make sure you fill out the form correctly so you can break even at tax time!

Passive Income: money earned on a regular basis with little or no effort required to maintain it

Portfolio Income: income from an investment sold at a higher price than you paid for it

Paper Asset: a representation (on paper) of stocks, bonds, currencies, mutual funds, etc.

Your JOURNAL

What taxes and withholdings take the biggest bite out of the amount of your paycheck?

_____

_____

_____

REMEMBER THIS   Add a ✓ next to each completed learning objective below.

○ You can describe the three types of income.

○ You can explain the taxes, standard withholdings, and common deductions that are taken out of an employee's paycheck.

THIS LESSON MAKES ME FEEL   Circle your response to what you learned.

😓 CONFUSED   😮 SURPRISED   🙂 THOUGHTFUL   🤩 CONFIDENT

Taxes don't have to be a scary thing. You can understand how the basic process works. — Anthony ONeal

GUIDED NOTES   While you watch the video, complete the section below.

1. The IRS is an agency of the _____ government.

2. Tax Day is _____ 15.

3. It's important to understand it's _____ money going to the government.

4. The total amount you owe is your tax _____.

5. There are two ways to file your taxes. Do it yourself or hire a _____ professional.

6. If you _____ money, you need to file a tax return.

7. A _____ form shows you how much you made during the previous year.

8. The average tax _____ is over $2,700.

ANALYZE AND REFLECT   After you watch the video, respond to the question(s) below.

1. Why is it important to file your income taxes before Tax Day? Provide two reasons.

_____

_____

_____

LEARNING OBJECTIVES

- Understand how and why federal income tax is collected.
- Identify ways to avoid paying too much or too little in taxes.

MAIN IDEA

Filing your federal tax return on time is how you (and the IRS) make sure the taxes you owe are settled each year—either with a refund or another payment.

Income Tax Basics

In the last lesson, you learned about the three different types of income and the taxes that are taken out of your paycheck. These are (of course) called **income taxes**—and they apply to any kind of income. If you're an employee working for a company, every paycheck you receive has taxes taken out. If you're a contractor or self-employed, you'll have to put aside money from each payday to go toward these taxes.

> **You can give yourself a raise each month if you do your taxes correctly.**
> — *Rachel Cruze*

The amount of tax withheld from your paycheck depends on Form W-4, which you fill out when you start working. Form W-4 estimates how much tax you'll owe based on your personal tax situation. But how does the government figure out how much tax you actually owe? Basically, the more money you make, the more you're going to pay in taxes.

So how do you know what rate you'll be taxed at? Your taxable income gets split between ranges called **tax brackets**, with the income that falls in each range getting taxed at a different rate. Sound confusing? It is. But tax tables, tax software, and tax professionals all make sure you're taxed the correct amount.

For the 2020 tax year, these tax rates ranged from 10% to 37%.[9] So to find your actual **tax liability**, you'd look at your taxable income compared to the year's brackets and apply the different rates for each range your income covers—adding them all up to get your total. The chart on the next page shows you how that works.

When spring rolls around, almost every citizen who earned income is required to fill out and turn in a federal **tax return** to the IRS—the Internal Revenue Service. This is what people mean when they talk about filing their taxes (we'll cover that in Lesson 5). The information on the tax return is balanced with the taxes taken out of your paycheck. If too much was taken out, you get a refund. If not enough was taken out, you have to pay more. The goal is to get as close to zero as you can.

Income Tax: tax paid out by anyone who earns an income

Tax Bracket: the income ranges in which tax rates apply

Tax Liability: the total tax a person or business has to pay

Tax Return: a report that a taxpayer has to submit annually to the government and is used to determine a person's tax liability

Did You Know?

The 2018 Tax Reform Law impacted tax rates and deductions for millions of Americans in a good way.

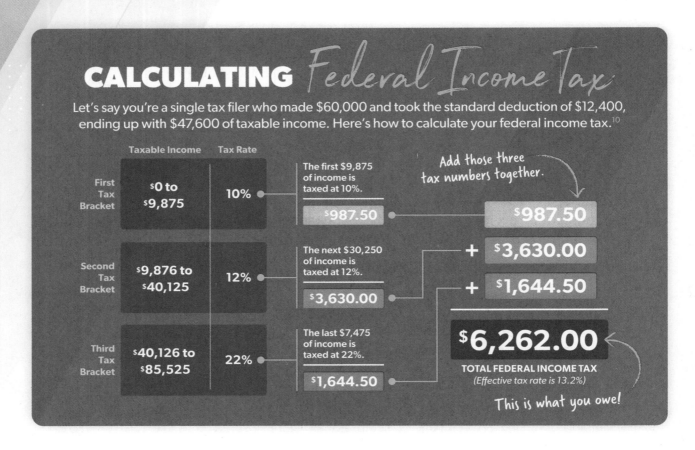

CALCULATING *Federal Income Tax*

Let's say you're a single tax filer who made $60,000 and took the standard deduction of $12,400, ending up with $47,600 of taxable income. Here's how to calculate your federal income tax.[10]

	Taxable Income	Tax Rate	
First Tax Bracket	$0 to $9,875	10%	The first $9,875 of income is taxed at 10%. **$987.50**
Second Tax Bracket	$9,876 to $40,125	12%	The next $30,250 of income is taxed at 12%. **$3,630.00**
Third Tax Bracket	$40,126 to $85,525	22%	The last $7,475 of income is taxed at 22%. **$1,644.50**

Add those three tax numbers together.

$987.50
+ $3,630.00
+ $1,644.50

$6,262.00
TOTAL FEDERAL INCOME TAX
(Effective tax rate is 13.2%)

This is what you owe!

Filing Deadlines

By the end of January, employers are required to provide the necessary tax documents to their employees. One of those is a year-end report called Form W-2. It lists your employer's information, how much you were paid, and how much they withheld in taxes and other deductions. (The IRS also has this information.) Once you have all your documents, you can start the tax return process.

The deadline for filing your tax return for the previous calendar year is usually April 15 each year—also called **Tax Day**. You can get an extension of up to six months if you request one before the deadline or are on active military duty. But your tax payments still have to be postmarked by the filing deadline or you might have to pay interest, penalties, or both. No, thanks!

Penalties

The IRS isn't too happy with people who don't file a tax return every year. They'll eventually get their money—plus penalties and interest.

If you don't file your taxes, you'll face a failure-to-file penalty. This is 5% of your unpaid taxes for each month your tax return is late. If you file more than 60 days late, the penalty is a minimum of $435 or 100% of the taxes you owe, whichever is less.[11] If you file your taxes but don't pay them, the IRS will charge you a failure-to-pay penalty. Generally, you'll be charged from 0.5% up to 25% of your unpaid taxes for each month you don't cough up the cash.[12] All the while, interest will be piling up on your unpaid taxes.

Bottom line: It's much better to just get your taxes done early each year and send

Did You Know?

The IRS reports over $1 billion in tax refunds go unclaimed each year![13]

Tax Day: the annual deadline for filing your income taxes; usually falls on April 15

them in by the filing date. You can make the process easier and more wallet-friendly by making sure your Form W-4 is filled out correctly. That way, you won't have to stress about a huge tax bill.

Refund or No Refund?

Speaking of tax bills, when it comes to filing taxes, a lot of people fall into one of two categories: "I don't like filing my taxes because I always have to pay more money every year" or "I don't like filing my taxes, but I do get a big refund every year."

Both of these scenarios mean you're doing your taxes wrong. If you set up your Form W-4 correctly, you shouldn't owe too much extra. If you do, that just means you underpaid your taxes throughout the year. You also shouldn't be getting a hefty refund—that means you're overpaying.

Getting a big tax refund is not winning with money. That was *your* money in the first place! But you can fix both of those issues by tweaking your Form W-4.

What's the fattest refund check you can get? $0.

— Anthony O'Neal

Then, there's a third category of people related to taxes: those who carefully fill out their Form W-4 so they don't have too much or too little withheld. They complete their tax returns before the deadline and get as close to zero owed and zero refunded as possible. Then they keep their money during the year and put it to work. That's the category you want to be in!

Did You Know?

The average tax refund in 2019 (2018 taxes) was $2,732.[14] That's almost $230 per month. If you invested that $230 each month over 40 years, it would grow to about $2 million!

The hardest thing in the world to understand is the income tax.

Albert Einstein
Physicist

Your JOURNAL

Why is getting a large tax refund or having to pay a large tax bill at the end of the year a sign of poor planning?

_____

_____

_____

REMEMBER THIS   Add a ✓ next to each completed learning objective below.

○ You understand why and how income tax is collected.

○ You can identify ways to avoid paying too much or too little in taxes.

THIS LESSON MAKES ME FEEL   Circle your response to what you learned.

😓 CONFUSED   😮 SURPRISED   🙂 THOUGHTFUL   🤩 CONFIDENT

LESSON VIDEO GUIDE

If you have a simple tax situation, online tax software can be a good option. —Dave Ramsey

GUIDED NOTES   While you watch the video, complete the section below.

1. Filing taxes is something that _____ has to do.

2. What you really want is no big tax _____ or big additional tax bills.

3. A tax professional is someone authorized by the _____ to prepare federal tax returns for other people.

4. A tax professional needs to be either an _____ agent (EA) or a Certified Public Accountant (CPA).

5. An _____ is when the IRS reviews your tax documents to make sure you reported them correctly.

6. If you're self-employed, you should set aside about 25% to _____ of your income.

ANALYZE AND REFLECT   After you watch the video, respond to the question(s) below.

1. List three things you should look for when hiring a tax professional.

_____

_____

_____

LEARNING OBJECTIVES

- Understand how and when to file your federal income taxes.
- Recognize the differences in the various tax reporting forms.

MAIN IDEA

Filing an annual federal tax return with the IRS (Internal Revenue Service) is one of those things most people dread but everyone has to do.

It's Tax Time!

Let's say you started your first job about 10 months ago and had taxes taken out of every paycheck all year. Now it's the end of January. You receive an email or letter from your employer. It's your Form W-2. That means it's time to file your taxes. Don't forget that the filing deadline is April 15.

Generally speaking, every American who earns an income and has tax deducted has to file a federal tax return each year. There are some exceptions, so it's always best to double-check. You definitely don't want to skip filing your taxes. The federal tax return allows taxpayers to calculate their tax liability, or the amount of taxes they should have paid in the previous year.

> **When you're self-employed, set aside 25–30% of your income for your taxes.**
>
> — Anthony O'Neal

Do you, as a high school student, have to file a tax return? If you earned more than $12,200 and had income tax taken out of

your paycheck, then yes! So, does that mean if you earned less than $12,200, you don't have to file a tax return? Technically, you don't have to. But if you had any taxes taken out of your paychecks, you would want to file a tax return so you could get that money—your money—back. It can get confusing, so it's always best to check with the IRS as well as a tax professional.

Getting Started

To get started with your tax return, you can download and print the tax return forms from the IRS website or use other online resources to fill out the forms electronically. If you need some help understanding it all, a tax professional can walk you through the process—for a fee.

Once you've completed all the forms, you can mail your tax return to the IRS or file everything electronically (called e-filing). E-filing is faster—both in getting your forms accepted by the IRS and taking care of payments or refunds. Tax software and online tax preparation sites offer free e-filing for most federal tax returns. Depending on where you live, you may also need to file a state tax return.

Did You Know?

Before 1943, Americans paid their income taxes quarterly or annually. The Current Tax Payment Act of 1943 required companies to withhold income taxes from employees' paychecks.

A Message From DAVE

MOST PEOPLE dread tax season every year because of all the paperwork. Thankfully, it doesn't have to be that way! Preparing your taxes can actually be a no-stress process if you do a little work on the front end. It just takes some organization and time. Keep two dates in mind: January 31 is when you should have all your W-2s, and April 15 is the filing deadline. If you keep all your important receipts and tax documents in a folder, it will make everything easier. And e-filing has really simplified the process of filing your taxes with the IRS.

Completing the Forms

One thing you can always count on during tax season is paperwork—and lots of it. And when it comes to the IRS forms, there are new ones every year. Thankfully, all of these forms come with detailed instructions that you can find online. Here's a quick look at the most common forms.

Form 1040 is the main form most people use to list income, expenses, and take the **standard deduction**, which benefits most people because of the 2018 Tax Reform changes. Form 1040 shows your tax liability as well as how much you still owe or how much you'll get back. **Tax schedules** are used for **itemized deductions** and to report other income. Here are the most common tax schedules:

Schedule	Usage
Schedule A	Itemize deductions like property tax, medical expenses, and charitable contributions
Schedule C	Report profits and losses from freelancing, side hustles, or contract work
Schedule SE	Calculate the Social Security tax for anyone who is self-employed

In addition to the tax schedules, there are a variety of numbered forms for reporting different types of income and payments. Here are the most common:

Form	Usage
Form 1098	Report mortgage interest
Form 1098-T	Report tuition payments
Form 1098-E	Report interest paid on student loans
Form 1099-MISC	Report amount a client paid you for freelance or contract work
Form 1099-INT	Report interest earned on savings and investments
Form 1099-DIV	Report dividends earned on investments

While you're young and your tax situation is fairly simple, you may just need your Form W-2 and Form 1040 to wrap up your tax filing. But as your wealth grows and you start investing and earning passive and portfolio income, you'll likely have to fill out or include information from a variety of these schedules and forms when you file. Yes, it can get confusing really fast! That's when you may need to get some help.

Did You Know?

With the 2018 increase in the standard deductions, most people do not have to itemize their deductions.

Standard Deduction: the dollar amount people can subtract from their income before the tax is calculated

Tax Schedule: a special tax form to report certain types of income or deductions

Itemized Deductions: a list of all eligible expenses that can be claimed to decrease taxable income

Tax Credits

While deductions lower your taxable income *before* you figure out the taxes you owe, **tax credits** lower your tax bill. Common credits are related to adoption, childcare, and health coverage. Tax credits can save hundreds on your tax bill, so do your research or talk to a tax professional.

Self-Employed Differences

Self-employed people also complete Form 1040. Usually, their income is reported on Form 1099-MISC instead of Form W-2. In addition to the main forms, they'll generally file Schedule C to report the profits and losses from their businesses.

The big difference for self-employed people is filing Schedule SE to figure out their Social Security taxes and reporting it on Form 1040. Since self-employed people don't have an employer paying half of their FICA taxes, they have to pay the entire 15.3% figure themselves—ouch! It's complicated, so self-employed folks should get a tax professional's help.

Taxes Are Important

Always keep your filed taxes for at least three years in case the IRS decides to **audit** (or check) your figures. Look—we get it. Audits, deductions, credits, and tax forms don't seem important now, but they will be when you're a working adult. Tax software will walk you through each step of filing your taxes by asking simple questions. And you always have the option of working with a tax pro! The bottom line: It's your job to make sure your tax return is *done right the first time!*

Tax Credit: an amount of money a taxpayer can subtract from the taxes they owe

Audit: an official IRS inspection of a tax return to make sure the income and deductions are accurate

---

Your JOURNAL   Why is it important to file your federal income taxes every year?

REMEMBER THIS   Add a ✓ next to each completed learning objective below.

○ You understand how and when to file your federal income taxes.

○ You can identify the various tax forms that are right for your situation.

THIS LESSON MAKES ME FEEL   Circle your response to what you learned.

CONFUSED   SURPRISED   THOUGHTFUL   CONFIDENT

LESSON VIDEO GUIDE

When you make more money, you are going to pay more in taxes. — Anthony O'Neal

GUIDED NOTES   While you watch the video, complete the section below.

1. If you own any property at all, you're going to pay _____ taxes.

2. If you receive an inheritance, you may have to pay an _____ tax.

3. A capital _____ tax is a tax you'll pay if someone leaves you a house and you sell it at a later time.

4. An _____ tax is another common type of inheritance tax.

5. A gift is anything of _____ for which the person doesn't get anything in return.

6. There is no limit to how much you can _____ to a 501(c)(3) nonprofit organization.

7. The gift tax limit is _____ per individual.

ANALYZE AND REFLECT   After you watch the video, respond to the question(s) below.

1. Why is it important to know the tax implications of giving away money or an inheritance?

   _____

   _____

   _____

LEARNING OBJECTIVE

Understand the various forms of wealth tax.

MAIN IDEA

In the United States, the more money you earn—actively or passively—the more you'll be required to pay in taxes.

Taxes on Wealth

Remember, paying taxes is just one of those certainties of life as a U.S. citizen. Another certainty is that the federal government is always going to find a way to get their taxes. In Lesson 2, we identified three types of income. All earned income is subject to tax.

The more money you make and the more types of income you have, the more complicated taxes can get. But don't let that stop you from working to build wealth. But it's important to understand how taxes can affect your wealth. As they say—more money, more problems! Or at least, more money creates more taxes.

What Is a Wealth Tax?

As the term suggests, a **wealth tax** is a tax on the wealth possessed by the people who live in a country. While a lot of developed countries choose to tax wealth, the U.S. has historically favored taxing income.

So when we're talking about types of wealth taxes, we're usually referring to taxes on assets. These assets include things like bank deposits, stock shares, real estate, and pension plans—among others. The tax is generally based on the value of those assets.

Examples of Wealth Taxes

While the United States doesn't currently have a wealth tax plan that taxes wealthy citizens as a percentage of their net worth, there are some taxes in place that are considered wealth taxes. Let's break down the most common ones.

> ## A tax professional can guide you in the right steps to take.
>
> — *Chris Hogan*

PROPERTY TAX

Property tax is the main source of revenue for local governments. Taxes on land, homes, and business property are all forms of property tax. These taxes are ultimately categorized as a wealth tax. Property taxes are recurring, meaning they have to be paid each year by the owner.

INHERITANCE AND ESTATE TAXES

If you receive an inheritance, there are three types of taxes that could potentially come into play: a capital gains tax, an inheritance tax, and an estate tax.

Did You Know?

The wealthiest 1% of Americans earn 21% of the total income but pay 38% of the total income tax. The top 10% pay 70% of the taxes.[15]

Wealth Tax: a tax based on the market value of owned assets

Property Tax: taxes paid by anyone who owns property, such as land, a home, or commercial real estate

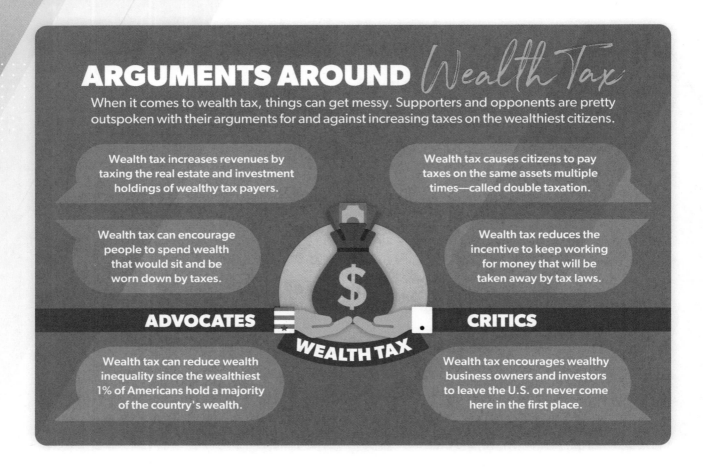

Capital Gains Tax: a tax on the positive difference between the sale price and the value of a gift when it was inherited

Inheritance Tax: a state tax on an asset an individual received from someone who has passed away

Definitions continued on next page

A **capital gains tax** is paid if you sell an inherited gift (like a house). A tax is paid on the difference between the selling price and the value when it was inherited.

An **inheritance tax** is a state tax that you would pay (with your own money) on an asset (property or money) you receive from someone when they pass away. There are only a few states that have this tax—and many of them have exceptions that don't require family members to pay.

An **estate tax** (also called a death tax), on the other hand, is taken out of the value of a deceased person's estate (their assets after their death). That way, you don't have to pay this tax. However, since the estate is paying the tax, it could reduce the value of your inheritance.

GIFT TAX

A **gift tax** is applied to the transfer of any money or asset (like a car) that you give to someone without getting something of equal value (or fair market value) in return. But don't worry about that donation you made last week—this gift tax doesn't kick in unless you're giving away serious money (think over $15,000).

Wealth Taxes Vary by State

Many of the taxes Americans pay are imposed at the state and local level. Wealth taxes, in particular, are often dependent on where you live. Federal estate taxes apply no matter where you live in the United States. There are some states that impose an additional estate tax on their residents.

Keep in mind that state tax laws can change often. So, when it's time to plan your estate or communicate with older family members about theirs, it's always a good idea to understand the tax rules in your state.

I've never met anyone who wins at money who doesn't give generously.

— Dave Ramsey

Giving and Taxes

It's true that building wealth may make your tax situation a little more complex—especially when you start having a variety of income streams. That's when you really start to build wealth.

Dave Ramsey often says, "Giving is the most fun you can have with money." And yes, it's easier to be generous with money when you're wealthy. Being extremely generous can create some tricky tax situations. Don't let that stand in the way of being outrageous with your giving. In fact, for those who choose to itemize deductions on their tax return, giving to charities and organizations helps lower your taxable income.

But long before you get to that point, adjusting your W-4 may help you find extra money in your budget. If you've been struggling with being generous because you just don't feel like you have the cash, this is a great chance to work that in. Same if you get a tax refund! Always look for ways to give back, because giving allows you to *be a blessing to others!*

Estate Tax: a tax that's imposed on a property owner's right to transfer the property to others after his or her death

Gift Tax: a tax on any asset that exceeds the yearly amount you can transfer to another person without compensation of equal value

---

Your JOURNAL

Do you think wealth taxes are a good idea? Why or why not? Defend your position.

_____

_____

_____

REMEMBER THIS   Add a ✓ next to the completed learning objective below.

◯ You understand the differences between the various types of wealth taxes.

THIS LESSON MAKES ME FEEL   Circle your response to what you learned.

 CONFUSED   SURPRISED   THOUGHTFUL   CONFIDENT

Chapter 10 Review

REVIEW KEY TERMS   Fill in the blanks below using the correct key terms from this chapter.

Gross Income	Excise Tax	Income Tax	Tax Credit
Net Income	Earned Income	Tax Bracket	Audit
Withholdings	Wage	Tax Liability	Wealth Tax
Fiscal Year	Minimum Wage	Tax Return	Property Tax
Deficit Spending	Salary	Tax Day	Capital Gains Tax
National Debt	Passive Income	Standard Deduction	Inheritance Tax
Consumption Tax	Portfolio Income	Tax Schedule	Estate Tax
Sales Tax	Paper Asset	Itemized Deduction	Gift Tax

1. Each year, taxpayers submit a(n) _____ _____ to the IRS with the goal of getting as close to zero as possible.

2. Due to recent tax reforms, most tax filers can just take the _____ _____ when filing their taxes.

3. The taxes you pay for snacks and other items at a gas station are an example of _____.

4. _____ is money you make from working at your job.

5. The 12-month period used for reporting financial activity is known as a(n) _____.

6. An example of a(n) _____ is the taxes you pay on the fuel you purchase for your car at a gas station.

7. If a long-lost relative or friend were to leave you a lot of money, you might have to pay a(n) _____.

8. Planning to spend more money than you actually have coming in is called _____.

9. _____ is money you make from your investments.

10. The IRS may conduct a(n) _____ of a person's tax return to check the accuracy of the figures.

1. Which form is used to calculate how much income tax is withheld from your pay?

   A. Form W-2

   B. Form W-4

   C. Form 1098

   D. Form 1099

2. _____ is your total pay before taxes and withholdings are taken out.

   A. Net income

   B. Earned income

   C. Passive income

   D. Gross income

3. What percentage of their income should a self-employed person set aside for taxes?

   A. 15–20%

   B. 20–25%

   C. 25–30%

   D. 30–35%

4. What federal payroll tax goes toward Social Security and Medicare?

   A. FICO

   B. FICA

   C. FACO

   D. FOCA

5. The total amount the U.S. owes to other countries and companies is called what?

   A. National debt

   B. Deficit spending

   C. Wealth tax

   D. National tax

6. April 15 of every year—the usual deadline to file your taxes—is also called what?

   A. Deadline Day

   B. Due Day

   C. Tax Day

   D. Equinox Day

Review **QUESTION**

What types of taxes and deductions are factored into the difference between your gross pay and your net pay?

_____

_____

_____

_____

_____

_____

Living on Your Own

Housing and Real Estate

In this chapter, you'll discover the financial costs related to having your own place to live, the differences between renting and homeownership, and what to do when you're ready to buy a house.

LESSON VIDEO GUIDE

Living on your own is great—just make sure you are smart with your money in the process.

—Anthony O'Neal

GUIDED NOTES   While you watch the video, complete the section below.

1. Write down three key takeaways from the conversation about living on your own.

    _____

    _____

    _____

2. Living on your own can be _____.

3. Rent should be no more than _____ of your monthly take-home pay.

4. You will need _____ insurance.

ANALYZE AND REFLECT   After you watch the video, respond to the question(s) below.

1. What are two things that worry you about living on your own? What are two things that you're excited about?

    _____

    _____

    _____

    _____

LEARNING OBJECTIVES

- Evaluate the cost-of-living expenses.
- Understand what it means to be house poor.

MAIN IDEA

When it comes to living on your own, you need to factor in the cost of living because you'll be responsible for paying for all the stuff you need out of your own income.

Living on Your Own

Freedom! Is that the first word that comes to mind when you think about what it will be like to live on your own? Of course! Independence is wonderful—but the truth is that enjoying your newfound freedom can be more expensive than you think.

Cost of living refers to the average cost of housing, food, clothing, and any other goods and services you need to maintain a certain **standard of living**. When your parents pay for and provide most of the things you need, it's tough to understand just how much those things cost. It's a good thing you're learning about budgeting and developing good money habits now instead of figuring it all out once you're on your own!

Moving out and living on your own are natural parts of growing up. After all, you don't want to be living with your parents when you're 30 years old! And your parents don't want that either.

How and when you move out can look really different depending on your plans after high school. Living in a dorm, renting an apartment, or even buying a house are big decisions. Really big decisions.

Moving Out

If you're planning to attend college and live on campus, you can ease your way into living on your own. Your room will be furnished, have internet, and come with a meal plan. You'll know how much your basic living expenses will be in advance.

Or you might choose to dive into independence by living off campus. You'll have to pay rent and utilities, buy furniture and other items, and do your own grocery shopping. And you'll have all kinds of transportation expenses like gas, insurance, and maintenance.

> **You're more prepared than you know to be able to live on your own.**
>
> — *Anthony O'Neal*

When you're done with school and join the workforce, you should rent until you can financially afford to buy a home. Rent a place that's affordable and close to your work. We'll talk about ways to keep your cost of living down later in this chapter.

Cost of Living: the average cost of the basic goods and services needed to sustain a certain standard of living

Standard of Living: the level of wealth, comfort, material goods, and necessities available to a group of people

The ache for home lives in all of us—the safe place where we can go as we are and not be questioned.

Maya Angelou
American poet

The Cost **OF LIVING ON YOUR OWN**

You probably can't wait to start living on your own. That's normal. You know what else is normal? All the costs associated with getting your first place! Here are some of the basics.

- **Security Deposit**
- **First Month's Rent**
- **Renter's Insurance**
- **Utilities Setup**
- **Furniture**

- **Sheets and Towels**
- **Kitchen Supplies**
- **Cleaning Supplies**
- **Groceries**
- **Transportation**

House Poor:
when someone spends so much of their income on the costs of homeownership that they struggle to reach other financial goals

Did You Know?

In 2018, 41% of homeowners had a paid-off mortgage or never had a mortgage.[1]

If you plan to enter the military after high school, that's an entirely different form of living on your own. Your living situation will vary depending on the branch of service and your rank. Your recruiting officer will be able to provide details about what to expect for living expenses.

No matter which path you choose, the money principles you're learning in this course will keep you on track: Save, always have a budget, stay out of debt, live on less than you make, and be generous.

Renting Isn't a Bad Thing

Yes, owning your own home is part of the American dream, but renting for a season of your life is a great first step. The day you'll become a homeowner probably feels like a long way off, but it's not a bad idea to learn a few things about homeownership early.

After all, your house will probably be your biggest asset—an important part of your personal financial plan and your total net worth. Renting is a low-risk way to figure out what you really want before you buy—like size, location, and how much yardwork you want to do. Knowing what you want is just the first part of making a wise home-buying choice. The next part is buying a home you can afford so that, instead of ending up **house poor** like most people, you buy a home that sets you up to win financially.

Get Started Today

This chapter will help you learn about the benefits of owning or renting a home, learn the legal terms of a lease agreement, and learn when and how to buy a house—all the basics of housing and living on your own! It's exciting, but there's a lot to know if you're going to do it the right way.

So how can you learn about the costs of living before you're responsible for covering them yourself? Just sit down with your parents or guardians and go through the monthly bills. Ask questions about how and when they pay the bills.

Do they have a budget? Sit with them as they write it out—or show them what you've learned about budgeting. Ask if you can sit in on their budgeting discussions each month because you want to learn how all of this works in real life.

The first thing I want you to do, before getting a place to live, is get on a budget.

— Anthony O'Neal

As you have budget conversations, find out which bills stay the same each month, which ones vary from month to month, which expenses take up most of their income, and how debt payments impact the budget. You could find out which expenses are seasonal or periodic, how they handle unexpected expenses, and what happens if they don't pay a bill on time.

Financial Responsibility

You've learned a lot about taking personal responsibility for your financial decisions and about being generous to others. So, what does renting or buying a home have to do with being generous? A lot, actually.

People who are house poor find it very difficult to be generous because most of their income is tied up in living expenses. So they don't have the ability to give money. Or they're working so much to make a mortgage payment that they have no extra time for volunteering. Financial responsibility lets you do both—

give money and time!

Did You Know?

25% of people who rent say their housing costs are 50% or more of their income and are a severe financial burden.[2]

Your **JOURNAL**

When you think about where you'll live after you graduate, what monthly living expenses do you think you'll have?

_____

_____

_____

REMEMBER THIS   Add a ✓ next to each completed learning objective below.

◯ You've begun to evaluate the cost of living on your own.

◯ You can explain what it means to be house poor.

THIS LESSON MAKES ME FEEL   Circle your response to what you learned.

😓 CONFUSED   😮 SURPRISED   🙂 THOUGHTFUL   🤩 CONFIDENT

LESSON VIDEO GUIDE

Renting is not a bad thing, but it should be temporary for most people.

—Anthony ONeal

GUIDED NOTES   While you watch the video, complete the section below.

1. Write down your top takeaways from the discussion with the real estate professional. Include the pros and cons of renting vs. buying.

   _____

   _____

   _____

2. It is possible to rent an apartment without a _____ score.

3. _____ is a good idea while you are paying off debt.

4. _____ is a good option for people who are debt-free.

ANALYZE AND REFLECT   After you watch the video, respond to the question(s) below.

1. When you graduate and find a place to live on your own, do you expect to rent or buy your home? Why?

   _____

   _____

   _____

LEARNING OBJECTIVES

- Analyze the differences between owning and renting.
- Understand how to evaluate whether renting is always cheaper.

MAIN IDEA

Deciding whether to rent or to buy a house is a big decision. It's important to know your financial situation so you can make the best choice.

A Place to Live

The two most common ways to pay for housing is to rent or buy. **Renting**, or leasing, simply means that you have an agreement with the property owner or landlord to pay a fixed amount of money (usually monthly) for a place to live. And, of course, buying a home means you pay an agreed-upon price to transfer ownership of a property from the seller to yourself.

There may come a time when you're financially ready to buy a house. But could renting still be the smarter option?

First, you have to decide if you can afford to buy. According to a survey of current renters, 77% say that having the money for a down payment and closing costs would be an obstacle to owning a home.[3] In addition, many have too much debt to buy a home.

On the other hand, being financially ready to buy a house doesn't always make buying the right choice. There are a lot of additional responsibilities that come with homeownership that might make renting a better option. In order to make the best choice for yourself at any given time, you have to consider several things.

Deciding to Rent or Buy

You'll have some financial boxes to check off before you're ready to buy a house. You should be completely out of debt, have a fully funded emergency fund of three to six months of expenses, and have enough cash saved for a down payment of 10–20%. You'll learn more about all of that in Lesson 4.

People get in such a hurry to buy. Renting, sometimes, is just patience.

— Dave Ramsey

But just because you've checked off those home-buying boxes, it doesn't mean you're ready to buy. If you've been married less than a year—wait. You need to learn how to live together as a married couple before you dive into a home purchase! If you just moved to a new area or don't plan on staying where you are for more than three years, renting is still the way to go. The next page breaks down the advantages and disadvantages of renting and owning.

Renting: periodic payments (usually monthly) by a tenant to a landlord in return for the use of a property

Did You Know?

62% of millennials rent a place to live.

38% of millennials have bought a home.[4]

RENTING *Vs* OWNING

When it comes to having a place to live, your first decision is whether to rent or to buy. Here are some of the most common advantages and disadvantages for each option.

ADVANTAGES

+ **MOVING** can be easier—just be super clear on your lease obligations.

+ **YOUR LANDLORD** takes care of paying for all the maintenance costs.

+ **UTILITY COSTS** for an apartment are often less expensive than for a house.

+ **INITIAL COST** (1–2 months' rent) is much lower than a down payment on a house.

+ **RENTER'S INSURANCE** to protect your stuff is very inexpensive.

+ **EVERY PAYMENT** brings you closer to owning your home totally free and clear.

+ **APPRECIATION** means your home will likely increase in value over time.

+ **TAX DEDUCTIONS** can be taken for mortgage interest and property taxes.

+ **RENOVATION** makes a house your own and can even increase its value.

+ **A PAID-OFF HOUSE** significantly adds to your total net worth.

DISADVANTAGES

– **RENT RATES** may go up year after year when you sign a new lease agreement.

– **NO FINANCIAL ADVANTAGES** like tax deductions, equity, or rising property value.

– **LESS FREEDOM** to make it your own. Landlords usually restrict renovations.

– **RELOCATING** can be difficult. Selling your house can take time and cost you money.

– **EMERGENCIES:** If your water heater or air conditioner breaks, you have to pay for it.

– **MAINTENANCE:** When you own your home, all the repair work is up to you.

Is Renting Always Cheaper?

On the surface, renting may seem like the cheaper option. But that's not always the case. Homeownership does come with big monthly expenses like maintenance, homeowner's insurance, and taxes—not to mention your monthly mortgage payment.

But if you look at the long-term costs, homeownership is the better deal most of the time. Why? Partly because of inflation—rent prices are subject to inflation just like all other goods and services. When you own a house, you don't have to worry about the landlord increasing your rent every year. If you get a **fixed-rate mortgage**, the principal and interest portion of your mortgage payments are locked in.

Plus, when your house's value goes up and your **mortgage principal** (the remaining balance of your loan) goes down, you're investing money in your house that you'll get back if and when you sell it.

If you're moving every few years or you're in a super expensive city (like San Francisco), renting would be the better option even though it might not be the cheaper option.

You can rent an apartment without a credit score.

— Anthony O'Neal

When it comes time to decide if you want to rent or buy, your ability to afford a home is just part of the decision. You'll learn more about how to rent a place to live or buy a house in the next two lessons.

> Home is the nicest word there is.
>
> Laura Ingalls Wilder
> American Writer

Fixed-Rate Mortgage: a mortgage with a set interest rate for a set number of years

Mortgage Principal: the amount borrowed (that has to be paid back) to purchase a home

---

Your JOURNAL

What details will you consider as you decide to rent or buy a home?

_____

_____

_____

REMEMBER THIS
Add a ✓ next to each completed learning objective below.

○ You can explain the costs and benefits of owning versus renting.

○ You can determine if renting is always the cheaper option.

THIS LESSON MAKES ME FEEL
Circle your response to what you learned.

 CONFUSED   SURPRISED   THOUGHTFUL   CONFIDENT

LESSON VIDEO GUIDE

The key is to shop around and find a place you can truly afford to rent. —Anthony O'Neal

GUIDED NOTES   While you watch the video, complete the section below.

1. _____ is the most significant factor in the price of rent.

2. _____ are things that provide convenience, comfort, or enjoyment in life.

3. More amenities usually mean _____ rent.

4. The larger the space and the _____ it is, the more it will cost you.

5. A lease agreement is a _____ contract between a landlord and a tenant.

6. The lease _____ will detail the length of time the lease is valid.

7. Your security deposit should be _____ to you when you move out.

8. The _____ is responsible for maintaining the building.

ANALYZE AND REFLECT   After you watch the video, respond to the question(s) below.

1. If you were leasing an apartment, would you consider a roommate? Why or why not?

_____

_____

_____

LEARNING OBJECTIVES

- Understand the legal components of a lease agreement.
- Explain the financial benefits of having a roommate and strategies to find one.

MAIN IDEA

Before you rent a place to live, it's important to understand what's involved with signing a lease agreement and finding compatible roommates.

Renting Your Home

So you've made the decision to move out on your own and rent. That's great! All of the money principles you're learning in this course are about to come in super handy! In this lesson, you'll learn how much rent you can afford, the components and obligations involved in a lease agreement, and how to choose roommates you can actually live with.

How Much Can I Afford?

Who doesn't want a stylish apartment to show off to your friends? But let's be practical. Style often comes with dollar signs! If you really want a glamorous apartment in a hot location, you have to first be able to afford the rent. And there's an easy way to figure out what you can afford. Your rent payment should total no more than 25% of your take-home pay. So if your take-home pay is $2,500 a month, your rent should be no more than $625 per month. Easy!

Why is 25% the magic number? You don't want too much of your take-home pay tied up in rent. You've got things to do! You need room in your budget for

food, gas, car maintenance, and utilities. If all your money goes toward rent, how will you save for emergencies or other goals—like a down payment to buy a house of your own? If you're spending more than 25% of your income on rent, you'll never get there!

> **Renting helps you save up money so you can buy a home the right way.**
>
> — *Chris Hogan*

Take the time to shop around and compare prices. Some apartments come with fancy **amenities** like a pool, fitness center, and granite countertops. Which of those things, if any, are truly worth paying higher rent? Hint: None of them are worth it if they stand in the way of saving money and reaching your goals!

The Lease Agreement

When you rent an apartment or any type of real estate, you'll sign a lease agreement with your landlord. You agree to pay the

Here's a Tip:

When is it a good idea to rent instead of buy?

1. When you're paying off debt.
2. When you're still building your emergency fund to 3–6 months of living expenses.
3. When you're saving up for a 10–20% down payment.

Amenities: things that help provide convenience, comfort, or enjoyment

Leasing Contract: a legal contract that allows the renter, or lessee, rights to the use of a property owned or managed by the lessor for a period of time

Legal Contract: an agreement made between two or more parties that is enforced by law

Acknowledgment Clause: the portion of a legal contract signed by both parties

landlord or property owner a certain amount of money in exchange for a place to live. Real estate **leasing contracts** are legal documents that allow the renter, also referred to as the tenant or lessee, rights to the use of a property owned or managed by the lessor (property owner) for a period of time—typically six months or one year.

Leasing contracts—also called lease agreements—are often long, complicated documents written in legal language. As intimidating as they are, it's important to read and understand your lease. Why? Because a lease agreement is a **legal contract.** That means anything in the contract, once you sign it, is enforceable by law. If you don't abide by the contract, it's referred to as breaking your lease—and that often comes with costly penalties.

What's in a Lease?

Most leases are pretty straightforward. They contain the following information:

- Landlord's and tenant's names
- Property address and unit number
- Rental term or the exact dates the lease agreement is valid
- Rent amount, due date, and late fees
- Security deposit terms, including reasons deductions may be made
- Rules about pets and any pet fees
- Tenant responsibilities (keep property safe from hazards, keep property clean, do not cause damage, etc.)
- **Acknowledgment clause** signed by both lessee and lessor

Since leasing contracts are legal contracts, you should take as much time as you need

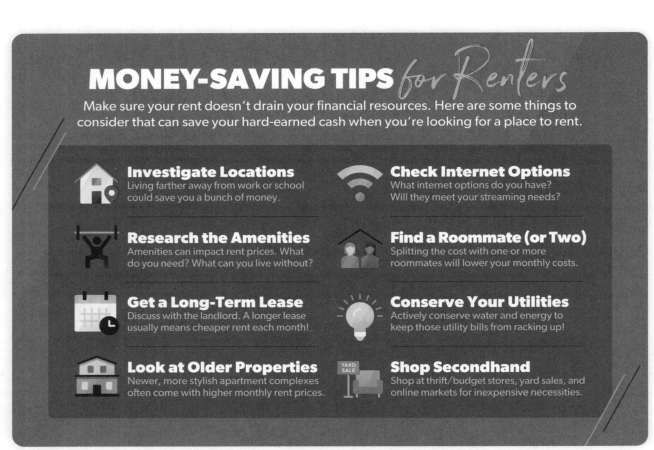

MONEY-SAVING TIPS *for Renters*

Make sure your rent doesn't drain your financial resources. Here are some things to consider that can save your hard-earned cash when you're looking for a place to rent.

Investigate Locations
Living farther away from work or school could save you a bunch of money.

Research the Amenities
Amenities can impact rent prices. What do you need? What can you live without?

Get a Long-Term Lease
Discuss with the landlord. A longer lease usually means cheaper rent each month!

Look at Older Properties
Newer, more stylish apartment complexes often come with higher monthly rent prices.

Check Internet Options
What internet options do you have? Will they meet your streaming needs?

Find a Roommate (or Two)
Splitting the cost with one or more roommates will lower your monthly costs.

Conserve Your Utilities
Actively conserve water and energy to keep those utility bills from racking up!

Shop Secondhand
Shop at thrift/budget stores, yard sales, and online markets for inexpensive necessities.

to read through the lease. You may even want a parent or an experienced adult in your life to look it over with you. The terms of your lease will inform you of your rights and responsibilities outlined in the rental agreement. It will also help you resolve any conflicts or problems that may come up during the term of the lease.

Consider Roommates

The tips on the bottom of the previous page can help you save money while you're renting. If you're having trouble finding a place you love that fits your budget, a roommate helps you solve that problem. Having a roommate (or two) can save you a lot of money and help you reach your financial goals more quickly. Of course, living with roommates has its challenges.

We all have our own habits. But you can find an awesome roommate if you take your time and you're honest about your likes and dislikes. Don't take for granted that just because someone's been your best friend since you were five years old that they'll be a great roommate.

There's nothing wrong with renting a place to live.

— Anthony ONeal

Ultimately, communication is key! It's impossible to predict every bump in the road. But if you're mature, respectful, and considerate of one another, you can work out any unexpected complications.

Did You Know?

49% of renters are under the age of 30.[5]

Your **JOURNAL**   What are some of the possible advantages and disadvantages of having a roommate?

_____

_____

_____

REMEMBER THIS   Add a ✓ next to each completed learning objective below.

◯   You understand the legal components of a lease agreement.

◯   You can explain the financial benefits of having roommates and strategies for finding a roommate.

THIS LESSON MAKES ME FEEL   Circle your response to what you learned.

😓 CONFUSED   😮 SURPRISED   🙂 THOUGHTFUL   🤩 CONFIDENT

LESSON VIDEO GUIDE

 Owning a home is a huge goal that a lot of people want to achieve and a dream that can be a reality for you. —Anthony ONeal

GUIDED NOTES   While you watch the video, complete the section below.

1. A _____ is a loan that people take out in order to buy a home.

2. A house is an asset that _____ in value over time.

3. A _____ rate means the interest rate on the loan won't go up.

4. The down payment is a _____ of the purchase price.

5. Write down four key takeaways from the home-buying process in the space below.

_____

_____

_____

_____

ANALYZE AND REFLECT   After you watch the video, respond to the question(s) below.

1. Why do you think owning a home is considered the American Dream for so many people?

_____

_____

_____

LEARNING OBJECTIVES

- Understand the financial criteria for buying a home.
- Explain how to choose the best type of mortgage.

MAIN IDEA

Homeownership is a wonderful financial goal, but it comes with a lot of extra costs and maintenance. You'll want to make sure you're ready before buying a house.

The Great American Dream

Owning your own home is a huge part of the American dream. As crazy as the idea may seem right now, one day you'll want to stop renting and buy a house. You'll see your friends buying homes, you'll love the idea of having a garage, and your dog will want a yard. And if you get married, your spouse may want a place to settle down.

In Lesson 2, you learned about the financial boxes you need to check off before you buy a home. Let's take a closer look and find out why they're so important.

First, be debt-free. Remember, **The Second Foundation** is to get out and stay out of debt. Buying a house can be super stressful when you don't have extra debt. But debt on top of your **mortgage** can put your home purchase at risk!

Next, have an emergency fund of three to six months of expenses saved. This can help you pay your mortgage and your bills if you lose your job for some reason.

Third, save a 10–20% **down payment**. That's a lump sum of money (a percentage of the total price of that home) paid by the buyer at the time of purchase. The bigger your down payment, the faster

you'll pay off your mortgage—and you'll avoid **private mortgage insurance (PMI)**.

Fourth, same as with rent, stay at 25% of your take-home pay for your mortgage payment. That leaves plenty of room in your budget to achieve other financial goals.

When you're ready to buy a house, only get a 15-year fixed-rate mortgage.

— Dave Ramsey

Finally, if you're not planning to stay in a place for more than three years, it's generally not a good idea to buy a house. And if you're not crazy about where you live, why would you buy a house there?

If you don't have all five of these things in place, hold off on buying a home and focus on your finances until you do!

A Home Mortgage

The very best way to buy a home is the same as any other purchase—with cash. Some people actually do that. But most people will need a home loan (aka mortgage).

The Second Foundation: Get out and stay out of debt.

Mortgage: a loan obtained for the purchase of a home

Down Payment: a lump sum of money, usually a percentage of the total price of that home, paid by the buyer at the time of purchase

Private Mortgage Insurance (PMI): insurance that protects lenders against loss if the borrower defaults on the loan; does not go toward paying down your mortgage at all

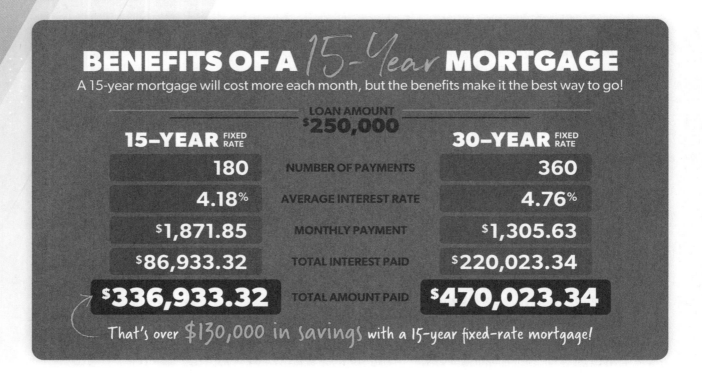

BENEFITS OF A *15-Year* MORTGAGE

A 15-year mortgage will cost more each month, but the benefits make it the best way to go!

LOAN AMOUNT
$250,000

15-YEAR FIXED RATE		30-YEAR FIXED RATE
180	NUMBER OF PAYMENTS	360
4.18%	AVERAGE INTEREST RATE	4.76%
$1,871.85	MONTHLY PAYMENT	$1,305.63
$86,933.32	TOTAL INTEREST PAID	$220,023.34
$336,933.32	TOTAL AMOUNT PAID	**$470,023.34**

That's over $130,000 in savings with a 15-year fixed-rate mortgage!

Equity: the increase in value of a home over time; the difference between the amount owed and what the home could be sold for

When getting a mortgage, many people only ask, "How much is the monthly payment?" They should also ask, "How much is the total cost of the loan?" We recommend a 15-year, fixed-rate conventional mortgage with a payment less than 25% of your take-home pay as the best way to buy a home. But what does that mean? Let's break it down:

15-year refers to the term, or length in years, of the mortgage. As the graphic above shows, with a 30-year mortgage, you'll end up paying almost twice the price of the house. Your monthly payments will be slightly higher with a 15-year mortgage, but it's worth it in the long term—and it helps you build **equity** faster. Equity is the difference between what your home is worth and how much you still owe on it.

Fixed-rate refers to an interest rate that's locked in and won't change for the life of your loan. Adjustable Rate Mortgages—or ARMs—have interest rates that can fluctuate from year to year. ARM loans can seem attractive with a lower initial rate, but there's more risk since the rate may go up and impact your payment.

Conventional refers to the type of mortgage. Most home loans are one of three types:

- *Conventional loans* are not secured by a government entity. They usually have the best rate and term, especially if you have a 20% down payment to avoid PMI.
- *FHA loans* are backed by the Federal Housing Administration and are very popular with first-time homebuyers or people with little or no down payment. FHA loans often cost way more money in the long run because of fees, restrictions, and other penalties.
- *VA loans* are backed by the Veterans Administration and are only available for active or former military members. VA loans have attractive terms and can seem like a good idea for people

who qualify. But, like FHA loans, the additional fees or terms actually make them a more expensive option.

Now you understand why we recommend a 15-year, fixed-rate conventional mortgage as your best long-term option!

Steps to Buying a Home

So, let's say it's a few years down the road and you're ready to buy a house—now what? We won't lie, the process can take a little time, but the steps are fairly simple:

1. *Get preapproved.* This lets you know how much a bank will loan you and shows sellers you're a serious buyer.
2. *Hire an agent.* Interview and find a pro you like who also knows their stuff.
3. *Find a home.* Stick to your budget and find a house you can afford!
4. *Make an offer.* Your agent can help you make a solid offer for the best deal.
5. *Get a home inspection.* This step will uncover major issues before you buy.
6. *Close on your home.* This is where you sign a lot of papers, pay, and become an official homeowner!

Buying a house is the only time it's okay to borrow money for a purchase.

— Anthony O'Neal

Just like any other form of debt, you'll want to get rid of a mortgage as fast as you can. Always remember to hate debt when you buy a house—it will help you keep the drive and passion to pay off your home early!

> Purchased with common sense, paid for in full, and managed with reasonable care, [real estate] is about the safest investment in the world.
>
> Franklin D. Roosevelt
> 32nd president of the United States

Did You Know?

Normally, the seller pays the agent commission for both the listing agent and the buyer's agent— usually 3% of the total sale price for each agent.

Your JOURNAL   How do you know when you're ready to buy a house?

_____

_____

_____

REMEMBER THIS   Add a ✓ next to each completed learning objective below.

◯   You understand the financial criteria for buying a house.

◯   You can explain how to choose the best type of mortgage.

THIS LESSON MAKES ME FEEL   (Circle) your response to what you learned.

😓 CONFUSED   😮 SURPRISED   🙂 THOUGHTFUL   🤩 CONFIDENT

Chapter 11 Review

Fill in the blanks below using the correct key terms from this chapter.

Cost of Living	Fixed-Rate Mortgage	Legal Contract	Mortgage
Standard of Living	Mortgage Principal	Acknowledgment Clause	Down Payment
House Poor	Amenities	Private Mortgage Insurance (PMI)	Equity
Renting	Leasing Contract		

1. If you're _____, your house payment or rent is more than you can afford and still pay your other bills.

2. The total amount still owed on a house is the _____.

3. You'll want to have a(n) _____ of 10–20% of the total cost of the house you want to buy.

4. _____ means you pay someone else each month for a place to live.

5. _____ refers to the average amount needed for housing, food, clothes, and other goods and services.

6. _____ is the difference between what a house is worth and what is still owed on it.

7. Apartment _____ such as a pool, fitness center, and other perks are nice but usually mean higher rent prices.

8. An apartment lease is a _____ for a set period of time.

FINISH THE SENTENCE Use what you've learned in this chapter to complete these sentences.

1. A fixed-rate mortgage means your payment and interest rate won't _____ _____.

2. Whether you're renting or buying, your monthly payment should be _____ _____.

3. Having a large house down payment (at least 20%) has benefits such as _____ _____.

4. Appreciation means that the value of a home you buy will continue to _____ _____.

1. When buying a house, you'll typically need a _____% down payment to avoid paying PMI.

   A. 10   C. 20

   B. 15   D. 25

2. The first step in buying a house is to find out how much a bank will loan you for the purchase—also known as being what?

   A. Preapproved   C. Prerecognized

   B. Preactivated   D. Preordained

3. Another word used for "renting" is:

   A. Buying   C. Investing

   B. Leasing   D. Owning

4. What does the A stand for in the home loan option referred to as an ARM?

   A. Adjustable   C. Adaptable

   B. Automatic   D. Administration

5. Whether you rent an apartment or buy a house, try to keep your monthly payment below _____% of your take-home pay.

   A. 20   C. 30

   B. 25   D. 35

6. A loan obtained for a home purchase is a(n):

   A. Equity   C. Lease

   B. Inspection   D. Mortgage

Review QUESTION

Describe the advantages and disadvantages of buying a home versus renting a home or apartment.

_____

_____

_____

_____

_____

_____

Plan for the Future

Investing and Retirement

This chapter dives into the basics of preparing for retirement, investing for the future by understanding the stock market and mutual funds, and planning to live a life bursting with generosity.

LESSON VIDEO GUIDE

When you are investing, time is your friend as long as you start early and remain patient. *—Chris Hogan*

GUIDED NOTES   While you watch the video, complete the section below.

1. You should invest _____ of your income for retirement.

2. Investing is a _____, not a sprint.

3. List the three ingredients needed to build wealth for your future:

   _____

ANALYZE AND REFLECT   After you watch the video, respond to the question(s) below.

1. If retirement is many years away, why is it important to start thinking about it now?

   _____

   _____

   _____

2. Why do you think so many adults wish they had started investing earlier?

   _____

   _____

   _____

LEARNING OBJECTIVE

- Understand what it means to have financial security in retirement.
- Understand basic investing terms and principles.

MAIN IDEA

Investing is saving money in a way that earns money so you can build wealth and reach your long-term financial goals, like saving for retirement.

Retirement Is Not an Age

We get it—retirement feels like it's a lifetime away and it's likely not on your radar right now. (We're talking *decades* down the road, right?) But here's the thing: Retirement isn't an *old* person thing, it's a *smart* person thing. The earlier you start to think about it—and plan for it—the more opportunities you have to make your retirement exactly what you want it to be.

> **When you have a real plan and work that plan with real effort, you'll get real results.**
>
> — *Chris Hogan*

You may know someone who is retired and living the dream. They travel and seem to have all the money they need. But you probably also know someone who is well past the usual age of retirement and is still working day in and day out to make ends meet. Starting early can be the difference between those two realities. **The Fifth Foundation** is to build wealth and give, and that's the focus of this chapter.

Investing Basics

Investing is basically saving money in a way that earns money through compound growth. That's what we mean when we talk about your money working for you. And that takes time. Investing is a long-term play—the longer the better.

When you invest, your goal is to earn a positive **return on investment (ROI).** In other words, you make money when your investments increase in value. Some investments do that better than others, but the fact is, all investments involve some level of risk. An investment's **risk-return ratio** helps you understand how risky that investment is compared to the return you can expect. We'll talk more about how that works in the next lesson.

Retirement Investing

Remember the example of Jack and Blake from Chapter 3? Jack ended up with a ton of money for retirement. Why? Because he had money, time, and investments that provided a solid return on his money with an acceptable level of risk. Early investing paid off for Jack, and it can for you too. Check out what Jack did:

The Fifth Foundation: Build wealth and give.

Investing: the process of setting money aside to increase wealth over time for long-term financial goals such as retirement

Return on Investment (ROI): measures the gain or loss generated on an investment relative to the amount of money invested

Risk-Return Ratio: relationship of expected return (profit you expect to make) compared to the amount of risk (amount you stand to lose if the price goes down) taken with a given investment

BUILD WEALTH FOR *Retirement*

In addition to an emergency fund and short-term savings goals, you need a long-term plan to build wealth for retirement. Remember, you won't need this money for a long time—so put that money to work for you! Here's what you need to build wealth for the future:

MONEY + **TIME** + **RATE OF RETURN** = **COMPOUND GROWTH**

MONEY	TIME	RATE OF RETURN	COMPOUND GROWTH
This is the starting point in order to build wealth for the future. You actually need to invest some money if you want to have any for retirement. If you put in zero, that's exactly what you'll have later.	The longer your money is in your investments, the more earning potential it will have. Why? It takes time for the money you invested to grow. That's why it's important to start early.	With investing, there will always be ups and downs in the market. Over the long term, though, you should see the value of your mutual funds growing, giving you a positive rate of return.	Compound growth is a millionaire's best friend. It's an explosion for your money. But in order for it to work, you have to invest consistently over time—and leave your money alone so it can grow!

REMEMBER JACK?

At age 21, Jack (mentioned in Chapter 3) started investing $200 per month using good growth stock mutual funds. He averaged an annual return of around 11% over the long term. The cool thing is that Jack only invested for nine years but ended up with *millions*. Why? He invested money consistently, gave it time to work, and chose investments with a solid, long-term rate of return. That's a winning formula!

Total invested over 9 years: **$21,600**	Total return after 46 years: **$2,547,150**

9 yrs · · · 19 yrs · · · 29 yrs · · · 39 yrs · · · 46 yrs

Imagine what would have happened if Jack kept investing each month!

The Value of Liquidity

Like we talked about in Chapter 8, **liquid assets** can easily be sold and turned into cash. Usually, the more liquid an asset is, the less return you can expect. Cash in the bank is very liquid—you can go to the bank and get it. But it's not growing very much. Real estate is not liquid because it takes time to sell and get the money. Retirement investments are different. While you can cash them out pretty easily, you'll get hit with expensive taxes and penalties if you do it too soon.

The Retirement Problem

Fifty or sixty years ago, retirement was built in to most people's career plans. You'd work for a company for 35 years or so, retire at 65, receive a pension, and live a comfortable life of recreation and travel.

Today, retirement isn't a certainty. Of non-retired Americans, 25% have no money saved for retirement and 49% said they aren't even confident they can reach their goals for retirement.[1,2]

When your money makes more than you do, you are officially wealthy.

— Dave Ramsey

A lot of adults will tell you that they regret not investing sooner for retirement. Don't let that be you! This is the perfect time for you to learn how to invest the right way because time is on your side. You'll be able to retire with dignity and change your family tree!

Liquid Asset: an asset that can be easily bought or sold

Here's a Tip:

When you're done paying for college, are debt-free other than your mortgage, and save three to six months of expenses in your emergency fund, you should invest 15% of your income for retirement.

Your JOURNAL

Why do most people your age never stop to think about retirement?

_____

_____

_____

REMEMBER THIS — Add a ✓ next to each completed learning objective below.

◯ You can explain what it means to have financial security in retirement.

◯ You understand the basic terms and principles related to investing.

THIS LESSON MAKES ME FEEL — Circle your response to what you learned.

😓 CONFUSED   😯 SURPRISED   🙂 THOUGHTFUL   🤩 CONFIDENT

LESSON VIDEO GUIDE

There are things you can invest in that are good for your future and there are things that are way too risky.

—Chris Hogan

GUIDED NOTES   While you watch the video, complete the section below.

1. A _____ fund allows investors to pool their money together to invest.

2. The _____ of the mutual fund will often tell you what's going on inside of it.

3. A "growth stock mutual fund" has stocks that are _____.

4. Your return comes when the _____ of the fund increases.

5. Do not buy mutual funds unless you are going to leave them alone for at least _____ years.

ANALYZE AND REFLECT   After you watch the video, respond to the question(s) below.

1. Why is it so important to avoid buying single stocks and invest in mutual funds instead?

   _____

   _____

   _____

2. Why does Dave recommend that you invest in mutual funds for at least five years?

   _____

   _____

LEARNING OBJECTIVES

- Explain the basic concept of the stock market.
- Evaluate the risk and return of various types of investments.

MAIN IDEA

You have a lot of options when you're investing, so it's a good idea to understand some basic principles that will help you choose the right investments for your goals.

The Stock Market

If you've ever watched the news, you've probably heard of the **stock market**. It's up! It's down! But what is it?

First, let's talk about **stocks**. Think of stocks like little building blocks. Each stock is an individual block that—together with a lot of other little blocks—makes up a company. So, when you buy a stock, you own a little piece of a company.

The stock market is a large group of financial markets from all over the world where people buy and sell these stocks. The stock market goes through periods of growth and decline—sometimes dramatic highs and lows. For many people, all of the ups and downs are terrifying.

Measuring the Market

As scary as it might sound, you actually want to use the power of the stock market to help your investments grow. There are smart ways to do that and not-so-smart ways to do that. The fact is, even successful investing is like a roller coaster with crazy ups and downs, twists and turns. But remember this: The only people who get hurt on a roller coaster are the ones who jump off! Stick with your plan. History shows that those ups and downs level out. You—and your investments—will be okay.

> **Stick with your investing plan whether stocks are up or down.**
>
> — Dave Ramsey

As an investor, how do you know how the stock market is doing? A **stock market index** measures a section of the stock market to give investors an idea of overall market performance. The most well-known stock market index is the Standard & Poor's (S&P) 500 that tracks the stock values of the top 500 companies on the New York Stock Exchange. Other market indexes like the Dow Jones and NASDAQ do the same thing with different groups of stocks.

The stock market has a strong history of upward and downward trends. There are actually names for those trends—**bull** and **bear markets**—that are described in an easy-to-understand way on the chart on the next page.

Stock Market: a financial market that trades shares of ownership of public companies

Stock: a security that represents part ownership or equity in a company

Stock Market Index: a measurement of a section of the stock market, typically a weighted average of the prices of selected stocks

Bull Market: when prices in a financial market are on the rise or expected to rise

Bear Market: when prices in a financial market experience a prolonged decline

BULL & BEAR *Markets*

Why are the ups and downs of the stock market referred to as bull and bear?

Bears use their claws to attack downward.

Bulls use their horns to attack upward.

Types of Investments

When it comes time for you to invest, you'll have a lot of options. Making sense of all those options can be a challenge. For each investment option, you'll want to weigh the level of risk compared to the possible returns on your money. The higher the risk, the greater your chance of losing a lot—or all—of your money. Here's some quick info about the most common investments:

- *Certificates of deposit (CDs)* are a type of savings account with a slightly higher interest rate because they have a longer savings commitment, like six months or a year. **RISK:** LOW **RETURN:** LOW

- *Money market accounts* are savings accounts with check-writing privileges. They're a great option for storing your emergency fund savings because they're very liquid, stable, and have a slightly higher interest rate than a typical savings account but may have certain restrictions. **RISK:** LOW **RETURN:** LOW

- *Single stocks* are investments in a single company and they're extremely risky!

Remember, when you buy a share of stock you're buying a small piece of the company. Your return comes as the company increases or decreases in value. If the company goes bankrupt or fails, there goes all of your money. **RISK:** HIGH **RETURN:** LOW TO HIGH

> Don't invest your money in single stocks—they're way too volatile.
>
> — *Chris Hogan*

- *Bonds* are sold by companies and governments. When you buy a bond, you're basically lending your money to the issuer for a certain period of time. They make regular interest payments to you and promise to pay back the bond (loan) at a set date—the maturity date. Your return is the fluctuation in price and the interest rate paid. **RISK:** MODERATE **RETURN:** MODERATE

- **Mutual funds** are made up of a pool of money from a group of investors to invest in stocks, bonds, money markets, and similar assets. We'll dig deeper into the different types of mutual funds in Lesson 3. The return on your investment comes as the value of the fund increases.
  RISK: MODERATE **RETURN:** LOW TO HIGH

- **Annuities** are very complex investments sold by insurance companies and often have high fees and charges. You pay a premium, and they promise to send you payments during retirement. Annuities have some appealing benefits, like no investment limits and guarantees on your investment that mean you won't lose money. **Fixed annuities** have low, fixed rates of interest. **Variable annuities** allow you to invest in mutual funds.
  RISK: LOW **RETURN:** MODERATE

- **Real estate** can be a great tool for helping you to build wealth, but it's a big commitment. You can make money by renting property or selling it for a profit.
  RISK: HIGH **RETURN:** LOW TO HIGH

What's Best?

Investing is the best way to build wealth and set yourself up for retirement. With so many options, what's the best one? That really depends on you and your tolerance for risk and possible money loss.

It's always a great idea to talk with an investing professional who can help you understand what you're investing in. And that really is the key to investing: Never invest in anything you don't understand. A simple, consistent investing strategy is all you need to reach—even exceed—your personal financial goals!

Fixed Annuity: annuity that offers low, guaranteed rates of interest and fixed income payments in retirement

Variable Annuity: a type of annuity that can vary in value based on the performance of the mutual funds inside it

---

Your **JOURNAL** Based on what you understand about risk and return, why is investing in single stocks a bad idea?

_____

_____

_____

REMEMBER THIS Add a ✓ next to each completed learning objective below.

◯ You have a basic understanding of how the stock market works.

◯ You can explain the risk and return of various types of investments.

THIS LESSON MAKES ME FEEL ⟨Circle⟩ your response to what you learned.

 CONFUSED   SURPRISED   THOUGHTFUL   CONFIDENT

LESSON VIDEO GUIDE

The main tools used to build wealth are 401(k), 403(b), and company-sponsored retirement plans. —Chris Hogan

GUIDED NOTES While you watch the video, complete the section below.

1. 401(k): Companies can allow their _____ to save for retirement.

2. 403(b): _____ can allow their employees to save for retirement.

3. A _____ IRA lets you invest pre-tax money.

4. A _____ IRA lets you invest post-tax money and grows tax-free.

5. A 401(k) and IRA are not investments, they protect your investments from _____.

6. _____ lowers risk.

ANALYZE AND REFLECT After you watch the video, respond to the question(s) below.

1. After learning the difference between Roth and traditional retirement plans—IRA, 401(k), and 403(b)—which type would you prefer? Why?

    _____

    _____

    _____

LEARNING OBJECTIVES

- Understand how pre-tax and after-tax investments work.
- Identify different types of retirement plans.

MAIN IDEA

Whether you work for a company or own your own business, there are plenty of retirement plans to help you make the most of your investment dollars.

Mutual Funds

In Lesson 2, you learned about different types of investments—some good, some not-so-good. Let's continue digging into one of the best options for your long-term investing goals: mutual funds. When you invest in a mutual fund, you're contributing to a pool of money that will be invested in a mix of stocks, bonds, money market accounts, etc.

People called *fund managers* decide what investments a mutual fund will include in its **portfolio** (collection of investments). Their goal is to meet the objectives in the fund's **prospectus**, a fancy word for a document that describes the details of a fund for a potential investor. It's also the fund manager's job to make sure the fund grows in value so that it provides capital gains (profit) and income for the people who invest in the fund.

A well-managed mutual fund can perform as well as, or better, than the stock market itself and reduce your risk. That's because mutual funds invest in hundreds of companies at once. That's a lot less risky than putting all your eggs in one basket with single stock investing.

It's a Marathon

As you saw with the Jack and Blake example in Chapter 3, successful mutual fund investing takes a long time—it's a marathon! Time is the key for compound growth to take effect. That's why mutual funds are such a great investment for retirement. But they're not a good option for your short-term savings or emergency fund. You don't want to risk a drop in the market wiping out a chunk of your emergency savings just when you need it.

> ## Investing is a marathon, not a sprint.
> — *Chris Hogan*

So how long are we talking about? To make the most of the ups and downs of the market and experience compound growth, we're talking 30 to 40 years! That's why you need to start early. And that's why you want mutual funds that keep up with or outperform the stock market. Before you invest, make sure a fund has done well for five to 10 years (or more).

Did You Know?

75% of millionaires make regular, consistent investing part of their ongoing personal finances.[3]

Portfolio: a list of your investments

Prospectus: a description of the investing strategy the mutual fund management company will use to invest your money

Common Retirement Plans

When you're investing for retirement, take advantage of savings plans like an **individual retirement arrangement (IRA)** as well as a company-sponsored **401(k)**. Both offer tax benefits that will make the most of the money you invest for the future. These types of plans are not actually investments—they simply protect your investments from taxes.

An IRA is a tax-advantaged account designed for retirement investing. You can invest in lots of things through your IRA, and as we said earlier, mutual funds are a great fit in your IRA. Because they're intended for retirement investing, if you take money out of your IRA before you're 59 1/2 you'll have to pay a penalty.

A 401(k) is a type of qualified retirement savings plan that many employers offer so employees can invest money from their gross pay (before taxes) toward retirement. The money you put in a traditional 401(k)

is pre-tax, so it grows tax-deferred. That means you don't pay taxes on that money until you take it out at retirement after 59 1/2 as shown in the graphic below.

Free Money

Some employers will also match an employee's contribution up to a certain amount. If your employer offers a full 4% match and you invest 4% of your pay in your 401(k), your employer will also contribute—or match—that same amount. That's free money!

For a lot of people, a Roth plan option can end up saving them a lot of money in taxes when they retire. Unlike a traditional IRA or 401(k) where you pay taxes when you take the money out, a Roth IRA or Roth 401(k) allows you to contribute from your net income after taxes are taken out. So you won't have to pay taxes on that money in retirement. And all of the growth is tax-free as shown in the graphic below!

Individual Retirement Arrangement (IRA): a tax-advantaged investing account that people use to save for retirement

401(k): a qualified retirement savings plan offered by a company to its employees who contribute money from their gross pay

Did You Know?

Nearly 8 out of 10 millionaires said the key to their financial success was investing in their company's 401(k) plan.[4]

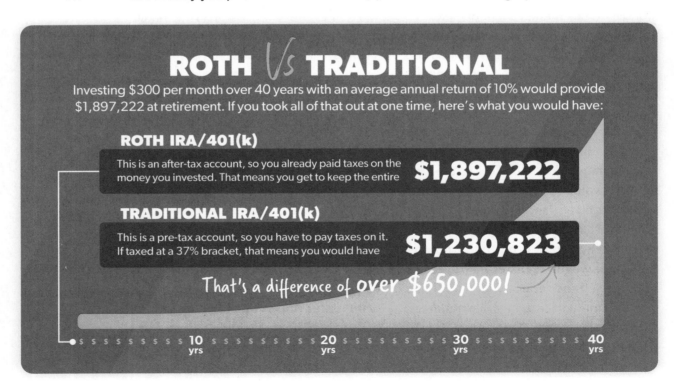

ROTH Vs TRADITIONAL

Investing $300 per month over 40 years with an average annual return of 10% would provide $1,897,222 at retirement. If you took all of that out at one time, here's what you would have:

ROTH IRA/401(k)

This is an after-tax account, so you already paid taxes on the money you invested. That means you get to keep the entire **$1,897,222**

TRADITIONAL IRA/401(k)

This is a pre-tax account, so you have to pay taxes on it. If taxed at a 37% bracket, that means you would have **$1,230,823**

That's a difference of *over $650,000!*

| 10 yrs | 20 yrs | 30 yrs | 40 yrs |

Other Retirement Plans

If you work for the government, a nonprofit, or are self-employed, there are still plenty of tax-advantaged retirement plans to help you reach your goals. These include:

403(b): This is a **qualified retirement savings plan** similar to a 401(k), but it is offered by nonprofit organizations, such as churches, hospitals, schools, and some government organizations.

457 plan: This is a nonqualified, tax-advantaged retirement plan offered to state and local government employees as well as some nonprofit employees. These plans are less common and allow employees to contribute pre-tax or after-tax dollars.

Simplified Employee Pension Plan (SEP): A retirement savings plan that allows people who are self-employed or own a small business to make contributions toward their retirement (and their employees' retirement) without the costs of a more complex qualified plan.

A 401(k) is a great plan to help you plan for retirement.

— Anthony O'Neal

When you're debt-free and have a fully funded emergency fund, it's time to participate in a tax-advantaged plan and a company match—if one is offered—with your employer. Remember, the sooner you start, the more time compound growth will have to work and the more *your funds can grow!*

Qualified Retirement Savings Plan: an employer-sponsored retirement plan that has a special tax treatment

Did You Know?

56% of American workers contribute to their workplace retirement plans.[5]

Your **JOURNAL**

What is the difference between investing with a traditional 401(k) and investing with a Roth 401(k)?

_____

_____

_____

REMEMBER THIS Add a ✓ next to each completed learning objective below.

◯ You can explain the difference between pre-tax and after-tax investing.

◯ You understand the differences between various retirement plans.

THIS LESSON MAKES ME FEEL Circle your response to what you learned.

 CONFUSED   SURPRISED   THOUGHTFUL   CONFIDENT

LESSON VIDEO GUIDE

When you invest, you need to make sure that you are spreading your money around.
— *Chris Hogan*

GUIDED NOTES   While you watch the video, complete the section below.

1. Diversification means to _____ around.

2. Diversify 25% across _____ types of mutual funds.

3. You need _____ in your investments.

4. What are some things with investing that you should NEVER do?

_____

_____

_____

ANALYZE AND REFLECT   After you watch the video, respond to the question(s) below.

1. If a mutual fund is already a form of diversification, why is it important to also diversify your investments into different mutual funds?

_____

_____

_____

LEARNING OBJECTIVES

- Understand the importance of diversification in your investing plan.
- Explain the differences between four types of mutual funds.

MAIN IDEA

Diversification helps to balance risk and improve your chances of building wealth when you're investing for long-term savings goals, including retirement.

What Is Diversification?

After all the information about the explosive growth your money can have through investing, you're probably ready to start piling up some investments and letting compound growth get to work. But hold up for a minute, because there's a crucial detail in all this investing business that you need to keep in mind: **diversification**.

> **Money is like manure. Left in one pile, it stinks—spread around, it will grow things.**
>
> — Dave Ramsey

Diversification helps limit your risk by using a mix of investment types in your portfolio. Instead of all your financial eggs being in one basket, you're spread out among many baskets. That's important because a good mix of investments can reduce your risk without sacrificing your chance to build wealth. Even when one or more of your investments doesn't do so hot, your others have the potential to make up the difference.

Diversify the Right Way

You've figured out that mutual funds are a good way to invest and you know that you should diversify. So, let's talk about putting those two concepts together. A mutual fund is already diversified in itself based on the different companies that make up the fund. But you should also diversify the types of mutual funds in your investing portfolio. You can do this by spreading your investments equally among four different types of mutual funds.

- **Growth stock mutual funds** *(mid-cap):* These funds buy stock in medium-sized companies that have experienced some growth and are still expanding. Growth stock mutual funds are usually predictable—meaning they don't have dramatic highs and lows.
- **Growth and income stock mutual funds** *(large-cap):* These funds are made up of large, well-established companies. When it comes to the risk-and-reward factor, these are fairly moderate.
- **Aggressive growth stock mutual funds** *(small-cap):* These funds aim to provide maximum long-term growth from stocks of primarily smaller companies. They're

Diversification: the practice of dividing the money a person invests among different types of investments in order to lower risk

Standard Diversification Plan:

25% Growth Stock Mutual Fund (Mid-Cap)

25% Growth and Income Stock Mutual Fund (Large-Cap)

25% Aggressive Growth Stock Mutual Fund (Small-Cap)

25% International Stock Mutual Fund

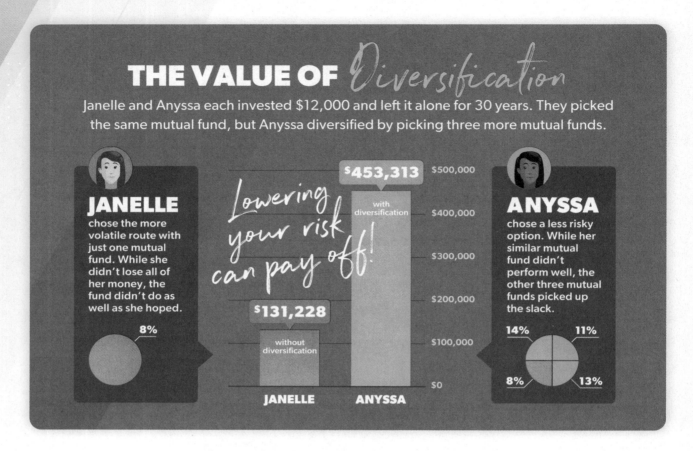

THE VALUE OF *Diversification*

Janelle and Anyssa each invested $12,000 and left it alone for 30 years. They picked the same mutual fund, but Anyssa diversified by picking three more mutual funds.

Lowering your risk can pay off!

$453,313 with diversification

$131,228 without diversification

$500,000
$400,000
$300,000
$200,000
$100,000
$0

JANELLE   ANYSSA

JANELLE
chose the more volatile route with just one mutual fund. While she didn't lose all of her money, the fund didn't do as well as she hoped.

8%

ANYSSA
chose a less risky option. While her similar mutual fund didn't perform well, the other three mutual funds picked up the slack.

14%   11%
8%   13%

---

the wild child of your portfolio because they can swing dramatically upward or dramatically downward—a lot. Think high risk with high potential return.

- ***International stock mutual fund:*** These funds invest in companies from around the world. Putting some of your money into international companies helps protect you if America's economy takes a hit. Plus, you get to invest in some big-name, non-U.S. companies. These may also be called foreign or overseas funds, but don't get them confused with world or global funds (a mix of U.S. and foreign stocks together). By spreading out your investments this way, you balance those high-risk investments with more steady and predictable ones.

Now, when you see large-, mid-, and small-cap, that refers to **capitalization**,

Capitalization: the total dollar market value of a company or how much a company is worth

which is a measure of how much a company is worth. A small-cap company is worth under $2 billion, mid-cap companies can range anywhere from $2–10 billion and large-cap companies are worth more than $10 billion—these are the Amazons, Facebooks, and Microsofts of the world.

Don't Do These Things

Okay, we've covered most of the things you *should* be doing with your investments. But what about things you should be sure *not* to do? It's pretty simple:

1. ***Never invest in something you don't understand.*** Dave uses the KISS rule for investing: Keep it simple, stupid! Don't get offended—we're not calling you stupid. Just make sure you understand where you're putting your money. If an opportunity seems too good to be true

or too confusing to understand, don't put your money there. Work with an investment professional to understand what you're investing in.

2. ***Never borrow from your retirement account.*** Taking a loan out of your 401(k) is never a good idea. Not only are you taking that money out of mutual funds where it's earning money, but you also run the risk of serious fees if you leave your company before paying it back in full. If you leave, you have to pay the loan back within a certain period of time or get hit with a penalty on top of the taxes that you'll owe for the early withdrawal.

3. ***Never invest purely for tax savings.*** If what you're investing in is primarily a tax deal, then it's probably not a good investment. Your motivation should be to make money, not save on taxes.

4. ***Never borrow money to invest.*** We've talked again and again about why you shouldn't borrow money to buy things that you can't afford. Don't borrow money for investing either.

You should never, ever take out a 401(k) loan.
— *Chris Hogan*

We've said it before and we'll say it again: Debt is not a wealth-building tool. It just adds more risk! Stay out of debt altogether so you have free rein with your income. Remember, your largest wealth-building tool is your income. Invest your income wisely to create a portfolio that will provide for your future needs.

Did You Know?

Almost 60% of young workers (ages 18–34) have taken money from their retirement account.[6]

$\mathcal{Y}our$ **JOURNAL**   Why is diversification important when it comes to investing for long-term savings goals, including retirement?

_____

_____

_____

REMEMBER THIS   Add a ✓ next to each completed learning objective below.

◯ You understand how diversification can help investments grow safely.

◯ You can explain four different types of mutual funds.

THIS LESSON MAKES ME FEEL   (Circle) your response to what you learned.

 CONFUSED   SURPRISED   THOUGHTFUL   CONFIDENT

LESSON VIDEO GUIDE

There are many people who retire at the age of 40, and there are some that retire at 70 or 75. —Chris Hogan

GUIDED NOTES   While you watch the video, complete the section below.

1. Retirement is not an age; it is a _____ number.

2. You get to decide when you want to _____.

3. _____ what your retirement is going to look like.

4. Get your _____ number.

5. Understand how much you need to invest each _____.

ANALYZE AND REFLECT   After you watch the video, respond to the question(s) below.

1. List three goals or dreams you have for your life that you would like to do when you retire.

   _____

   _____

   _____

2. Why is it important to start making retirement plans early in life?

   _____

   _____

MAIN IDEA

Knowing what to expect in retirement will help you create a solid financial plan now that will provide for your needs—and allow you to be generous—in retirement.

Planning for Retirement

What's your dream retirement look like? This is a question you should ask yourself in all stages of life, because it will determine how you set up your plans for the future. No matter what your retirement dream is, you've got to lock in on it. Can you see that dream in a crystal-clear, high-definition picture? It's all possible—but you've got to plan.

Retirement isn't an old people thing. It's a smart people thing.

— *Chris Hogan*

Retirement planning is the process of figuring out how much money you'll need in retirement to do the things you want to do—and then creating a plan to help you get there. Sure, your 401(k) or IRA make up a part of this plan, but we're talking about the big picture here. To get to that high-definition picture, ask yourself questions like: *What do I want to do in retirement? When do I want to retire? How much money will I need to save by the time I retire? How will I cover medical expenses and long-term care in retirement?*

Start by figuring out how much money you'll need in retirement based on these questions, then work with a financial advisor to create a plan to get you there. Remember that retirement isn't an age; it's a financial number. You could retire and live life on your terms much earlier than age 67—it just takes a little planning and a lot of hard work.

Income During Retirement

As you work on your plan, you'll need to analyze where you'll have money coming in and where you'll have money going out. Here are the most common sources of income you could have during retirement.

- ***Retirement Accounts and Investment Returns:*** If you invest enough through your adult life, your investments should generate enough of a return to provide retirement income that's similar to what you had when you were working. Three out of four millionaires (75%) said that consistent investing over a long period of time was the reason for their success.[7]

Did You Know?

How many Americans develop a long-term plan for their money?[8]

████████ **92%**
of millionaires

██████ **60%**
of the general population

Retirement Planning: the process of figuring out how much money you'll need in retirement and creating a plan to get there

- *Social Security:* We identified Social Security as one of the payroll deductions in Chapter 10. Many people rely on Social Security for income during their retirement years. You can start taking Social Security payments when you turn 62 years old—but you'll only get 75% of your full monthly benefit. Why? Because, for anyone born after 1960, full retirement age is 67. So if you start taking benefits at 62, you'll get a reduced amount since you started drawing on the benefits early.

  If you start taking Social Security when you turn 67, you'll get 100% of the monthly benefit. But if you can hold off until you turn 70, you'll actually get 125% of the monthly benefit. So if you're in a solid financial position, waiting a little longer could pay off—literally.

  Just remember that Social Security is meant to supplement your income in retirement, not replace it. According to the Social Security Administration, Social Security benefits are only meant to replace about 40% of your income from when you were working.[9]

- *Real Estate:* If you own rental property, you'll have some passive income thanks to rent payments. But you'll also want to budget for property management too.
- *Inheritance:* If you're going to inherit a large amount of money, that needs to be included in your plan. Don't bank on it as a key part of your plan but accept it as a blessing.

Retirement Expenses

You'll have some basic expenses during retirement, so it's a good idea to plan for them. Remember that 15-year mortgage? A paid-for home in retirement means a lower cost of living and greater financial security. But even without a mortgage payment, you'll still need to pay utility bills, property taxes, insurance, and maintenance.

Other basics include food, clothing, personal items, transportation, medical expenses, and even entertainment. You'll need to consider your spending patterns to estimate how much you'll spend in these categories in retirement.

And of course, you can't forget taxes. You'll continue to pay taxes in retirement.

A Message From CHRIS

YOU KNOW what gets me fired up? Talking about retirement. Now, I know what you're thinking: *Retirement? Seriously?* Let me put it this way: Retirement isn't an *old* people thing—it's a *smart* people thing. It's about sacrificing now so you can live your dreams later. Do you want to travel the world, or spend time with family, or serve your community? Whatever it is, you need to hear me: The earlier you plan for your future, the better. If you get started now, you'll really rock your retirement. A dream without a plan is simply a wish, so roll up your sleeves and let's get to work!

You can expect to pay taxes on **dividends**, interest income, or capital gains. Some sources of income, like a Roth IRA, are not subject to income taxes in retirement. It's important to estimate the amount of taxes, both state and federal, you'll pay in retirement so you can budget for it.

Estate Planning

At some point, you'll also need to start **estate planning.** This is an important part of everyone's financial plan because it helps others know what you would like to do with your money, property, and possessions after you die. Granted, nobody likes to talk about that, but it's a reality in life. Not talking about it won't make it not happen.

The first place to start an estate plan is with a **will**. A will is just a legal document that says who will get your stuff when you die. A will lets you make those decisions ahead of time.

Everyone over the age of 18 needs a will.

— Dave Ramsey

Start Early

Remember, it's never too early to start working on your retirement plans. Compound growth needs two things: money and time. You can take care of the first part with good budgeting and saving habits, and you can take advantage of the second by starting to work toward your financial goals now. Don't put it off. You can be a millionaire too!

Dividend: a distribution from the net profits of a company to its shareholders

Estate Planning: preparation of tasks to manage an individual's assets after death

Will: a legal document listing how a person wants their assets distributed after their death

---

Your JOURNAL

What are the benefits of thinking about retirement expenses now?

_____

_____

_____

REMEMBER THIS   Add a ✓ next to each completed learning objective below.

◯   You can explain the different sources of income for retirement.

◯   You understand the importance of estate planning in your overall financial plan.

THIS LESSON MAKES ME FEEL   Circle your response to what you learned.

😓 CONFUSED   😮 SURPRISED   🙂 THOUGHTFUL   🤩 CONFIDENT

6 | Outrageous Generosity

LESSON VIDEO GUIDE

You save and you budget and you get out of debt so that you can live, and give, like no one else. —Dave Ramsey

GUIDED NOTES   While you watch the video, complete the section below.

1. Giving is the most _____ that you'll ever have with money.

2. Generosity is not an act or a thing you do, it is a _____ quality.

3. Generosity is a _____ to be others-centered.

4. The average American family gives _____ of their household income.

5. Practice the idea of being a _____ rather than a taker.

ANALYZE AND REFLECT   After you watch the video, respond to the question(s) below.

1. Dave teaches that generosity is a character quality and not an act you do. In your own words, explain what he means.

   _____

   _____

   _____

2. What are two ways you can be generous with your time or money today?

   _____

   _____

LEARNING OBJECTIVES

- Explain the benefits of being generous.
- Understand the tax requirements and benefits of charitable contributions.

MAIN IDEA

While it sounds completely unbelievable, giving really is the most fun you can ever have with money!

Build Wealth and Give

You've learned to save, budget, avoid debt, and invest. Now let's talk about giving. If you follow **The Five Foundations** you've learned, you *will* achieve wealth. How exciting is that? Super exciting!

But managing money isn't just about getting rich. Money magnifies who you are. If you're a stingy person, you'll be even more stingy when you have a lot of money. If you're a generous person, you'll be even more generous when you have more money to give. We can't complete a class on personal finance without talking about the value of helping others—of being outrageously generous. That's why **The Fifth Foundation** is build wealth and give.

Giving to Others

Giving is one of the most important and rewarding parts of your financial journey. You might only be one person, and you may not have a lot of money, but you *can* make a difference! Since you're going to make sure that you stay debt-free, you'll have much more money to spend, invest, and give. The money you give creates more joy than it could ever buy!

After you've spent so much time working on your finances, it could be easy to get caught up in your wealth and get wrapped up in getting yourself all of the things "you deserve" for your hard work. Generosity is the cure for this selfishness that we're all prone to have.

> **You've got to live like no one else so later you can give like no one else!**
>
> — *Dave Ramsey*

When you see how great the need is for some people, it's easier to be grateful for what you have. It's okay to have money and nice stuff, just don't let your stuff have you! Giving turns that spotlight away from yourself and allows you to focus on others.

As you're working toward your financial goals, like saving your $500 emergency fund or cash for your car, money to give may seem hard to come by. That's when you can find creative ways to give. You can give your time, talents, knowledge, or your service to help other people.

The Five Foundations:

Save a $500 emergency fund.

Get out and stay out of debt.

Pay cash for your car.

Pay cash for college.

Build wealth and give.

We make a living by what we get; we make a life by what we give.

Winston Churchill
UK Prime Minister,
1940–1945, 1951–1955

Some people give time, some money, some their skills and connections, some literally give their life's blood. But everyone has something to give.

Barbara Bush
Former First Lady of the United States

Did You Know?

In one year, over 77 million Americans volunteered almost 7 billion hours of time worth $167 billion in economic value to various organizations![11]

A Change of Focus

Our culture can be so "me" focused—just look at all the selfies on social media! But a powerful thing happens when you serve others: You stop focusing on yourself. You stop being consumed by your own struggles, looks, and the things you want. When you give to others, you're saying, "Right now the needs of this person matter more." That's why giving is so powerful! It moves you from selfish to selfless.

Each person you give to creates a new story and a new thrill. Your giving could be money, but it could be so many other expressions of selflessness. In a way, giving is a lot like compound growth—you put something in, but you get much more out! Try it! When you're in line at a coffee shop, offer to pay for the coffee of the person behind you and see how it makes you feel. That feeling and the feeling of the person receiving your generosity is much more valuable than the $5 you'll spend. It's a feeling that never gets old.

Tips for Donating Money

1. Be proactive in your giving. Take time to identify causes or charities that matter to you.
2. Check the charity's commitment to accountability and transparency.
3. Research the charity's financial records and see how much of their funds go to salaries and the cost of running the organization. You should feel confident that the money you give is being used to actually help people—not being spent on administrative costs.
4. Concentrate your giving on just a few organizations so your donations can have a real impact through them.
5. Make a long-term commitment to support your favorite charities.

Charitable Giving Benefits

While your primary motivation for giving should be the simple desire to help others, there can be financial benefits for you as well. You might be eligible for some tax

BE *Generous* NOW

Here are some practical ways you can start becoming more generous today.

Donate Clothes
Give your used clothes to a homeless shelter.

Assist a Senior
Do something helpful for a senior adult.

Make a Friend
Meet and eat lunch with someone new.

Tutor Others
Help a peer or younger child with schoolwork.

Help a Neighbor
Rake leaves, shovel snow, or clean gutters.

Care for a Soldier
Send a note and a care package to a soldier.

Volunteer Time
Help at a ministry or an animal shelter.

Run for a Cause
Run a 5k for your favorite charity.

Thank a Teacher
Thank a teacher who has impacted your life.

deductions as a result of your charitable giving. Here are some things to know:

- A gift (money or personal property) to a qualified **charitable organization** may entitle you to a charitable contribution deduction on your income taxes if you itemize deductions.
- Most charitable organizations, but not all, qualify for a charitable contribution deduction on your taxes.
- A contribution to a qualified charity is deductible in the year in which it is given.
- There are limits to how much you can deduct for giving, but the limits are very high.
- Certain rules exist for non-cash, personal property donations (like giving a car).
- You should document your charitable contributions if you plan to deduct them on your tax return.

Your Legacy

You can make a lot of money and be wildly successful. You can go after your dreams and accomplish each and every one of them. But what does it all mean if you're the only one benefiting from it?

Giving is the most fun you can have with money.

— *Dave Ramsey*

If you're giving of yourself, then you're building a legacy to be proud of. That's your impact on the world—and it shows the world what really matters to you. Now, get out there and start living and *giving like no one else!*

> **Charitable Organization:** an organization set up to provide help and raise money for those in need

> The best thing about giving of ourselves is that what we get is always better than what we give. The reaction is greater than the action.
>
> Orison Swett Marden
> American author

Your JOURNAL

When have you been impacted because someone else demonstrated generosity toward you or your family?

_____

_____

_____

REMEMBER THIS   Add a ✓ next to each completed learning objective below.

○ You understand the benefits of being generous.

○ You can explain the tax requirements and benefits of charitable giving.

THIS LESSON MAKES ME FEEL   Circle your response to what you learned.

 CONFUSED   SURPRISED   THOUGHTFUL   CONFIDENT

Chapter 12 Review

Fill in the blanks below using the correct key terms from this chapter.

Investing	Stock Market Index	Fixed Annuity	Capitalization
Risk-Return Ratio	Portfolio	Variable Annuity	Dividend
Liquid Asset	Prospectus	401(k)	Estate Planning
Stock Market	Bull Market	Diversification	Will
Stock	Bear Market	Retirement Planning	Charitable Organization
Return on Investment (ROI)	Individual Retirement Arrangement (IRA)	Qualified Retirement Savings Plan	

1. An extended time of falling stock values is referred to as a(n) _____ .

2. Cash in a bank savings account is a good example of a(n) _____ .

3. Your collection of investments is called your _____ .

4. Preparing a will is just one aspect of effective _____ .

5. The S&P 500 is one example of a(n) _____ .

6. Owning _____ means you own a small piece (or pieces) of a company.

7. A fund manager uses a(n) _____ to outline an investing strategy.

8. A(n) _____ is a payout of net profits from a company to shareholders.

FINISH THE SENTENCE   Use what you've learned in this chapter to complete these sentences.

1. When it comes to investing, one of the most important things to remember is never invest _____
_____ .

2. Capitalization (cap) refers to the total value of a company described in one of these three ways: _____
_____ .

1. _____ refers to the monetary gain or loss of an investment over time.

   A. ROY

   B. ROI

   C. IRA

   D. IRO

2. Which of the following is not considered a true retirement plan?

   A. IRA

   B. 401(k)

   C. SIP

   D. 403(b)

3. When it comes to picking investments, the higher the _____, the greater your chance of losing money.

   A. Return

   B. Risk

   C. Interest rate

   D. Index

4. Which of these investment accounts will provide tax-free withdrawals at retirement?

   A. 401(k)

   B. 457

   C. 403(b)

   D. Roth IRA

5. For a majority of millionaires, where did their money for retirement come from?

   A. Social Security

   B. Inheritance

   C. IRA/401(k)

   D. Real estate

6. Giving your money, time, or property to an organization that helps other people who are in need is called _____ giving.

   A. Charitable

   B. Legacy

   C. Financial

   D. Organizational

Review **QUESTION**   Explain why diversification is such an important concept when it comes to investing for your future.

_____

_____

_____

_____

_____

_____

The Flow of Money

Global Economics

This chapter examines how the global economy impacts your personal financial decisions and how different global economic systems influence decisions about goods and services that are used around the world.

Macroeconomics and Global Activity

LESSON VIDEO GUIDE

Global economics plays a huge role in your day-to-day life, and your actions impact the global economy.

—Chris Hogan

GUIDED NOTES   While you watch the video, complete the section below.

1. Global Economics: the study of how different _____ of the world work together.

2. Microeconomics: how money works at the _____, group, or company level.

3. Macroeconomics: how money works for the overall economy of a _____.

4. Goods are things that you can see and _____.

5. Services are _____ that someone does for someone else.

6. Recession: GDP must _____ for two consecutive quarters.

7. Economic _____ is when the value of a country's goods and services goes up.

ANALYZE AND REFLECT   After you watch the video, respond to the question(s) below.

1. Why do you think so many things are made in other countries? Provide two reasons.

_____

_____

_____

LEARNING OBJECTIVES

- Understand the difference between macroeconomics and microeconomics.
- Describe how the factors of production, economic sectors, and chain of production all work together.

MAIN IDEA

Every day, in one form or another, you're participating in global economics through the choices you make and the money you spend.

The Big Picture

We get it. Global economics may not be on your list of favorite subjects. After all, what does *global* economics have to do with *personal* finance? While understanding big economic concepts may not seem as important as learning how to create a personal budget, what insurance you need, and how to invest, the truth is the global economy impacts every aspect of your life.

Economics is your intentional decisions with your money.

— *Chris Hogan*

At its core, economics is a study of consumer choices (including yours) and how and why we make those choices. And while you're just one consumer, the science of economics recognizes the patterns of hundreds, thousands, millions—even billions—of consumers around the world making their own choices about what to eat, wear, listen to, and use. There's a lot to cover, so let's dig in!

Economics 101

When we talk about **global economics**, we're talking about how all the different countries of the world handle their money. And it's not just about countries—as individuals, we're all connected too. That global connectivity is known as **economic interdependence**, and it describes how many companies and even countries around the world depend upon one another. Most of that interdependence comes through trade, which we'll cover in Lesson 4.

The global impact of this economic interdependence can be seen when one country suffers an economic hardship—a natural disaster, war, or even the pandemic of 2020—and the economies of other countries feel the effects too.

You need to understand two big, but important, words as you're learning about global economics: **macroeconomics** and **microeconomics**. Macroeconomics is the science, or study, of the whole economy—or big picture economics. Microeconomics is the science, or study, of the behavior of people, individual businesses, or markets.

Global Economics: the study of how the economies in all parts of the world operate

Economic Interdependence: the relationship between two or more countries dependent on one another for goods or services

Macroeconomics: the study of the big economic picture through various economic indicators

Microeconomics: the study of behavior in small economic units like businesses and individuals

326

GETTING TO *Market*

To successfully produce the incredible variety of goods and services available today, each country's economy relies on factors of production, economic sectors, and the chain of production to make sure those goods and services are available for global consumers.

FACTORS OF PRODUCTION

A country's economy is built on the value of finished goods and services. To get that supply of goods and services, a country needs four basic economic building blocks:

LAND

refers to physical land where a farm, factory, or company is located as well as natural resources needed for a product.

CAPITAL

refers to all the man-made objects like tools, machinery, buildings, equipment, and chemicals needed for production.

LABOR

refers to the work done by individual people or an entire workforce in order to produce a product.

ENTREPRENEURSHIP

refers to the ability to combine the other three factors of production to produce and deliver a product or service.

An economy needs these four things to produce anything!

ECONOMIC SECTORS

A nation's economy is divided into large sectors based on the type of activity, industry, characteristics, or kind of work performed.

Knowledge and skill-based activities and careers

1 PRIMARY
Companies that extract and harvest natural products from the earth like raw materials and basic food. This includes mining, fishing, and agriculture.

2 SECONDARY
Companies that produce finished goods using raw materials. This includes processes such as refining, manufacturing, processing, and construction.

3 TERTIARY
Companies in the sales and service industry including retail, wholesale, restaurants, tourism, banking, health care, transportation, and law.

4 QUATERNARY
Intellectual activities often associated with technological innovation, education, media, libraries, government, and scientific research.

CHAIN OF PRODUCTION

Many of the products you enjoy follow a series of production steps directly related to the economic sectors. For example:

  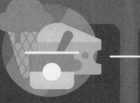 

Your favorite milk products start here. Raw milk is collected from dairy cows that have been fed and raised on farms across the country.

The milk goes to a processing plant and is made into a variety of different things, packaged, and shipped to stores everywhere— including your favorite one.

Stores and restaurants stock, sell, and use milk, butter, yogurt, cheese, cottage cheese, sour cream, and ice cream so you (and others) can enjoy them.

Research and development departments create and test new flavors, packaging options, healthy varieties, and education for consumers.

Thinking *Globally*

TO THINK GLOBALLY means a lot more than just buying stuff from around the world—it means recognizing we're all part of a global community. Just as the financial markets of the world are interdependent, we're connected together as human beings. We have a lot of opportunities to financially support others through international giving organizations. Have you ever thought about what the world might be like without people and organizations that help others in need? There are charities that feed children and care for orphans, organizations that rescue people from slavery and addiction, groups that provide job training, and so many other things. Donations of money and time help these organizations meet the needs of people around the world—and you can be a part of those solutions today.

Inflation: the persistent rise in the cost of goods and services over time

Deflation: the general reduction of prices in an economy over time

Gross Domestic Product (GDP): the total market value of all finished goods and services produced in a country in a given period of time

Economic Indicators: key statistics used to analyze a country's economy

Standard of Living: the level of wealth, comfort, material goods, and necessities available to a group of people

Economic Indicators

Macroeconomics studies broad economic events, such as **inflation** and **deflation**, the rate of economic growth, price levels, national income, **gross domestic product (GDP)**, and changes in employment rates. These are called **economic indicators** and they provide important statistical information that indicates whether an economy is healthy or in decline.

So, what good is all that information? Economists study the data from economic indicators and make predictions about where the economy is headed. Investors and governments use those predictions to figure out what they should do next. Macroeconomics is not a perfect science. With variables like inflation, government regulation, and social preference, economic theory can only go so far.

What Is GDP?

GDP is short for gross domestic product. GDP represents the total value of all the finished goods and services produced in a country for a specific period of time, like three months or a year. GDP is one of the economic indicators used to determine whether the economy of a country is growing or shrinking. It's a good way to judge the economic health of a country.

Economic Development

Countries around the world vary widely in their wealth and availability of services. A country's **standard of living** is determined by a lot of factors including income levels, availability of affordable housing, the average quantity (and quality) of the goods and services for sale, access to health care, and access to education.

Countries are generally divided into two categories based on economic development: developed or developing. To figure out whether a country is developed or developing, economists look at a lot of indicators, like GDP, per capita income, level of industry, and standard of living, as well as other non-economic criteria, like technology, education, personal freedom, poverty level, availability of clean water, and an adequate food supply.

Developed countries have a highly progressed economy with a strong, modern technological foundation. They also use more of the world's resources, such as oil, than developing countries. People who live in developed countries usually drive cars and power their homes with electricity and gas. This includes countries like the U.S., Canada, France, Italy, Japan, and Germany.

Developing countries don't have access to the same kinds of resources and technology. They're typically agriculturally based, have a less stable economy, less industrialization, and a lower standard of living. But they're making efforts to move forward—that's why they're called developing countries. This includes countries like Argentina, Peru, China, and the Philippines. This chart reflects a few of the differences between both categories:

Measure	Developed	Developing
Unemployment rate	Low	High
Poverty rate	Low	High
Infant mortality rate	Low	High
Birth rate	Low	High
Life expectancy	High	Low
Standard of living	High	Low

That's a lot of information to soak in. The bottom line is that you—an individual consumer in the United States—play a role in global economics by the decisions you make with your money every day.

Developed Country: one with a high level of economic growth, industrialization, and a higher standard of living

Developing Country: one with less economic development, an agriculture-based economy, less industrialization, high population, and high level of unemployment

---

Your JOURNAL

How does the global economy impact you as an individual worker and consumer?

_____

_____

_____

REMEMBER THIS Add a ✓ next to each completed learning objective below.

○ You understand the difference between macroeconomics and microeconomics.

○ You can explain how the factors of production, economic sectors, and chain of production all work together.

THIS LESSON MAKES ME FEEL (Circle) your response to what you learned.

 CONFUSED   SURPRISED   THOUGHTFUL   CONFIDENT

LESSON
2 | Economic Systems

LESSON VIDEO GUIDE

Economic systems are all about freedom and choices. As an entrepreneur, I want to be able to choose.
— Dave Ramsey

GUIDED NOTES   While you watch the video, complete the section below.

1. The desire for _____ is built into the human spirit.

2. Economic System: the organized way of managing _____, buying, and selling.

3. List the four types of economic systems:

   _____

   _____

   _____

   _____

ANALYZE AND REFLECT   After you watch the video, respond to the question(s) below.

1. Dave mentions how economic systems are about freedom and choices. With that in mind, if you were given the opportunity to start your own country, which economic system would you choose and why?

   _____

   _____

   _____

LEARNING OBJECTIVES

- Compare and contrast the characteristics of different economic systems.
- Explain how specialization allows countries to participate in global trade.

MAIN IDEA

Every country, including the United States, has a unique economic system that impacts the financial decisions of that country and its citizens.

What's an Economic System?

You've probably heard people say things like, "The economy's in good shape," or, "The economy's in bad shape," and wondered what that means. While it might be obvious that every country's economy is different, you may wonder how.

An **economic system** is the way in which a country uses their resources for production and how they distribute goods and services throughout the nation. Every country has a unique economic system that includes its leadership, the way it makes decisions, and how the citizens of a country buy stuff. A country's economic system is identified by the way these things interact.

While each country's economy is unique, economic systems around the world share many characteristics. We can categorize four basic types of economic systems based on those characteristics.

Traditional Economy

A traditional economy focuses entirely on goods and services that are directly related to beliefs, traditions, and customs. It's the most basic and ancient type of economy. Primary industries, especially fishing and farming, would be most common in traditional economies. Traditional economies typically don't have individual workers specializing in one task.

Traditional economies generally have very little waste, but also very little left over (surplus). You may be surprised to learn that large parts of the world—rural and underdeveloped countries—still operate under a traditional economy.

People in power can't make other people wealthy—you have to do that yourself.

— Dave Ramsey

Command Economy

In a command economy, a centralized power—typically the government—controls, or commands, most of the aspects of production, trade, and income. This type of economy is commonly found in communist countries. That's why communism is often described as a political and economic system.

Economic System: an organized way in which a nation or country manages all their buying, selling, and production

Top 10 Global Economies:

1. United States
2. China
3. Japan
4. Germany
5. United Kingdom
6. India
7. France
8. Italy
9. Canada
10. Brazil [1]

Socialism: economic and political theory promoting collective or government ownership and control of the means of production and distribution of goods

Capitalism: economic and political system in which trade and industry are controlled by private owners for profit

You might hear the terms **socialism** and communism tossed around like they're the same thing. But socialism isn't an economic system. It's a theory supporting the idea of collective or government ownership and control of the production and distribution of goods. So you could say a command economy is based on socialist theory.

Since the government is at the center of a command economy, it controls what can be made, the quantity, and the price. Important industries like utilities and railroads may also be controlled. In theory, a command economy can create enough jobs, goods, and services for its citizens—but it never really works.

The mismanagement of resources often causes shortages. There's little innovation and no reward for starting a business. Also, command economies have an unmotivated labor force because workers are often required to take government-assigned jobs.

Market Economy

In a market economy, everything takes place within the market—the places where things are sold, bought, and traded. In a free market economy, businesses and households are free to act in their own self-interest to determine how to use their resources, what goods to produce, and who buys them. Consumers are free to buy the things they want and at the price they're willing to pay. You might hear a market economy referred to as **capitalism** or a free enterprise system. We'll cover market economy concepts in Lesson 3.

In a pure market economy, there's no government involvement—the opposite of a command economy. The truth is, a pure market system is theoretical because no truly free market economy exists. There's some level of government regulation in every capitalist nation, including the United States. But there's a defined separation between the market and the government.

Mixed Economy

Most countries have what's called a mixed economic system—a mix of traits of the other systems (see the graphic below). Some countries, like China, have a lot of government involvement and lean more toward a command economy. Other countries lean heavily toward a free market

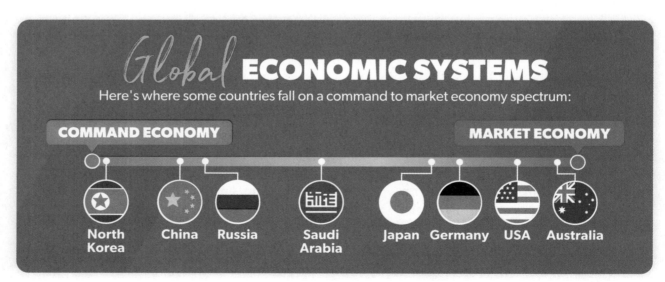

Global ECONOMIC SYSTEMS

Here's where some countries fall on a command to market economy spectrum:

COMMAND ECONOMY   **MARKET ECONOMY**

North Korea   China   Russia   Saudi Arabia   Japan   Germany   USA   Australia economy with less government control except in key industries like defense. But the government is still usually involved in regulating business by enforcing laws to prevent a **monopoly** and define a legal minimum wage, for example.

Capitalism gives you and me the best shot at prosperity.

— Dave Ramsey

The United States operates with a mixed economic system where businesses are free to create, produce, and sell what they want and at the prices they decide. Consumers are free to determine what types of things they want to buy as well as how much they're willing to pay. In turn, the government collects taxes to pay for a variety of programs and services including public education, the postal service, the armed forces, and other social services.

Specialization

Few countries have enough resources and/or production to be completely self-sustaining. **Specialization** allows a country to focus on producing a limited range of goods or services more efficiently. Many countries specialize in producing things native to their region and then trade with other countries for the other goods and services they need. Specialization on a macroeconomic level is the basis of global trade. On a microeconomic level, specialization allows workers to use their unique talents to contribute to the economy.

Monopoly: an industry or commodity that's dominated by one corporation that manipulates prices; an extreme result of free-market capitalism without government regulation

Specialization: when a nation or individual concentrates its efforts in producing a limited variety of goods or services

---

Your **JOURNAL**   In what ways do you benefit from living in a country with a mixed economic system that leans more toward a market economy?

_____

_____

_____

REMEMBER THIS   Add a ✓ next to each completed learning objective below.

○ You can compare and contrast the characteristics of different economic systems.

○ You can explain how specialization allows countries to participate in global trade.

THIS LESSON MAKES ME FEEL   Circle your response to what you learned.

😓 CONFUSED   😮 SURPRISED   🙂 THOUGHTFUL   🤩 CONFIDENT

3 | The U.S. Economy

LESSON VIDEO GUIDE

Competition helps ensure that the best goods or services are provided to you at a lower price. —Dave Ramsey

GUIDED NOTES   While you watch the video, complete the section below.

1. Capitalism focuses on the _____ businesses produce and sell items.

2. The fuel behind capitalism is _____, private ownership, and a motivation to make a profit.

3. Law of Supply and Demand: _____ go up when there's a shortage or down when there's a surplus.

4. Competition is good because it protects _____ from being taken advantage of.

ANALYZE AND REFLECT   After you watch the video, respond to the question(s) below.

1. Think of a product you recently purchased that you really wanted. How might the law of supply and demand have impacted the price? Do you believe you paid a fair price or too much? Did you have a choice to pay a different price from a competing brand?

_____

_____

_____

_____

_____

MAIN IDEA

The U.S., for the most part, is a free market economy driven by supply and demand, profit motive, and competition.

It's Your Economy

Remember, a pure market economic system has free markets and zero government control. The U.S. has a mixed economic system that leans more toward a market economy. It's true that the amount of government regulation and control in the U.S. economy is often widely debated among voters and politicians. But the fact is, the U.S. is mostly a free market—and since it's where you live as a worker and consumer, it's important to understand how the U.S. economy works.

> **We (the U.S.) have the greatest economic system in the history of mankind.**
>
> — Dave Ramsey

Supply and Demand

Remember, in a command economy, a central government controls the resources, production, distribution, and prices. But in a free market economy, natural market forces drive everything—and that's a good thing. The most prominent drivers in a free market are **supply and demand**. Supply refers to how much of a certain product, commodity, or service suppliers are willing to make available at a particular price. Demand refers to how much of that product, item, commodity, or service consumers are willing and able to buy at a particular price.

The **law of supply and demand** is an economic theory that explains the interaction between sellers and buyers for goods or services. The theory helps us understand how the supply (or availability) of a particular product and the demand (or desire) for it affects the price. Generally, low supply and high demand increases the price of an item, while high supply with low demand decreases the price.

Government regulation isn't needed with a free market because consumers and producers (buyers and sellers) will act in their own self-interest so that supply meets demand and prices will eventually stabilize. A market that reaches that point is in a state called **equilibrium** as seen in the graphic on the next page.

Supply and Demand: how the availability of a product or service, and how much it's desired by consumers, affects the price

Law of Supply and Demand: an economic theory that explains the interaction between the sellers of a resource and the buyers for that resource

Equilibrium: the state in which market supply and demand match each other, resulting in price stability

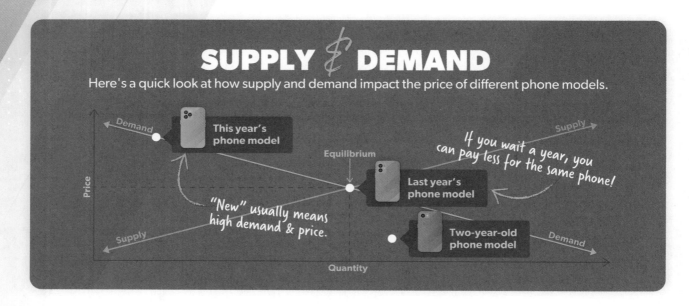

SUPPLY & DEMAND

Here's a quick look at how supply and demand impact the price of different phone models.

Profit and Competition

Two other driving forces characterize a free market: profit motive and competition. Businesses exist to make enough revenue (the money they earn) to cover and exceed their cost of business (investment) so they end up with a profit (surplus money). That's called **profit motive**—the desire and goal to make a profit—and you won't find it in a command economy where the government controls all industries. Trying to make a profit is not greedy, it's trying to stay in business. Businesses that don't make a profit aren't around very long.

Another market driver that doesn't exist in a command economy is **competition**. In a free market, anyone can become an entrepreneur and own a business—that's competition. For example, if you opened a restaurant, you would be competing for customers—and their dollars—with thousands of other restaurants.

The great thing about competition in a free market is that it encourages every business to provide high-quality products, services, atmosphere, and experiences that will get customers talking on social media and in their circle of friends. A key to competition, in many ways, is prices that appeal to the people buying those items. Customers don't want to spend a lot of money on a low-quality item if they can find better quality at a lower price somewhere else. At the same time, customers are often willing to spend more for better quality.

Doing the right thing attracts customers—and keeps them.

— Dave Ramsey

Think about the things you prefer to buy, eat, and wear, the places you choose to get those things, and the prices you're willing to pay. Your decisions as a consumer impact the profit and competition drivers of all kinds of businesses in our market economy. And everyone's different—we all buy different things. Aren't you glad we don't all have to buy, eat, and wear the exact same things? Yep, that happens in a command economy.

Profit Motive:
the desire to make money as the result of a business venture

Competition:
when businesses compete for a share of profit

Did You Know?
There are over 660,000 restaurants in the United States—with new ones added every year.[2]

The Business Cycle

The **business cycle** describes the natural rise and fall of economic growth in a country over time. Economists use the four stages of a business cycle—expansion, peak, contraction, and trough—to analyze the economy. While they can't tell exactly when each stage will happen, there are signals that indicate where the economy is.

Expansion is an economic growth stage where GDP is increasing, the stock market is in a bull market, unemployment levels drop, and the economy has a steady flow of money. An expansion stage can last for years.

Peak identifies the point at which the economy reaches its maximum level of growth—GDP growth is at its highest level, inflation is rising, and other economic indicators stop growing. Then the economy's growth starts to reverse. The month that the business cycle transitions from expansion to contraction is the peak stage.

Contraction, or recession, is the third phase. It begins at the peak and ends at the trough. During contraction, GDP growth falls, unemployment levels begin to rise, income is stagnant or in decline, and there is a decline in the stock market as seen in a bear market.

Trough is the period between contraction and the transition to another cycle of expansion. It's identified by the lowest point, or bottoming, in the business cycle and marks the end of the recession and the start of a financial turnaround.

Business Cycle: describes the rise and fall in production output; it is generally divided into four stages: expansion, peak (prosperity), contraction (recession), and trough

Did You Know?

The COVID-19 pandemic of 2020 resulted in the deepest global recession since World War II.[3]

Your JOURNAL

How have you seen the impact of supply and demand on the things you have purchased recently?

_____

_____

_____

REMEMBER THIS   Add a ✓ next to each completed learning objective below.

○ You understand the interaction of supply, demand, and price.

○ You understand the effect of profit motive and competition on a market economy.

○ You can describe the various parts of a business cycle.

THIS LESSON MAKES ME FEEL   Circle your response to what you learned.

😓 CONFUSED   😗 SURPRISED   🙂 THOUGHTFUL   🤩 CONFIDENT

LESSON VIDEO GUIDE

Your negotiating power in trade depends on the quality and quantity of your resources. — Chris Hogan

GUIDED NOTES While you watch the video, complete the section below.

1. An _____ is a resource that a country produces and sells to another country.

2. An _____ is a resource that a country buys from another country.

3. Economic Interdependence: a system by which many countries economically

   _____ on one another.

4. Scarcity occurs when there's a _____ demand and a low supply.

5. _____ resources include both renewable and nonrenewable resources.

6. _____ capital is made up of knowledge, skills, and talents of people in a country.

ANALYZE AND REFLECT After you watch the video, respond to the question(s) below.

1. Chris Hogan mentioned how the United States has a lot of natural resources available. Explain how this contributes to our GDP. What are some natural resources that we have to offer to other countries?

   _____

   _____

   _____

LEARNING OBJECTIVES

- Recognize the role of exports and imports on the global economy.
- Understand how natural resources are tied to global economics.
- Describe how scarcity impacts personal and global decision-making.

MAIN IDEA

We're not just members of a local community, we're also connected on a global level—and that comes with benefits and responsibilities.

Global Trade

On some level, you're already an expert on global trade. You buy things that come from all around the world. Really. Have you checked your labels lately? You probably don't think about it much, but the choices you make about what and when you buy— and how much you want to spend—have an impact on the resources, workers, and overall economies of other countries.

When you start to dig into global economics, one of the big concepts is **global trade**. Trade is the buying and selling of various goods and services. Trade can take place between producers and consumers within an economy, different countries within the same continent, or between countries around the globe.

International trade allows countries to expand their markets, resulting in greater competition and lower prices for consumers. A good example of this is all your options for buying a car. You can choose between an American-made car or go with a foreign-made option. You can buy a compact, midsize, SUV, or truck. Or you might want to buy an electric car.

A product that's sold to the global market is an **export** and a product that's bought from the global market is an **import**. Over the last couple of centuries, international trade has grown significantly and completely transformed the global economy. In fact, about one fourth of the total global production of all goods and services is exported to other countries.[4]

> **When the economy is growing, that trickles down to us in affordable goods.**
>
> — *Chris Hogan*

Economic Interdependence

The constant importing and exporting of goods and services contributes to economic interdependence. You learned in Lesson 1 that this is when one country depends on another country for something (like oil)—and that country may depend on another country for something else. It's a big web of interdependence!

Global Trade: the exchange of capital, goods, and services between different countries

Exports: resources, materials, and goods a country produces and sells to another country

Imports: resources, materials, and goods a country buys from another country

ECONOMIC *Resources*

It takes resources—both natural and human—to create products and services.

RENEWABLE
can be used again and again

NONRENEWABLE
once you use them up, they're gone

HUMAN CAPITAL
knowledge and skills that provide economic value

You're a resource too!

Protectionism: governmental actions that restrict trade with the intent to protect local businesses from foreign competition

Tariff: a tax imposed on the goods and services imported from another country

Product Standards: criteria and specifications related to the health, safety, and compatibility of goods and services

Subsidy: payment from the government to producers to lower their cost to produce or increase the quantity produced

Definitions continued on next page

That interdependence, however, can lead to times when countries have to evaluate their trade with other countries. **Protectionism** is when governments take action and enact policies that restrict international trade. The purpose of protectionism is just like it sounds—to protect local businesses and jobs from foreign competition. When it comes to protectionism, there are four types of policies that can be implemented: tariffs, product standards, government subsidies, and quotas. Here's a quick rundown:

Tariffs are a tax (or duty) paid on a particular class of imports or exports. That just means a country would have to pay more to get another country to take their items. Governments charge and collect tariffs to make the price of imports as much as or more than the price for nationally made items. The goal is to get consumers to support their own economies by buying items made in their own country.

Product standards are restrictions placed on goods for a variety of reasons, such as product safety, health standards, substandard materials, or product labeling.

Governments will sometimes offer **subsidies** (payments) to help lower the cost of production so businesses can keep their prices low and competitive but still be profitable. For example, in the United States some farms that produce corn, soybeans, wheat, cotton, or rice are provided agricultural subsidies to help them produce their crops.

Trade **quotas** limit the number of products that can be imported during a set period of time. Limiting the supply of competitive foreign products often raises prices and allows local businesses to benefit. An **embargo**—an official ban on trade with a country—prohibits trade altogether and is the most severe type of quota.

The Challenge of Scarcity

Because resources are limited and society's demand for resources is endless, **scarcity** is a fundamental economic problem. Scarcity occurs when there's greater demand for something than what's available. Lack of access to clean drinking water is just one example of scarcity that people around the world experience every day. Imagine how different your daily life would look if you had to find clean water each day.

Another real example of scarcity happened during the COVID-19 pandemic. A bunch of things were hard to find, including toilet paper, disinfecting wipes, hand sanitizer, and masks.

Rationing is a process to control the amount of goods or services being used. Sometimes this happens as the result of a natural disaster that leads to scarcity. At other times, if the government fears there may be a shortage of something, they may ration it.

Let's go back to the example of water. In some parts of the western United States where it doesn't rain much, cities may implement water rationing to limit the amount of water residents use. That would mean you could be fined for washing your car or watering your lawn.

Living on less than you make is critical to success.

— Dave Ramsey

We're All Connected

We're all global citizens. Your daily choices can have an impact—positive or negative—on the rest of the world. Use everything you've learned in this course to go and

make a difference!

Quota: a government-imposed restriction on the number or value of imported or exported items

Embargo: a government order that restricts or prohibits trade

Scarcity: limited resources and an unlimited demand by a population

Rationing: a limit placed on the distribution of resources in high demand but in short supply

Your JOURNAL

How do exports and imports help the economy of a country?

_____

_____

_____

REMEMBER THIS Add a ✓ next to each completed learning objective below.

◯ You can explain the role of exports and imports on the global economy.

◯ You understand how natural resources are tied to global economics.

◯ You can describe how scarcity impacts personal and global decision-making.

THIS LESSON MAKES ME FEEL (Circle) your response to what you learned.

😓 CONFUSED   😯 SURPRISED   🙂 THOUGHTFUL   🤩 CONFIDENT

Chapter 13 Review

REVIEW KEY TERMS   Fill in the blanks below using the correct key terms from this chapter.

Global Economics	Developed Country	Profit Motive	Tariff
Macroeconomics	Developing Country	Competition	Product Standards
Microeconomics	Capitalism	Business Cycle	Subsidy
Inflation	Monopoly	Global Trade	Quota
Deflation	Specialization	Exports	Embargo
Economic Indicators	Supply and Demand	Imports	Scarcity
Standard of Living	Equilibrium	Protectionism	Rationing
Economic System	Economic Interdependence	Law of Supply and Demand	Gross Domestic Product (GDP)
Socialism			

1. Product standards, subsidies, and quotas are examples of _____ policies.

2. _____ impacts pricing based on the availability of a product and the consumer desire for it.

3. A characteristic that sets _____ apart as an economic and political system is the private ownership of businesses.

4. _____ is experienced when demand meets insufficient resources.

5. _____ happens when multiple countries rely upon one another for goods and services.

6. _____ includes the study of individual purchasing decisions.

7. Fewer available resources and a lower standard of living are characteristics of _____.

8. A(n) _____ is the way in which a country uses their resources and distributes goods and services.

9. A(n) _____ is a product or service a country sells to another country.

10. In order to help sell more domestic products, a country might charge an extra tax, or _____, on imports.

1. Which of the four economic sectors includes education, the government, and scientific research?

    A. Primary

    B. Secondary

    C. Tertiary

    D. Quaternary

2. Which of the following is not considered a factor of production?

    A. Land

    B. Labor

    C. Competition

    D. Capital

3. Controlling the use of a product or service is known as what?

    A. Scarcity

    B. Rationing

    C. Subsidy

    D. Tariff

4. When consumer demand for a product is met by the available supply, the market has reached _____.

    A. Scarcity

    B. Deflation

    C. Equilibrium

    D. Expansion

5. What term is used to describe when economic growth is at its highest point?

    A. Expansion

    B. Peak

    C. Contraction

    D. Trough

6. The total value of all the goods and services sold by a country is known as what?

    A. GDP

    B. GPA

    C. DGP

    D. PGA

Review **QUESTION**   Identify and describe at least three key elements of capitalism that you would see in a market or mixed economic system.

_____

_____

_____

_____

_____

_____

What's the number one thing you learned about money through this course?

_____

_____

Take a look at the table of contents. Which two chapters were your favorites?

1. _____

2. _____

LOOKING FOR THE GLOSSARY OR SOURCES?

Visit **ramseyclassroom.com** for these and other
curriculum materials and resources.